Mel Bay Presents

FAVORITE OLD-TIME
AMERICAN SONGS FOR DULCIMER

BY MARK NELSON

2 3 4 5 6 7 8 9 0

© 2004 BY MEL BAY PUBLICATIONS, INC., PACIFIC, MO 63069.
ALL RIGHTS RESERVED. INTERNATIONAL COPYRIGHT SECURED. B.M.I. MADE AND PRINTED IN U.S.A.
No part of this publication may be reproduced in whole or in part, or stored in a retrieval system, or transmitted in any form
or by any means, electronic, mechanical, photocopy, recording, or otherwise, without written permission of the publisher.
Visit us on the Web at www.melbay.com — E-mail us at email@melbay.com

Foreword

In putting together this collection I had in mind the old American practice of making a sampler – those endearing needlework designs showing off various stitches and techniques. I wanted to present a sampling of the best Old-Time and Favorite American Songs for dulcimer players working in schools, churches, hospitals, nursing homes and other public performances spaces, or for anyone wishing to expand his or her repertoire and brush up on a few old chestnuts.

There's a little of everything here – sentimental old hearth songs, laments and lullabies, ballads and play-parties, the sacred and profane. The overwhelming majority come from pre-industrial rural traditions, because this is the kind of music that seems to go well with homemade music making in any age. What is more, I have tried to include a large number songs from the homeland of the dulcimer. Sometimes nothing sounds better than a song that was played on the instrument a hundred years' gone.

Some have called the Appalachian Mountain dulcimer America's only native-born musical instrument. While this may be stretching things a bit, it is certainly true that this wonderful sweet-voiced instrument took it's present form in the hills and hollers of the Southern mountains. As with much of our culture, it has been transformed by the simple fact of being used.

Like the dulcimer, these songs may be considered wholeheartedly American even though once upon a time they, too, may have come from across the sea. Consider "America (My Country 'Tis of Thee)" – American through and through — but known in England as "God Save the Queen." "The Two Sisters?" It goes back at least as far as Medieval Norway. Even "Red River Valley" may be a transplant from our neighbor to the north.

That's not to say all of our music is adopted; nothing speaks deeper to the American soul than a lone voice singing "Nobody Knows the Trouble I've Seen." And who else but an American would boast "Hallelujah, I'm a Bum?"

One thing this is not is a work of scholarship. Don't look for extensive notes or definitive settings from obscure locales. I make no apologies — rather I present songs that I enjoy and that I like to sing. They come from a variety of sources; some written, most not. Over many years of playing and singing in kitchens and campgrounds and festival hallways, I've changed some beyond recognition. If you take them to heart you'll change them, too — it's what makes a song a living thing.

I have sung these songs for years – they never fail to bring a smile, sometimes a tear, often a memory and always a sense of pride. I hope that you use this book to carry them on.

Mark Nelson
Applegate Valley, Oregon
Winter, 2003
www.Mark-o.com

Table of Contents

Foreword 2
A Note to the Dulcimer Player 6
Reading Musical Notation 7
How to Read Tablature 9
Songs Listed by Tuning 12

The Unquiet Grave – Ballads and Story Songs
Jenny Fair Gentle Rosemarie 16
Barb'ry Allen 18
The Lady From York 19
The King's Daughter Fair 20
The Banks of the Ohio 22
The Unquiet Grave 23
The Farmer's Curst Wife 24
Fennario 26
The Two Sisters 28
One Morning in May 30
Lady Mary 32
The Devil's Questions 34
Little Mattie Groves 36

Chickens Crowin' on Sourwood Mountain — Songs From the Southern Highlands
Shady Grove 39
Sourwood Mountain 40
The Cuckoo 42
Tom Dooley 43
Groundhog 44
Same Old Man 46
Omie, Let Your Bangs Hang Down 47
Cold Rain and Snow 48
Cindy 50
Cripple Creek 52
Oh, Death 54
Old Joe Clark 56
Chickens are a-Crowin' 58

Little Old Sod Shanty – Songs of The Frontier
When First Unto This Country 60
Red River Valley 61
In the Good Old Colony Days 62
The Young Man Who Wouldn't Hoe Corn 64
The Sow Took the Measles 66
Kansas Boys 68
Alsea Girls 69
Home on the Range 70
Acres of Clams 72
Bury Me Not on the Lone Prairie 75
Beulah Land 76
Dakota Land 77
Sweet Betsy From Pike 78
Little Old Sod Shanty 80

The Shantyman's Life – Working on the Land and Sea
- John Henry 84
- Haul Away, Joe 86
- The Little Brown Bulls 88
- Boatman Dance 90
- The Glendy Burke 92
- Shenandoah 94
- The Shantyman's Life 96
- The Erie Canal 98
- Whopee Ti Yi Yo 100
- The Drunken Sailor 102
- The E-Ri-E 104
- Blood Red Roses 106
- Pie in the Sky 108
- The Greenland Whale Fishery 110

I'm a Rambler, I'm a Gambler — Songs of Good Times and Bad Whiskey
- Darling Cory 113
- Frankie and Johnnie 114
- Bonnie Black Bess 116
- Camptown Races 118
- I'm a Rambler and a Gambler 120
- Handsome Molly 121
- Jack o' Diamonds 122
- Jimmy Crack Corn 124
- Hallelujah, I'm a Bum 126
- Don't Let Your Deal Go Down 128

Nearer, My God, To Thee – Songs of Faith and Hope
- Wondrous Love 130
- Little David, Play on Your Harp 132
- He's Got the Whole World in His Hands 133
- Amazing Grace 134
- Let My People Go 136
- Hold On 137
- Poor Wayfaring Stranger 138
- Simple Gifts 140
- Steal Away 142
- Nobody Knows the Trouble I've Seen 144
- I'm On My Way 146
- All Night, All Day 148
- Nearer, My God, To Thee 150
- There's a Little Wheel a-Turnin' 152

My Country, 'Tis Of Thee – Songs of Freedom and Strife
- The Girl I Left Behind Me 154
- When Johnny Comes Marching Home 156
- Eating Goober Peas 158
- Yankee Doodle 160
- All Are Talking of Utah 162
- The Yellow Rose of Texas 164
- The Texas Rangers 166

The Battle Hymn of the Republic 168
Dixie 170
Follow the Drinking Gourd 172
Tenting Tonight 174
America (My Country 'Tis of Thee) 176

It's Love, Oh Careless Love — Songs of the Restless Heart

Aura Lee 178
Beware, Oh Take Care 180
Down in the Valley 182
Wedding Dress 183
My Bonnie Lies Over the Ocean 184
On Top of Old Smoky 186
There's More Pretty Girls Than One 188
The Buggerboo 190
Careless Love 192
The Riddle Song 194
The Wagoner's Lad 196
Oh, Can't You Hear That Turtle Dove 198
Old Dog Tray 200
Silver Threads Among the Gold 202

Froggie Went a-Courtin' — Just for Fun

Polly Wolly Doodle 206
The Crawdad Song 208
Quit Kickin' My Dog Around 210
Rueben and Rachel 212
Froggie Went a-Courtin' 213
Fod 214
Turkey in the Straw 216
Clementine 218
I Wish I Was a Mole in the Ground 220
Old Dan Tucker 222
Little Liza Jane 224
Go Tell Aunt Rhody 226
Shoo, Fly, Don't Bother Me 227

About the Author 228
Alphabetical Song List 230

A Note to the Dulcimer Player

This collection represents some of my favorite songs, arranged to fit on the dulcimer with a minimum of fuss. In most cases the arrangements are well within the range of the novice and advancing player. Well, perhaps one or two may give even experienced musicians a run for their money — but you can't blame a boy for having fun.

Many of you have asked for a song book in one specific tuning. Rather than limit things, I have included arrangements in most of the common tunings. Once in while, the only way to get the song to fit was to wrestle it onto to the instrument by coming up with a unique tuning arrangement. As I said, I find that sort of thing to be a lot of fun. But fear not, the overwhelming majority of the songs don't stray far from familiar territory.

These days the dulcimer world seems to be pretty well divided into two camps: those who tune to D-A-D (sometimes called *Mixolydian* tuning) and those who tune to D-A-A (*Ionian* tuning). If you are a fan of either one you will find plenty here to keep you busy.

That being said, you'll gain even more from this book if you twist those tuning knobs a little. Some of the old-time songs use scales and tonalities that can only be experienced in certain tunings. If you don't already have one, invest in an inexpensive digital tuner and learn how to use it. Better still, work with a teacher to train your ear. Believe it or not, tuning is a skill that gets easier with practice.

I have included a generous helping of old style songs that use various modes. What's a mode? Simply put, a mode is a scale. The familiar major scale (think *Do Re Mi Fa So La Ti Do*) is actually called the *Ionian* mode. The dulcimer's fingerboard is designed to play music based on this and other modes: the *Dorian, Aeolian, Mixolydian* and all the rest. Each has a distinct sound as well as a distinct mood – just compare the haunting *Dorian* melancholy of "Wondrous Love" with the jaunty *Ionian* feel of "Little David, Play on Your Harp."

Nowadays many dulcimer players resist learning songs in the old modal tunings. That's a shame, since they are missing out on a wealth of wonderful repertoire. The dulcimer is a folk instrument – you can rest assured that people who played it 100 years ago didn't know *Mixolydian* from *MixMaster*. So do take the time to play through those songs that use unfamiliar tunings or scales. You may find a whole new voice for your instrument.

When I first learned to play the dulcimer, it was common to play with a noter – a short piece of wood held in the fretting hand. To my ear, nothing sounds better than an ancient modal melody accompanied by the whistle of the noter and the ringing of the drone strings. I have included a number of arrangements that lend themselves beautifully to this most typical of dulcimer styles. In general, anytime you see a song with the entire melody written on one string, feel free to use a noter and let the remaining strings sound as drones. Good examples are found in each section; you may wish to give "The Devils' Questions," "Wondrous Love," and "On Top of Old Smoky" a try.

Please refer to the sections on reading notation and tablature if you need brushing up on these important skills. But above all, have fun. After all, doctors *practice*, we musicians get to *play*.

Reading Musical Notation

Although it is not necessary to know how to read musical notation to play the songs in this book, knowledge of a few musical symbols will greatly enhance your enjoyment.

Since the TAB will give you the correct pitches on a properly tuned dulcimer, you really only have to worry about the rhythm of a particular piece.

Music is divided into **measures**, each of which contains the number of beats delineated by the **time signature**:

 4/4 means four beats per measure, each quarter note counts as 1 beat.

 3/4 is three beats per measure, each quarter note counts as 1 beat.

 6/8 has six beats per measure, with an eighth note getting the beat.

Occasionally alternate symbols are used for the time signature. **Cut Time** (¢) is another way of writing 2/2; and **Common Time** (C) is the same as 4/4.

Each beat can be further divided into smaller and smaller units:

o — The longest note is the whole note; it is the equivalent of four quarter notes, or four counts.

𝅗𝅥 — The half note is equal to two quarter notes.

♩ — The quarter note gets one count.

♪ — Two eighth notes equal a quarter note.

𝅘𝅥𝅯 — The sixteenth note is half as long as the eighth note; so two sixteenths equal one eighth, four sixteenths equal a quarter, and sixteen equal a whole note.

Rests correspond to each of the different note values.

A dot placed next to a note (or rest) lengthens it by one half of its value. For example:

Ties are used for notes that are held for their combined values:

   This figure would be held as long as three eighth notes.

Triplets are groups of three notes that are played in the space of two.

For example, three eighth note triplets

would be played in the same amount of time as two eighth notes:

Repeat signs: repeat the enclosed phrase one time before going on to the next measure. (Note that often the first section of a song only has the sign at the end of the phrase. This is a convention of writing folk tunes; treat it just as if the first sign was there.)

This sign means play the measures under the sign on the first time through and then go back to the beginning of the section. On the repeat you skip over the first ending and play the second ending.

D.C. — From the Italian, **Da Capo**, meaning "Head." This sign directs you to go back to the beginning of the music.

D.S. — **Dal Segno**, or "to the sign," tells you to look for the symbol (𝄋) and play that section next rather than returning to the beginning.

A **fermata** is the symbol to hold a note just a little longer than its value. It is used to add expression to your playing.

Chord symbols are given for all of the songs; these may be played on guitar, autoharp, dulcimer, etc. Remember that the chords used often represent one of several alternative harmonies to the melody; feel free to change them if you'd like.

How to Read Tablature

All of the music is written in standard notation and tablature for a dulcimer with three courses of strings. If your dulcimer is set up with four equidistant strings, simply tune one of them as an extra drone. Tunings appear at the beginning of each song. Some of the songs require an extra, or 6 1/2, fret, most do not.

Tablature, or TAB, is a ancient system of musical notation where lines represent the instrument's strings and the fingering positions are indicated by numbers. In the following example, the bottom line is the melody or treble string (or strings, if your dulcimer has doubled melody strings), the middle line represents the middle string, and the top line is the bass. The letters on the right tell you how to tune each string:

```
         D
    T 4  G  0 1 2 3
    A
    B 4  D           0 1 2 3
```

The numbers tell you which fret to play, with 0 being the unfretted, or open string, 1 the first fret, 2 the second and so on.

In the above example, you first play the open middle string, then fret the same string at the first fret, second fret, and then the third fret. You then jump over to the treble string (or strings) and do exactly the same thing – play the open string, then fret it at the first, second and third frets. If you hear a G major scale, you did it right.

Since some strings are left blank, it is up to you whether to play them as drones (open strings) or to avoid them all together. It has become common when writing dulcimer TAB to leave off notating drone strings so the page doesn't get cluttered up with a bunch of zeros.

TAB doesn't give any indication of how long to hold each note; for that refer to the staff above the TAB. (If you are unfamiliar with standard musical notation see the previous section.)

Fingerings have not been indicated to allow each player to develop a personal style – experiment with different fingerings to see what works best for you. Ornaments such as hammer-ons, pull-offs and slides are not included for the same reason. Get the gist of the tune first, then look for places to add slides, hammer-ons and pull-offs.

Remember, if a string is left blank, that usually means you can play it as a drone or not; the choice is yours. The only exception would be when the open string would clash with the melody – in that case a little deft picking will allow you to avoid the offending note. Let your ears be your guide.

Feel free to use a noter for any songs with the melody written entirely on one string.

About The Tunings Used in this Book

Here's a quick run down on the different tunings I've used, and why:

D-A-D
Probably the most common dulcimer tuning, D-A-D is great for chords and easy transpositions into the common fiddle tune keys. This tuning is used for songs in D major (*Ionian* mode), D *Mixolydian*, G major, E minor and A minor.

C-G-C
If you can play in D-A-D, you can play in C-G-C. It's exactly the same tuning but with the pitches lowered a full step. I love the increased warmth of my dulcimer when I tune it down. C-G-C is handy for songs in C, F, D minor and G minor; sometimes better keys for singers than those associated with D-A-D.

D-A-A
In the last few years, this tuning is again gaining popularity because so many fiddle tunes are in the key of D major. D-A-A is great for noter-style playing.

C-G-G
Just like D-A-A, but with the strings slacked down a full step. If you have light gauge strings on your instrument, those two G's may flop around a little. Try a heavier set.

D-A-C
A tuning that gives you the *Aeolian* mode in the key of D. The scale starts on the 1st fret of the melody string. Tune the open melody string to the same note as the bass string held at the 6th fret.

D-A-G
Gives the *Dorian* mode in the key of D starting at the 4th fret. You'll find a G on the third fret of the bass string; tune the open melody string down to this pitch.

D-G-D
Sometimes called *Reverse Ionian*, D-G-D is a versatile tuning that gives you the keys of G major, G *Mixolydian*, D *Dorian*, and E *Aeolian* (natural minor) with a minimum of fuss.

A-A-D
I use this tuning a lot for *Dorian* mode songs and fiddle tunes in the key of A. From D-A-D, simply loosen your bass string until it's an octave below the middle string.

A-A-A
Tune the bass an octave below the middle string, then tune the melody string to the middle string. Great for noter style tunes in A major and *Mixolydian* songs like "Old Joe Clark."

E-A-C
Sometimes you have to make up a new tuning in order to wrestle a particularly obstinate song onto the dulcimer. This weird and wonderful setting of "Hold On" is one such song. E-A-C, which gives you an A minor chord when you strum the strings, is a type of *Phrygian* mode tuning in the key of A.

Transposing

As any singer knows, songs often must be transposed to fit an individual's voice. Therefore, the keys and arrangements included in this book must be taken only as suggestions. Generally they were chosen to lay on the dulcimer with a minimum of fuss, so they may indeed work for your voice. If not, you may wish to transpose them to a more suitable key.

Guitar players have it easy — they just slap on a capo. Unfortunately, placing a capo on a dulcimer not only changes the key, but also the mode and the fingering.

The important thing is not to confuse *tuning* with *key*. *Key* refers to the home pitch of a given scale. So a song in the key of G major is played using the notes G — A — B — C — D — E — F# — G. A *tuning* is a combination of pitches on the open strings of your dulcimer. It is possible to play in the key of G major in a number of different dulcimer tunings, including, but not limited to, D-G-D, D-A-D, D-G-G, G-G-G, and G-B-D.

Dulcimer tunings arose out of necessity. The original instrument was played with a melody accompanied by *drone*, or unstopped strings. The player would simply find a pitch that matched her voice and tune the melody strings so that the key note landed on the proper fret for the type of scale, or *mode*. One mode, called the *Ionian*, is familiar as the major scale; others include the *Dorian*, *Aeolian* and *Phrygian* (all minor to varying degrees), the *Mixolydian*, *Lydian* and *Locrian*. These names come from ancient church music; mountain people had various names for both modes and tunings, such as *Mountain Minor*, or "Old Joe Clark" tuning. Old-time music still retains these echoes of an earlier time using old scales that don't quite fit into our modern harmonic structure.

Over time, players began to experiment with new techniques, such as harmony and chordal accompaniment, superimposing new features onto many of the older tunings. For example, D-A-D tuning is sometimes called *Mixolydian*. While it is true that it gives a *Mixolydian* mode beginning on the open D string, the tuning is often used to play in different keys and modes. A quick glance at the arrangements in this book revels this tuning used for songs in G major ("Beulah Land"), E minor ("Chickens Are a-Crowin'"), D major ("Turkey in the Straw") and D *Mixolydian* ("Don't Let Your Deal Go Down").

To aid to transposition, all related tunings are identical as far as how they are fingered. So a tune written in D-A-D tuning can easily be transposed down to C-G-C without any change in fingering. Likewise, a song in C-G-G would be easily played in D-A-A, bringing it up from the key of C to the slightly higher key of D.

In fact, most tunings may be moved as much as 1 and 1/2 steps up or down without too much strain placed on the instrument or its strings.

Both D-A-D and C-G-C tunings allow easy transpositions up a fourth – simply slap a capo across the third fret and play away.

Larger transpositions; say from the key of C to the key of G, require a little more thought. Since retuning a dulcimer up to G-D-G is likely to break strings, finding a way to play the song in a different tuning is essential. A common method involves simply moving from one tuning family to another – in this instance from C-G-C (*Mixolydian*, or I-V-I) to D-G-D (*Reverse Ionian*, or V-I-V). Naturally the melody would need to be refingered on different strings to accommodate the difference in pitch. The best way to do that is to learn the song well enough to play it by ear. From there, transposing to a different tuning is simple.

Songs Listed by Tuning

Here's a handy way to approach the book – play through all the songs in a favorite tuning. Sure cuts down on the knob twisting!

Remember that the D-A-A and C-G-G tunings are fingered exactly the same. If you wish, you could play through all of the songs arranged in these two tunings without retuning your dulcimer. Of course, the actual pitches will sound higher or lower than written, but the melodies will ring true. Likewise the D-A-D and C-G-C tunings share the same fingering and may be played in either tuning. Just make sure you let your accompanist know that you are playing in a different key from that written so he or she will play the proper chords.

So why didn't I simply arrange all the songs in one or the other tuning? For a couple of reasons. In the first place, not everybody is comfortable singing in the keys associated with D-A-A and D-A-D – tuning to C opens up some nice possibilities. What's more, guitarists, banjo players and autoharpists will enjoy the chance to play out of different chord positions. But to tell you the truth, I just like the sound of the dulcimer when it is tuned down to C or A. With practice, I'll bet you do, too.

D-A-A
All Are Talking of Utah
Amazing Grace
Barb'ry Allen
The Devil's Questions
Down in the Valley
Fod
I Wish I Was a Mole in the Ground
Kansas Boys/Alsea Girls
The King's Daughter Fair
Little David, Play on Your Harp
Little Liza Jane
Little Old Sod Shanty
On Top of Old Smoky
Polly Wolly Doodle
Rueben and Rachel
The Sow Took the Measles
Sweet Betsy From Pike
There's a Little Wheel a-Turnin'
Tom Dooley
When First Unto This Country

C-G-G
The Buggerboo
Eating Goober Peas
Go Tell Aunt Rhody
Groundhog
Silver Threads Among the Gold
There's More Pretty Girls Than One
The Wagoner's Lad
Whopee Ti Yi Yo

D-A-D
Acres of Clams
All Night, All Day
America (My Country 'Tis of Thee)
The Banks of the Ohio
The Battle Hymn of the Republic
Beulah Land/Dakota Land
Blood Red Roses
Bonnie Black Bess
Bury Me Not on The Lone Prairie
Careless Love
Chickens Are a-Crowin'
Darling Cory
Dixie
Don't Let Your Deal go Down
The Drunken Sailor
The E-Ri-E
The Erie Canal
Fennario
Follow the Drinking Gourd
Froggie Went a-Courtin'
The Glendy Burke
The Greenland Whale Fishery
Hallelujah, I'm a Bum
He's Got the Whole World in His Hands
In the Good Old Colony Days
Jack o' Diamonds
John Henry
Lady Mary
Let My People Go
The Little Brown Bulls
My Bonnie Lies Over the Ocean
Nobody Knows the Trouble I've Seen
Oh, Can't You Hear That Turtle Dove
Old Dog Tray
Poor Wayfaring Stranger
Quit Kickin' My Dog Around
Shenandoah
Shoo, Fly, Don't Bother Me
Steal Away
The Texas Rangers
Turkey in the Straw
The Two Sisters
When Johnny Comes Marching Home

C-G-C
Aura Lee
Beware, Oh Take Care

Camptown Races
Clementine
The Farmer's Curst Wife
Frankie and Johnnie
Home on the Range
I'm a Rambler and a Gambler
Jimmy Crack Corn
Nearer, My God, To Thee
Omie, Let Your Bangs Hang Down
One Morning in May
Pie in the Sky
Red River Valley
The Riddle Song
Simple Gifts

D-G-D
Cindy
The Crawdad Song
Cripple Creek
The Girl I Left Behind Me
Handsome Molly
I'm On My Way
Old Dan Tucker
Sourwood Mountain
Tenting Tonight
Yankee Doodle
The Yellow Rose of Texas
The Young Man Who Wouldn't Hoe Corn

D-A-C
The Cuckoo
Jeannie Fair Gentle Rosemarie
Little Mattie Groves
The Unquiet Grave
Shady Grove

D-A-G
Haul Away, Joe
The Shantyman's Life
Wedding Dress
Wondrous Love

A-A-D
Cold Rain and Snow
The Lady From York
Oh, Death
Same Old Man

A-A-A
Boatman Dance
Old Joe Clark

E-A-C
Hold On

Cold blows the wind on my true love,
And gently falls the rain.
I've never had but one true love,
And in greenwood he lies slain.

Ballads and Story Songs

Jenny Fair Gentle Rosemarie

Now sweet William to get him a wife,
Jenny fair gentle Rosemarie,
And there is Nancy and she's very bright,
And the dew flies over the green valley,
And there is Nancy and she's very bright,
And the dew flies over the green valley.

Now sweet William to the church has gone,
Jenny fair gentle Rosemarie,
He might have done better to have left her alone,
And the dew flies over the green valley,
He might have done better to have left her alone,
And the dew flies over the green valley.

Now sweet William comes in from the plow,
And he says, "Dear wife, is your dinner done now?"

She calls sweet William a paltry whelp.
"If you want any dinner you can get it yourself."

Down the barn sweet William did go,
And down with his best wether did throw.

He wrapped the skin upon his wife's back,
And with two sticks went whickety whack.

Now sweet William comes in from his plow,
And says, "Dear wife, is your dinner done now?"

She draws the table and spread the board,
And it's, "Oh dear husband," at every word

Ever since then she's been a good wife,
And I hope she'll remain so the rest of her life.

A slightly shortened version of The Wife Wrapped in Wether's Skin.
Although it may not hold up to today's standards, it has long proved popular among country folk.
(Or at least the men.) Shakespeare's The Taming of the Shrew *is another telling of the same tale.*

Barb'ry Allen

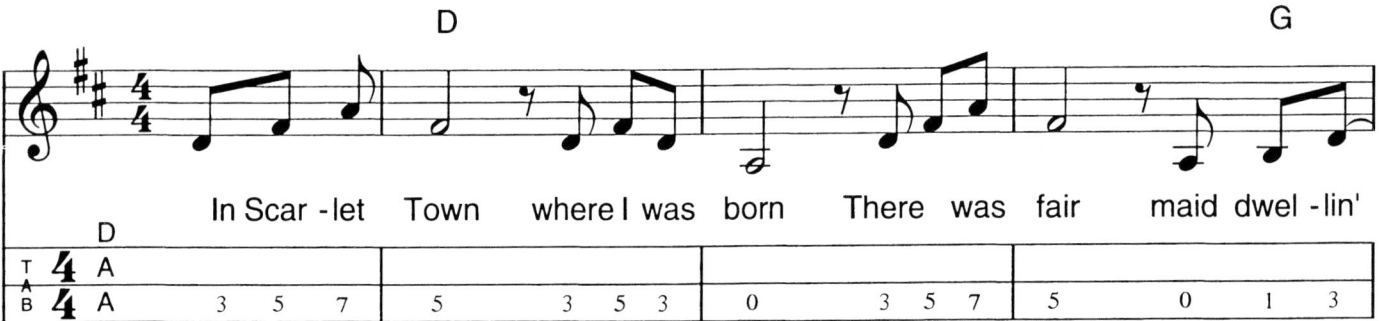
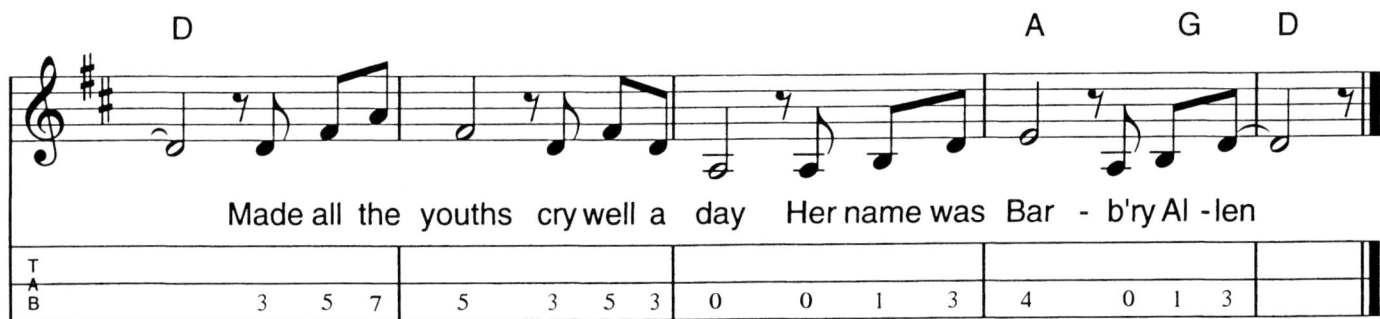

In Scarlet Town where I was born
There was a fair maid dwellin';
Made all the youths cry well a day,
Her name was Barb'ry Allen.

It was in the springtime month of May
When green buds were a swellin'
Young William Green, from the North Country
Fell in love with Barb'ry Allen.

He sent his man down to her then,
To the place where she was dwellin'.
"Come quick, come quick, my master's sick,
If your name be Barb'ry Allen."

Then slowly, slowly, raise she up
And slowly she drew nigh him.
And all she said, when she got there,
"Young man I think you're dyin'."

"Oh yes I'm sick, so very sick,
Death o'er my frame is stealin'.
But better by thee, I still may be,
One kiss from you could cure me."

Then slowly, slowly, raise she up,
And slowly, slowly, left him
And sighin' said, she could not stay,
Since death, of life, had left him.

As she was walkin' o'er the moor
She heard his death bell tollin',
And ev'ry peal, did again reveal,
"Hardhearted Barb'ry Allen."

Then it's "Father, Father, make my grave,
And make it long and narrow.
Young William died for me today,
I'll die for him tomorrow."

Then she was laid in the old church yard
And he was laid beside her.
Above his grave a red rose grew,
Above hers, a green briar.

And still they grew, and still they grew,
Till they could grow no higher.
And then they twined in a true love's knot,
The red rose and the briar.

One of the best-loved ballads, Barbara Allen was mentioned by the English diarist Samuel Pepys in 1665. I transcribed this haunting melody many years ago from an Appalachian singer whose name I have unfortunately lost.

The Lady From York

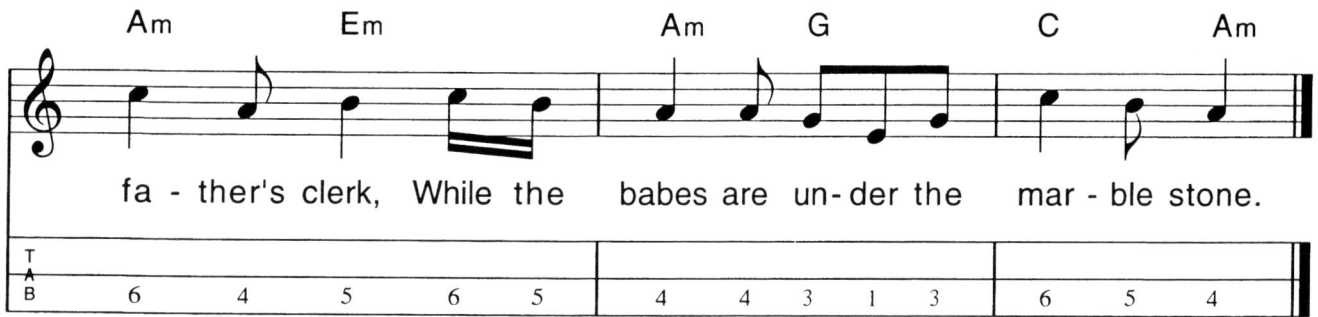

A great lady lived all in York.
Allay, allay, and all alone,
A great lady lived all in York,
And she was much loved by her father's clerk,
While the babies are under the marble stone.

She went into the deep oak wood,
And birthed her babes as best she could.

She leaned on the oak, she leaned on the thorn,
And under the sky her babes were born.

She took her dress off o'er her head,
To wrap up her babes when they were dead.

She walked up in her father's hall,
The fairest maid amongst them all.

She looked out o'er her castle wall,
And saw two little boys a-playin' ball.

"Come, pretty boys, if you were mine,
I'd dress you up in silk so fine."

"Oh mother dear, when we were thine,
You robbed us of our life divine."

"But now we in the ground do lie,
And you have the fires of hell to try."

A version of The Cruel Mother, *this ballad tells the story of a high born young lady who attempts to hide the evidence of her unwise tryst through murder most foul. As with all good ghost stories, her deed comes back to haunt her. My version is an amalgam of several texts.*

The King's Daughter Fair

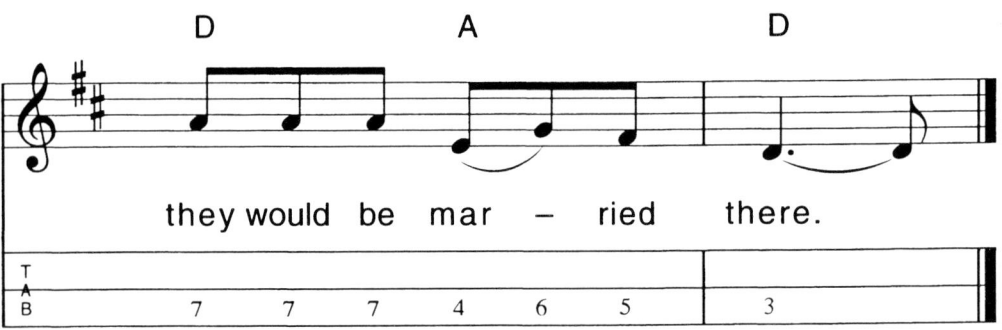

There was a noble English lad,
Who courted a king's daughter fair.
He promised to take her to the north country,
And they would be married there.

"Now you must get me some of your father's gold
And some of your mother's fee,
And two of the finest horses in these stables
Where there are thirty and three."

She mounted on her milk-white steed;
He rode the dappled gray.
They rode till they came to the salt sea shore
A little before it was day.

"Mount off, mount off from your milk-white steed,
Mount off, mount off," said he,
"For it's six king's daughters I've drowned here
And the seventh one you shall be."

"Now you must take off you silken dress
And give it unto me,
For I think it looks too rich and too rare
To rot in the salty sea."

"Well, if I must take off this silken dress,
You must turn your back unto me,
For I don't think it fit that a ruffian like thee
An undressed lady to see."

He wheeled himself around about
And bitterly she did weep.
She caught him by the coat collar
And plunged him into the deep.

"Take hold, take hold of my finger, my love,
Take hold with your lily-white hand,
And I will make you my own true love
And the fairest in the land."

"Lie there, lie there, lie there," said she,
"Lie there instead of me,
For if six pretty fair maids you've drowned here
The seventh one drownéd thee."

She mounted on her milk-white steed,
She led the dappled gray.
She rode till she came to her father's house,
A little before it was day.

The parrot rose up in the castle so high
And unto Polly did say,
"Oh where have you been, my pretty Polly?
You tarry so long before day."

"Oh hush, oh hush, oh hush," said she,
"Don't you tell no tales on me,
And your cage shall be lined with the glittering gold
And hang from the green willow tree."

The king rose up in the castle so high
And unto the parrot did say,
"Oh what is the matter, my pretty parrot?
You prattle so long before day."

"Nothing's the matter with me, kind sir,
Nothing's the matter, I say.
But there were two white kittens that bothered me so
I called Polly to drive them away."

"Well done, well done, well done," said she,
"Well done, well done," said she.
"Now your cage shall be lined with the glittering gold
And hang in the green willow tree."

A variant of Lady Isabel *and the* Elf-Knight *wherein a clever young woman outwits her evil seducer. Surprisingly, she is more concerned that her father's pet parrot may give her away for leaving home without permission than that she has just turned the tables on a murderer!*

The Banks of The Ohio

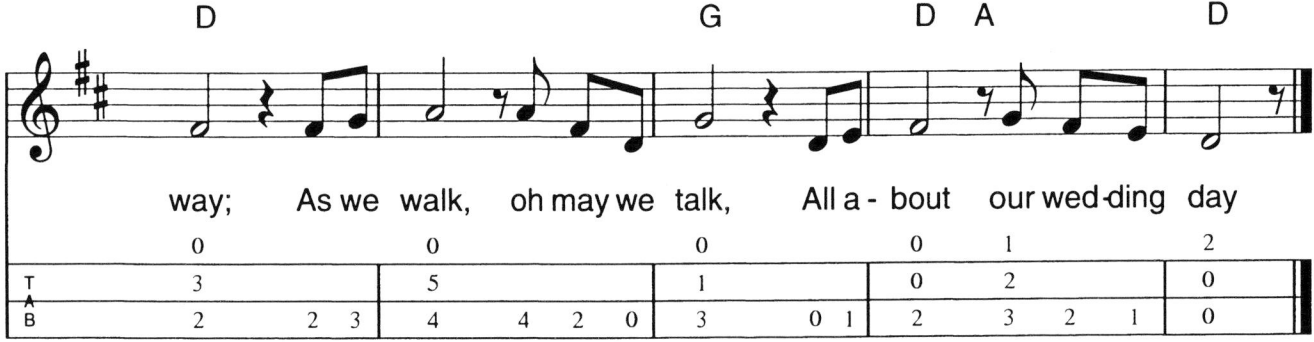

I asked my love to take a walk,
Just to walk a little way,
And as we walk, oh may we talk
All about our wedding day.

CH
Only say that you'll be mine,
And in my home we'll happy be,
Down beside, where the waters flow,
Down by the banks of the Ohio.

I took her by her lily-white hand,
I dragged her down to the river bank,
And there I pushed her in to drown,
And I watched her as she floated down.

I came home at half past one,
Thinking about the deed I'd done;
I had murdered the only girl I love
Because she would not marry me.

The very next day, at half past four,
The sheriff's men knocked on my door,
Sayin', "Young man, it's time to go,
Down to the banks of the Ohio."

This wholly American murder ballad seems to be made up from fragments of many earlier songs. Although the murderer isn't identified here, I've heard these kind of songs called "Willie Ballads" because so often that's the young rake's name. So let this be a warning, don't ever go down to the river with Willie!

The Unquiet Grave

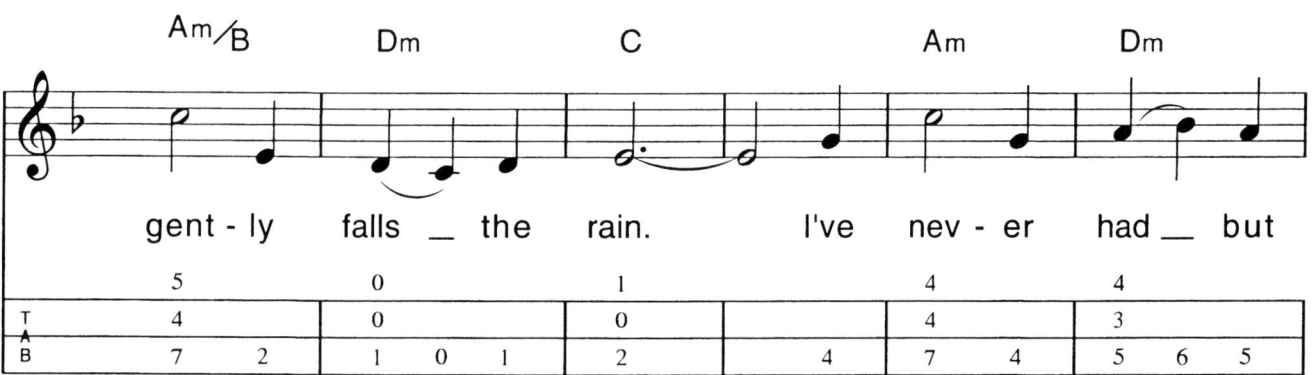
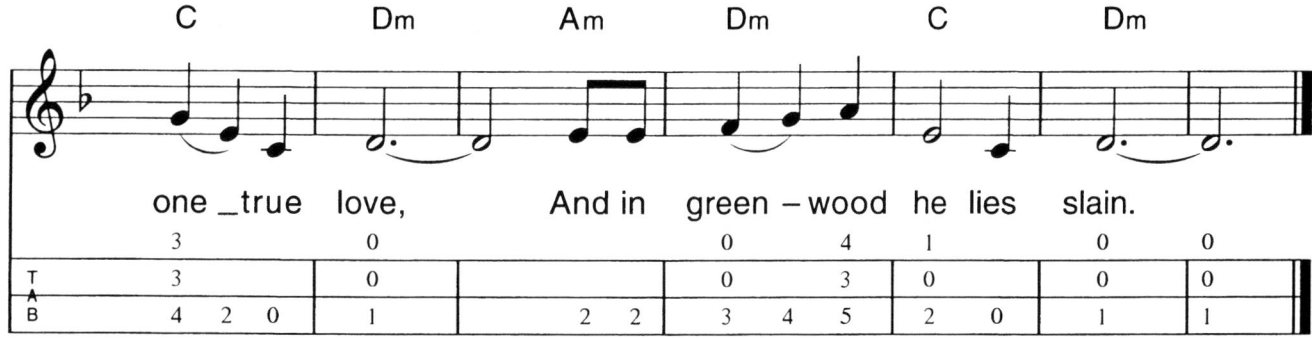

Cold blows the wind on my true love,
And gently falls the rain.
I've never had but one true love,
And in greenwood he lies slain.

I'll do as much for my true love
As ever a young girl may.
I'll sit and mourn all on his grave
For twelve month and a day.

When twelve months and a day had passed,
The ghost did rise and speak,
"Who sits weeping on my grave
And will not let me sleep?"

"Tis I, tis I, your own true love
Who keeps you from your sleep,
Just one kiss from your cold clay lips
Is all that I would seek."

"My breast is cold as any clay,
My breath is earthly strong,
And if you kiss my cold clay lips
Your time it won't be long."

"How oft on yonder grave, sweetheart,
Where we were wont to walk,
The fairest flower that e're I knew
Has withered to a stalk."

Excessive mourning disturbs the dead;
a common theme expressed uncommonly well in this Appalachian setting of the English ballad.

The Farmer's Curst Wife

There was an old farmer who lived on hill
If he ain't moved away he's living there still,
And hi diddle-um diddle-i-day
Diddle-um diddle-i-day.

The Devil came up to the farmer one day,
Sayin', "One of your family I'm taking away."

"Take my wife, with all my heart,
And I hope by golly that you never part."

He put the old lady into a sack,
And away they went, clickety clack.

When the Devil got to the fork in the road
He said, "Old woman you're a heck of a load."

When the Devil got her up to the gates of Hell,
It's "Stoke up the fires, we'll bake her well!"

Up came a little devil with a ball and chains,
Out came her foot and she's kicked out his brains.

Then nine little devils went climbing the wall,
Sayin' "Take her back, daddy, she'll murder us all!"

The old man was peepin' out of a crack
When up comes the Devil a' bringin' her back.

This proves that the women are better than men;
They can go down to hell and come back again.

Another one that is far older than it may appear. Versions of this ballad have turned up in places as far afield as Scandinavia, Rome and even India. Like a great many songs popular on both sides of the Atlantic, it was documented by the great ballad collector Francis Child.

Fennario

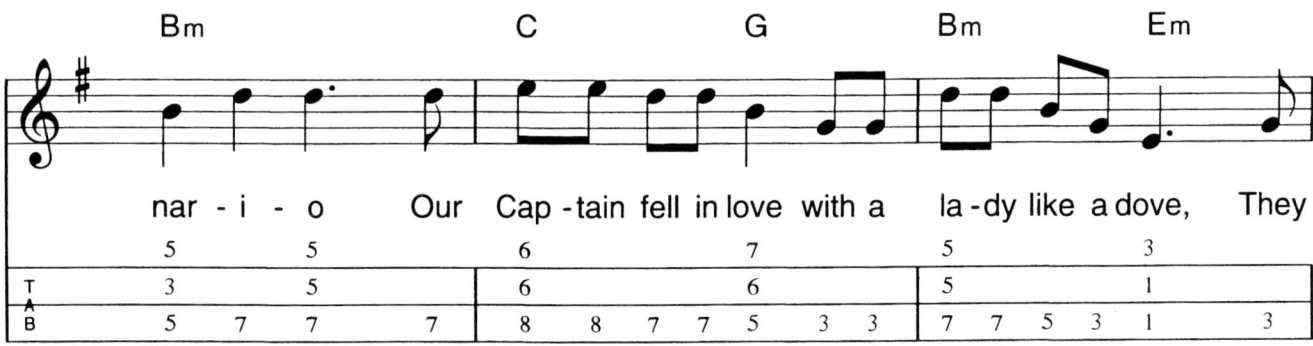
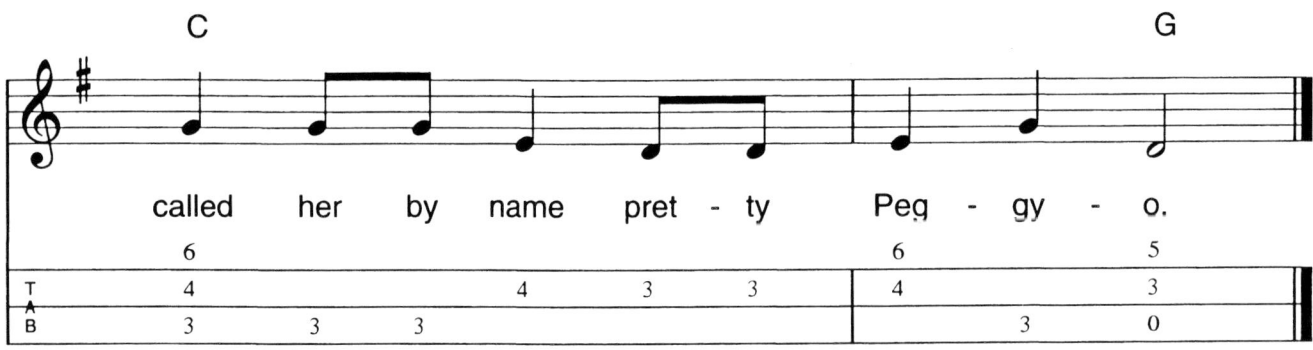

As we marched down to Fennario,
As we marched down to Fennario;
Our captain fell in love with a lady like a dove
They called her by name pretty Peggy-o.

What will your mother think, pretty Peggy-o?
What will your mother think, pretty Peggy-o?
What will your mother think, when she hears the coins clink,
And the soldiers all marching before ye, oh.

In a carriage you will ride, pretty Peggy-o,
In a carriage you will ride, pretty Peggy-o,
In a carriage you will ride, with your true love by your side
As fair as any maiden in the country-o.

Come skipping all down the stairs, pretty Peggy-o,
Come skipping all down the stairs, pretty Peggy-o,
Come skipping all down the stairs, combing back your long yellow hair,
And bid your farewell to sweet William-o.

Sweet William is dead, pretty Peggy-o,
Sweet William is dead, pretty Peggy-o,
Sweet William is dead, and he died for a maid,
The fairest maid in the country-o.

If ever I return, pretty Peggy-o,
If ever I return, pretty Peggy-o,
If ever I return, all your cities I will burn,
Destroying all the ladies in the country-o

Ballads always seem to leave out more than they tell; maybe this is why they can be so powerful. Why is the narrator so intent on destroying all the ladies? After all, it wasn't he who died of a broken heart. Or was it?

The Two Sisters

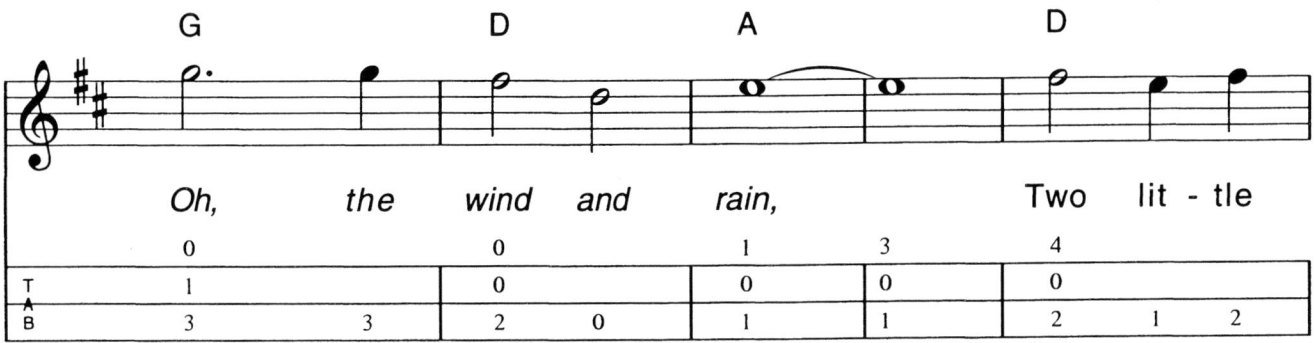
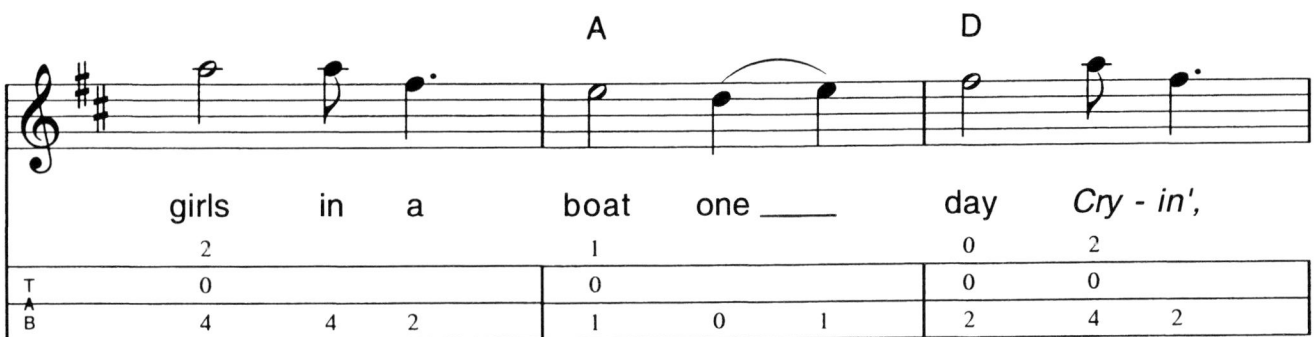
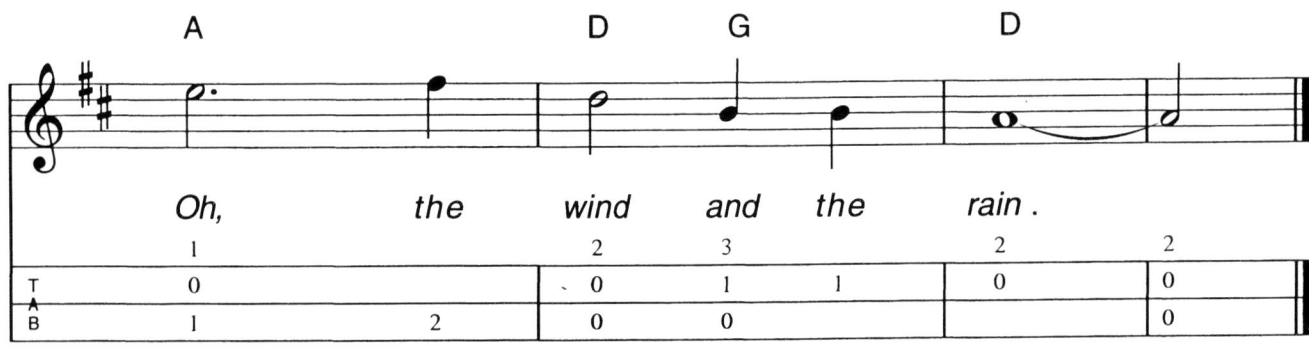

There were two little girls in a boat one day,
  Oh, the wind and the rain.
Two little girls in a boat one day.
  Cryin' oh, the wind and the rain.

And they floated down by the old mill dam,
  Oh, the wind and the rain.
They floated down by the old mill dam.
  Cryin' oh, the wind and the rain.

Charles Miller came out with his long, long hook,
  Oh, the wind and the rain.
Miller came out with his long long, hook.
  Cryin' oh, the wind and the rain.

And he hooked her in by her long yellow hair,
  Oh, the wind and the rain.
He hooked her in by her long yellow hair.
  Cryin' oh, the wind and the rain.

He made fiddle strings from her long yellow hair,
  Oh, the wind and the rain.
He made fiddle strings from her long yellow hair.
  Cryin' oh, the wind and the rain.

He made fiddle pegs from her long finger bones,
  Oh, the wind and the rain.
He made fiddle pegs from her long finger bones.
  Cryin' oh, the wind and the rain.

But the only song that the fiddle would play,
  Oh, the wind and the rain.
The only song that the fiddle would play was,
  Oh, the wind and the rain.

A tantalizing fragment from a far older tale of love, jealousy, murder, and revenge. In some versions the magical instrument is a harp which sings by itself and fingers the perpetrator, so to speak.

One Morning in May

As I was out walking one morning in May,
I spied a fair couple a-making their way,
The one was a maiden, a maiden so fair,
And the other was a soldier, a brave volunteer.

"Oh where are you going my pretty fair maid?"
"Just down by the river, just down by the shade,
Just down by the river, just down by the spring
To see the waters gliding and hear the nightingales sing."

They hadn't been sitting but an hour or so
When he drew from his knapsack a fiddle and bow,
And the tune that he played made the valleys to ring.
"Oh, hark," cried the maiden, "Hear the nightingales sing!"

"And now," said the soldier, "it's time to give o'er."
"Oh no," cried the maiden, "won't you play one tune more?
For I'd rather hear your fiddle and the touch of one string
Than to see the waters gliding and hear the nightingales sing."

"Oh," cried the maiden, "won't you please marry me?"
"Oh no," cried the soldier, "that never can be.
I've a wife back in Ireland and children twice three,
Two wives and the army's too many for me."

"I'll go home to Ireland and stay there one year,
I'll spend all my money on whiskey and beer;
But if ever I return it will be in the spring,
To see the waters gliding and hear the nightingale sing."

A most beautiful tribute to the power of a well-played tune. It's found all over the English-speaking world –
There's even a setting where the fiddler's a Texas cowpuncher.

Lady Mary

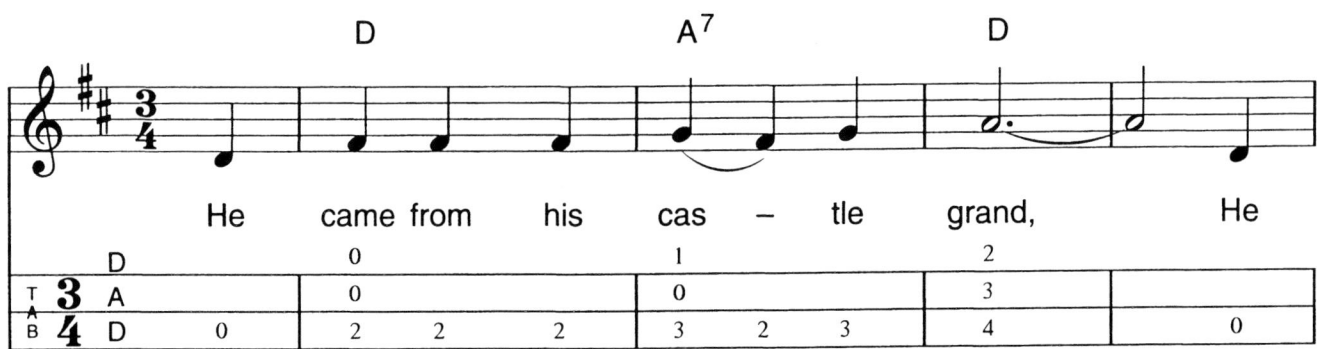
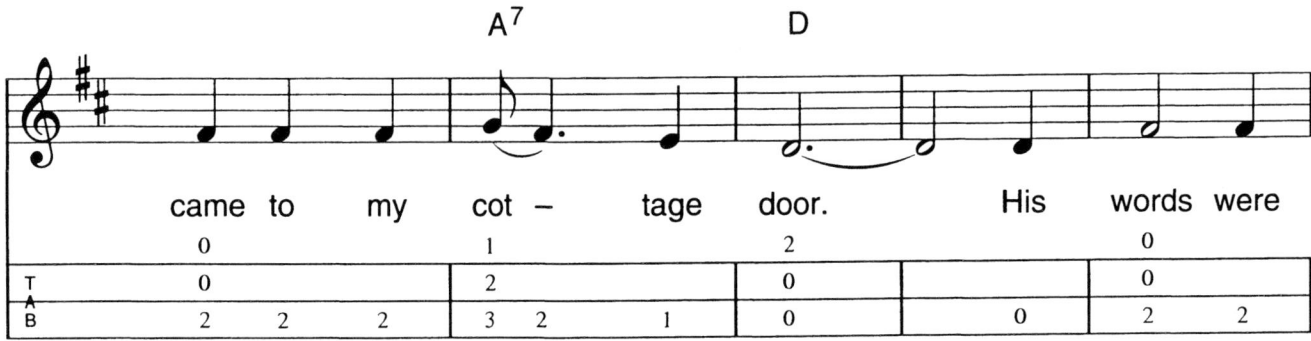
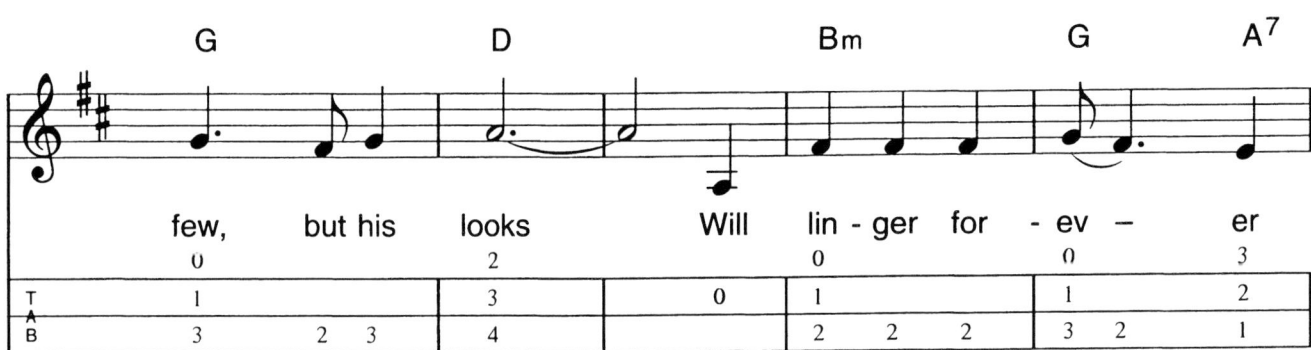
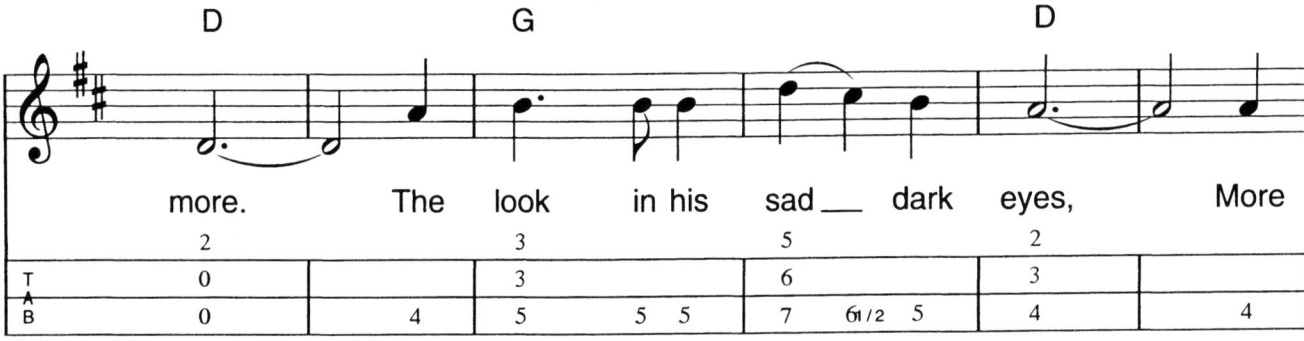

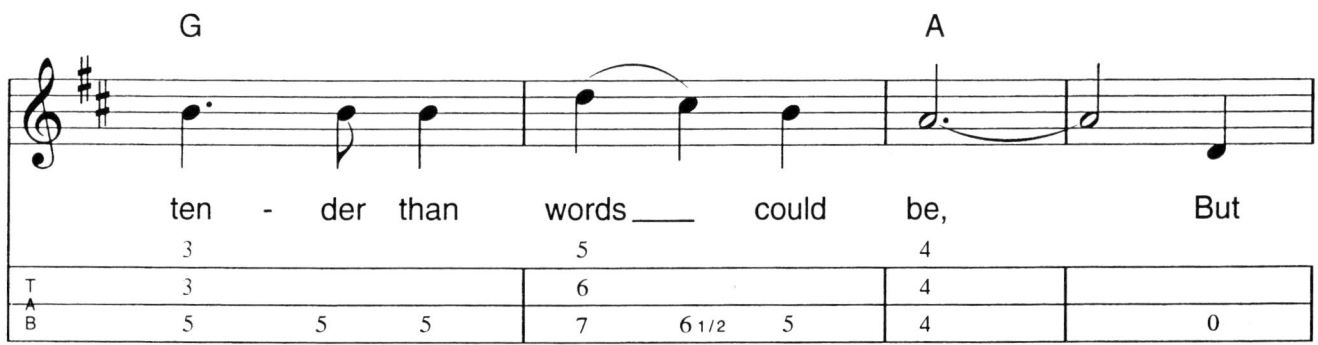
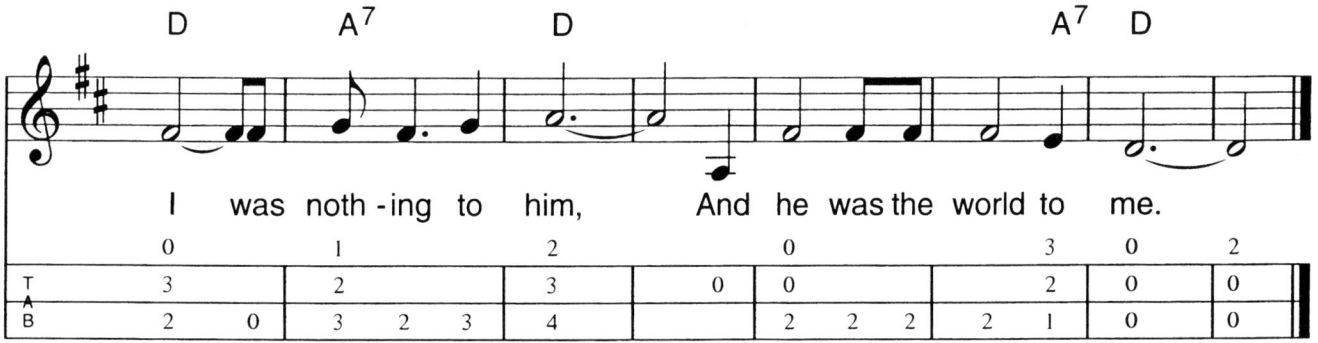

He came from his castle grand,
He came to my cottage door.
His words were few, but his looks
Will linger forevermore.
The look in his sad dark eyes,
More tender than words can be,
But I was nothing to him,
And he was the world to me.

There in the garden she stands,
All dressed in satin and lace,
Lady Mary so cold and so strange
Who finds in his heart no place.
He knew I would be his bride
With a kiss for a lifetime fee.
But I was nothing to him
And he was the world to me.

And now in his palace grand
On a flow'r strewn cot he lies.
His beautiful lids are closed
All over his sad dark eyes.
All among the ladies who mourn,
Why should I a mourner be?
For I was nothing to him,
And he was the world to me.

A lovely old ballad of true love wronged. I'd first heard this sung as a western song, only recently have I learned it is also found in the Ozarks.

The Devil's Questions

If you don't answer my questions well, Sing nine-ty nine and nine-ty, I'll car-ry you off to my home in hell And you are the fair-est __ bon-nie.

If you don't answer my questions well
    Sing ninety nine and ninety,
I'll carry you off and I live in hell,
    And you are the fairest bonnie.

Oh, what is whiter far than milk,
    Sing ninety nine and ninety,
And what is softer than the silk?
    And you are the fairest bonnie.

The snow is whiter far than milk,
    Sing ninety nine and ninety,
And down is softer than the silk.
    And you are the fairest bonnie.

Oh, what is louder than a horn,
    Sing ninety nine and ninety,
And what is sharper than a thorn?
    And you are the fairest bonnie.

The thunder's louder than a horn,
    Sing ninety nine and ninety,
And death is sharper than a thorn.
    And you are the fairest bonnie.

Oh what is higher than a tree,
    Sing ninety nine and ninety,
And what is deeper than the sea?
    And you are the fairest bonnie.

Heaven is higher than a tree,
    Sing ninety nine and ninety,
And hell is deeper than the sea.
    And you are the fairest bonnie.

And now I have answered your questions well,
    Sing ninety nine and ninety,
So get you off to burn in hell.
    And I am the fairest bonnie.

One of the best-loved ballads in the world. A young maid meets the Devil by the side of the road and bests him at his own game. Whose to blame her for boasting in the final verse?

Little Mattie Groves

Noter Style

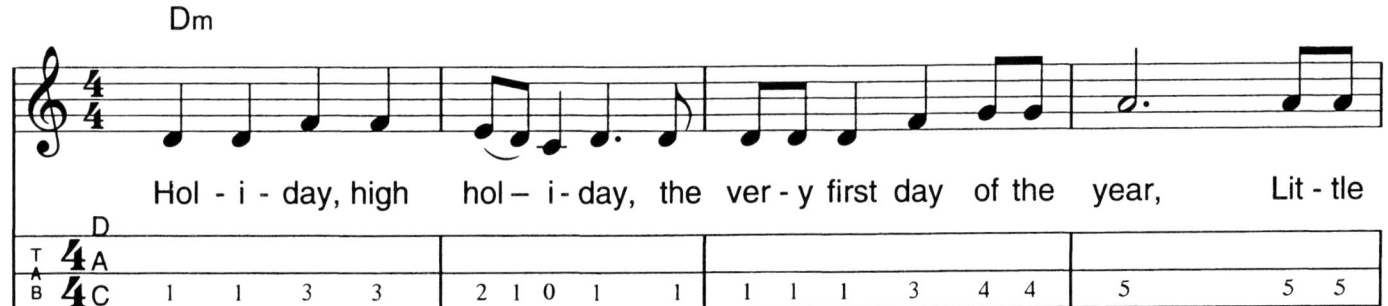

Holiday, high holiday,
The very first day of the year;
Little Mattie Groves he went to church
Some holy words to hear.

The first was a lady wearing black
Came into the hall,
And then came in Lord Arling's wife
The fairest of them all.

Then up spoke Little Mattie Groves
And this was her reply,
"You must come home with me tonight
All in my arms to lie."

"Little Mattie Groves, with me come stay,
I'll hide you out of sight,
And serve you there beyond compare
And sleep with you this night."

"I cannot go, I dare not go,
I fear not, for my life.
I can see by your middle ring
You are Lord Arling's wife."

"It's true I am Lord Arling's wife,
I can't deny it all,
But he's gone south to fair England
The flower of them all."

Her footy page did listen well
To all that they did say
And off to tell Lord Arling's shame
He quickly sped away.

He ran till he came to the waterside;
He buckled his breast and swam.
Until at last he came before
Lord Arling and all his men.

"What news, what news, my bonnie boy,
What news bring you to me?
What wrong has fell my house and lands,
While I have been away?"

"No wrong has fell your house and lands
While you have been away,
But Mattie Groves is in the arms
Of your fair lady gay."

"If this be false," Lord Aling cried,
"As I know it to be;
I'll raised up a scaffold high
And hangéd you shall be."

"Lord Arling, should what I've said
Prove false as false could be;
You may raise a scaffold high
And hangéd I shall be."

Lord Arling called to him his men
To gather and to go,
But bound them not a word to speak
And not a horn to blow.

The foremost one among the men
Knew little Mattie well;
He raised his horn up to his lips
And blew it loud and shrill.

"What's this, what's this," cried Mattie Groves.
"What's this that I do hear?
I hear the horn of Arling's men
The sound that I most fear!"

"Lie down, lie down, little Mattie Groves,
And keep my back from cold.
It's nothing but my father's horn
That calls the sheep to fold."

First they fell to huggin' and a-kissin'
And then they fell asleep,
And when they woke at the break of day
Lord Arling stood at their feet.

"How do you like my feather bed
And how do you like my sheets?
And how do you like my fair lady
Lies in your arms asleep?"

"It's well do I like your feather bed,
And well do I like your sheets,
But it's better do I like this fair lady
Who lies in my arms asleep."

"Get up, get up little Mattie Groves,
And all your clothes put on,
I'll never have it said in fair Scotland
That I slew a naked man."

"I'll get up," said Mattie Groves,
"Though I fear will cost my life,
You have got two bitter swords,
And I have a pocket knife."

"It's true I have two bitter swords,
They cost me dear in purse,
But you shall have the better one
And I shall have the worse."

"And you shall strike the very first blow
And kill me if you can,
But I shall strike the very next blow
And kill you if I can."

The very first blow that Mattie struck
Wounded Arling sore,
The very next blow that Arling struck,
Little Mattie struck no more.

"Get up, get up my gay lady,
Put on your pretty clothes,
Tell me who it is that you love best;
Is it me or Mattie Groves?"

She lifted up little Mattie's face
And kissed it cheek and chin,
"It's Mattie Groves I'd rather kiss
Than you or all your kin."

He took his wife by her lily-white hand
And led her through the hall;
He's cut off her head with his bitter sword
And kicked it against the wall.

"Woe to me," Lord Arling cried,
"Why stayed you not my hand?
Today I've killed the fairest folk
That lived in all Scotland."

A dramatic telling of Little Musgrave and Lady Barnard, one of the great ballads of the English-speaking world. Long as it is, even this version leaves out much. Once-upon-a-time, ballads provided entertainment full of great stories, strong characters and twisting subplots.

Chickens crowin' on Sourwood Mountain
Hey de ding dong doodle um day...

Songs from the Southern Highlands

Shady Grove

Noter Style

Shady Grove, my true love;
Shady Grove my darlin'
Shady Grove, my true love
I'm goin' back to Harlan.

Went to see my Shady Grove,
She was standing by the door,
Shoes and her stockings in her hand
Little bare feet on the floor.

Wish I had a high brown horse,
Corn to feed him on;
Pretty little girl to stay at home
And feed him when I'm gone.

Shady Grove, my little love,
Shady Grove, I know.
You are the darlin' of my heart,
Stay till the sun goes down.

When I was a little boy
I played with a pocket knife,
Now that I'm a full-grown man
I'm lookin' for a wife.

When I was first learning to play the dulcimer in Southern California I used to practice out under a tree in a park. One day a lanky stranger from Kentucky appeared out of nowhere. He whittled me a noter and taught me this song: "If you're gonna play the dang thing, the least you could do is play it right!"

Sourwood Mountain

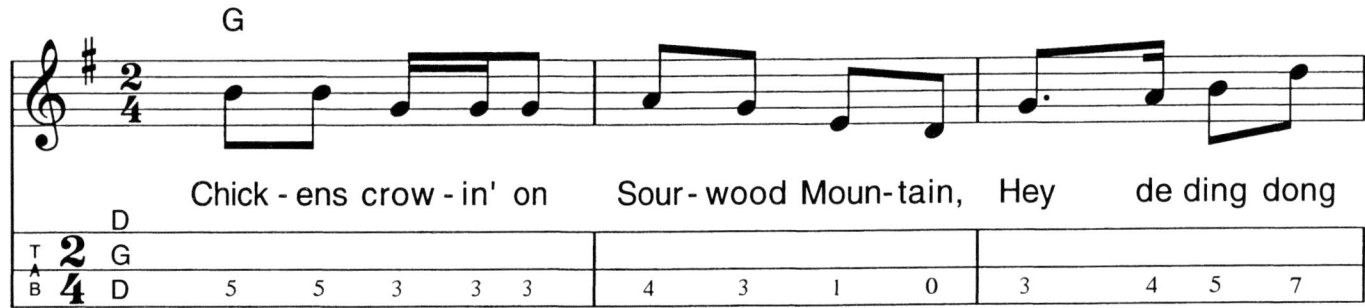

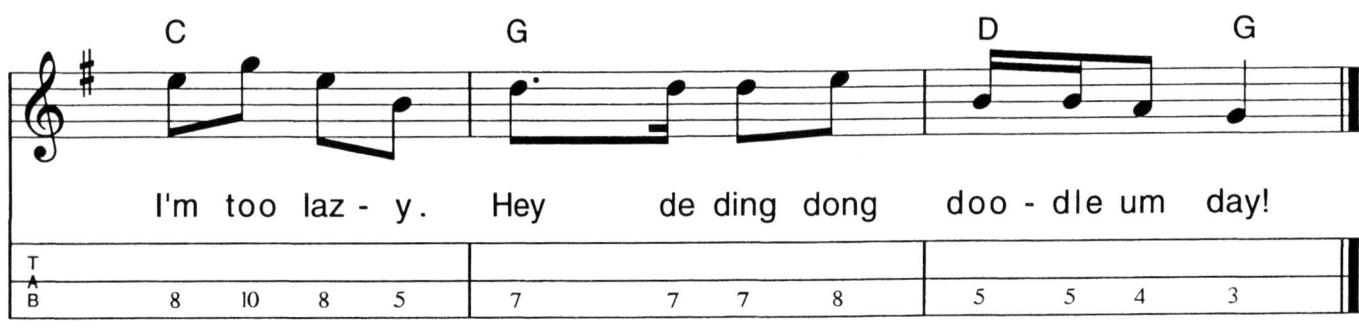

Chickens crowin' on Sourwood Mountain
Hey de ding dong doodle um day,
So many pretty girls I can't count 'em!
Hey de ding dong doodle um day.

My true love's a blue-eyed daisy,
Hey de ding dong doodle um day,
She won't work 'n' I'm too lazy.
Hey de ding dong doodle um day.

My true love's a blue-eyed daisy,
She don't kiss me, I'll go crazy!

My true love's a blue-eyed dandy;
She's as sweet as taffy candy.

My true love lives up the holler,
She won't come, and I won't foller.

It used to be you heard this song everywhere. If a hometown revue, radio comedy, or big Hollywood movie needed to set the tone for a rural wingding, Sourwood Mountain *was likely part of the soundtrack.*

The Cuckoo

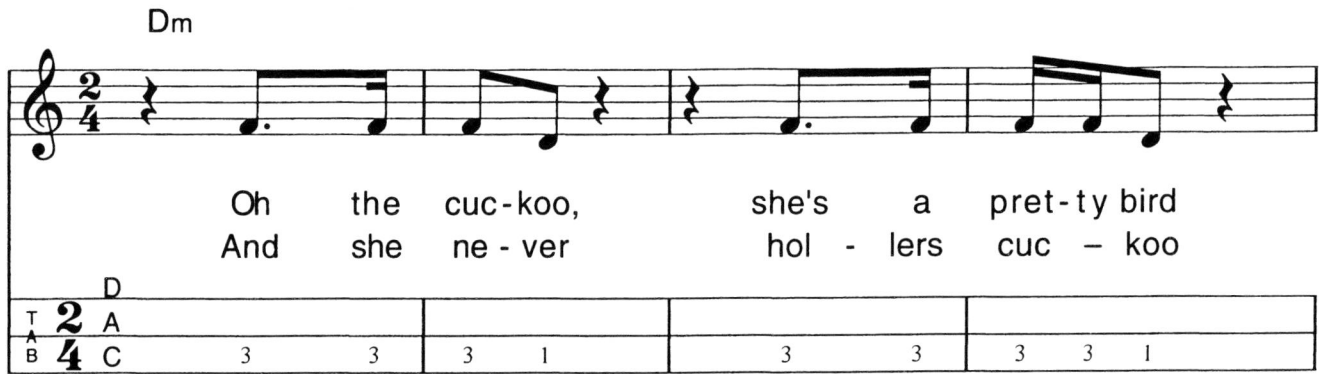
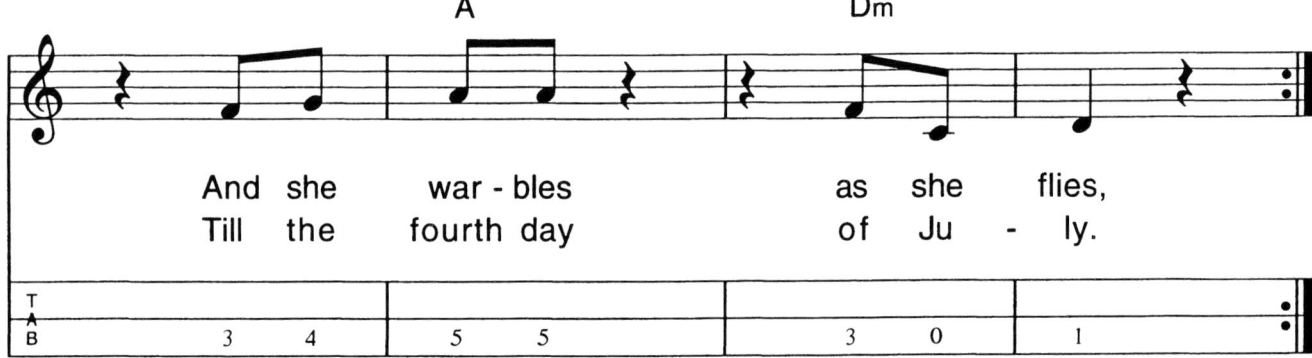

Oh the cuckoo, she's a pretty bird
And she warbles as she flies.
And she never hollers cuckoo
Till the fourth day of July.

Gonna build me a log cabin
On a mountain so high,
So I can see Willie
As he goes on by.

Sometimes I wonder
What makes women love men;
I look back and I wonder
What makes men love them.

Jack of diamonds, Jack of diamonds,
I know you from old;
You've robbed my poor pockets
Of my silver and gold.

I've played cards in England
I've played cards in Spain;
I'll bet you five dollars
That I'll beat you this game.

Oh, the cuckoo, she's a pretty bird;
I wish she was mine.
And she never drinks water,
She always drinks wine.

Related to any number of British and American songs and ballads, The Cuckoo *is the quintessential old-time mountain song. It is best sung with a high lonesome voice to an austere accompaniment. I have always wondered what was so special about Willie that he shows up in so many great songs.*

Tom Dooley

Hang your head, Tom Dooley,
Hang your head and cry,
Killed poor Laura Foster,
You know you're bound to die.

You took her on the mountain,
As God almighty knows,
Took her to the mountain,
And there you hid her clothes.

You took her to the roadside,
Where you begged to be excused,
Took her to the roadside,
And there you hid her shoes.

You took her to the hillside,
To make her your wife,
Took her to the hillside,
And there you took her life.

You dug a grave four feet long,
Dug it three feet deep.
Throw'd the cold clay on her,
And tramped it with your feet.

Take down my old fiddle
And play it all you please,
This time tomorrow
It'll be no use to me.

This time tomorrow,
Where do you reckon I'll be?
If it hadn't be for the sheriff
I'd a-been in Tennessee.

The song that launched the folk revival of the 60's.
Tom Dooley was a real murderer from North Carolina, where the song exists in several forms.
The verse about the violin harks back to the story of Quince Dillon, who fiddled his way out of the gallows.

Groundhog

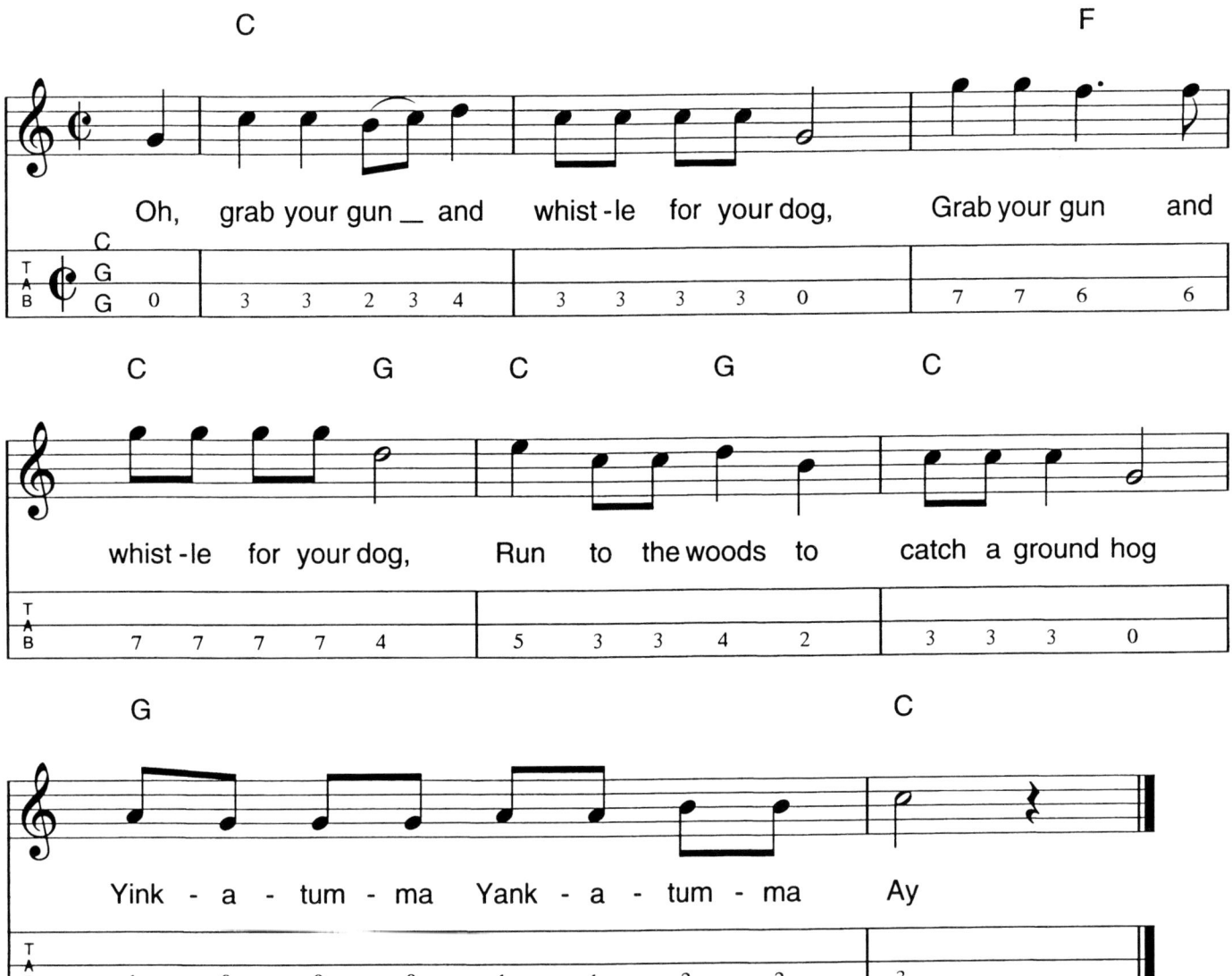

Oh, grab your gun and whistle for your dog,
Grab your gun and whistle for your dog,
Run to the woods to catch a ground hog.
Yink-a-tum-ma, Yank-a-tum-ma Ay

That old woman was the mother of us all,
That old woman was the mother of us all,
Feed us on whistle pig soon as we could crawl.
Yink-a-tum-ma, Yank-a-tum-ma Ay

Up come Jonah from the plough,
Catch that whistle pig, catch him now.

Treed him in a rock, treed him in a log,
Doggone, boys, he's a big ground hog.

Skin that whistle pig, save the hide,
Makes the best shoe strings ever been tied.

Put him in a pot, put it on to bile,
Smells so good you could smell him a mile.

Up comes the baby with a snigger and a grin,
Ground hog gravy all over his chin.

Up comes sister, happy as a crane,
Said she'd eat them red-hot brains.

Eat up that whistle pig, all they could hold,
Till there's none left in the bowl.

February the Second is quite possibly a remnant of an ancient round of European rural holidays celebrating the changing seasons. Although other holidays like Christmas and Halloween have succumbed to astonishing levels of commercialization, Groundhog Day remains blissfully simple.
The rodent sees his shadow, or not. That's about it.

Same Old Man

Noter Style

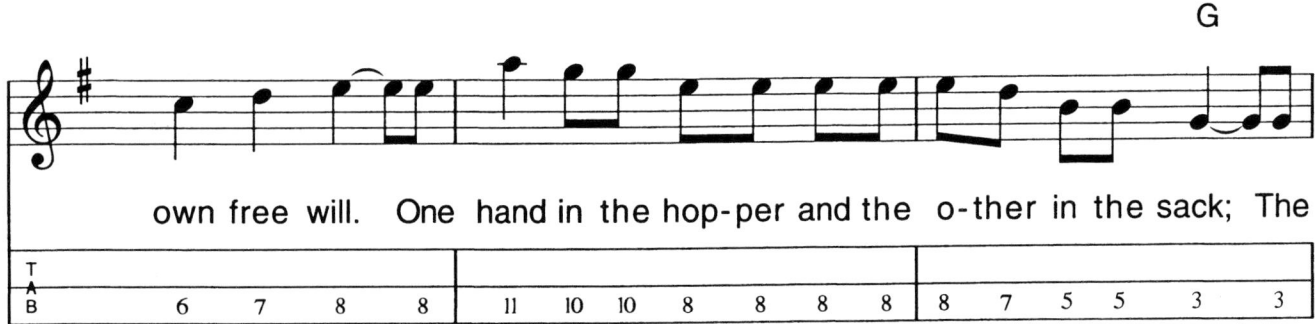
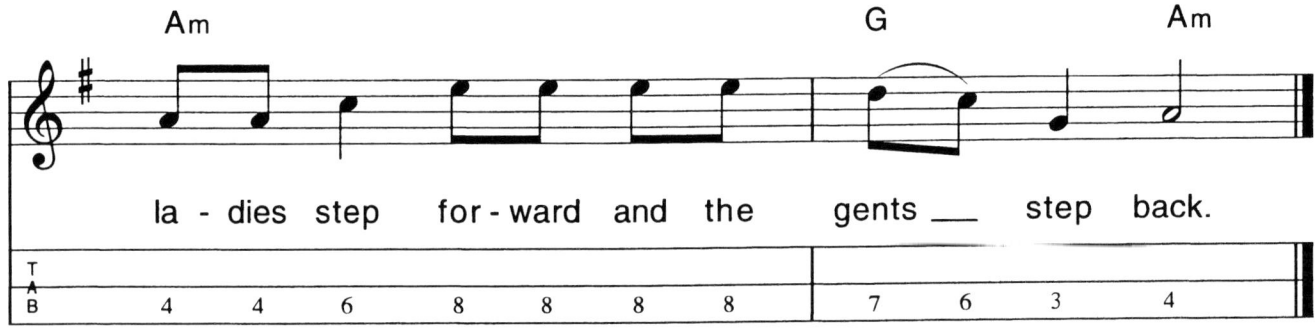

Same old man workin' at the mill
And the mill turns around of its own free will.
One hand in the hopper and the other in the sack;
The ladies step forward and the gents step back.

Up spoke the little leatherwing'd bat,
"I'll tell to you the reason that,
The reason that I fly by night,
Because I've lost my heart's delight."

Up spoke the raven as he flew,
"If I were a young man I'd have two;
If one got saucy and wanted to go,
I'd have a new string for my bow."

Up spoke the owl with his head so white,
"It's a lonesome day and a lonesome night,
I thought I heard a pretty girl say,
Court all night and sleep all day"

Up spoke the lonesome turtle dove,
"I'll tell you how to win her love.
Keep her up both night and day;
Never give her time to say you nay."

A lively play-party song. Dancing may have been a sin to some, but there was never any harm in just acting out the words of the song. Though I have heard many different sets of words sung to this tune these seem to echo something deeper from a far off time.

Omie, Let Your Bangs Hang Down

Little Omie, let your bangs hang down;
Little Omie let your bangs hang down.
Let your bangs hang down,
Let them drag along the ground,
Little Omie let your bangs hang down.

It's, "Daddy, where you been so long?
Daddy, where you been so long?"
When I come 'round the hill
With a five dollar bill,
It's, "Daddy, where you been so long?"

This one's a mystery to me. I think it's a cross between a couple of very different songs, the murder ballad Omie Wise *and* I Wish I was a Mole in the Ground. *Or maybe its just about a young girl who wouldn't cut her hair.*

Cold Rain and Snow

Noter Style

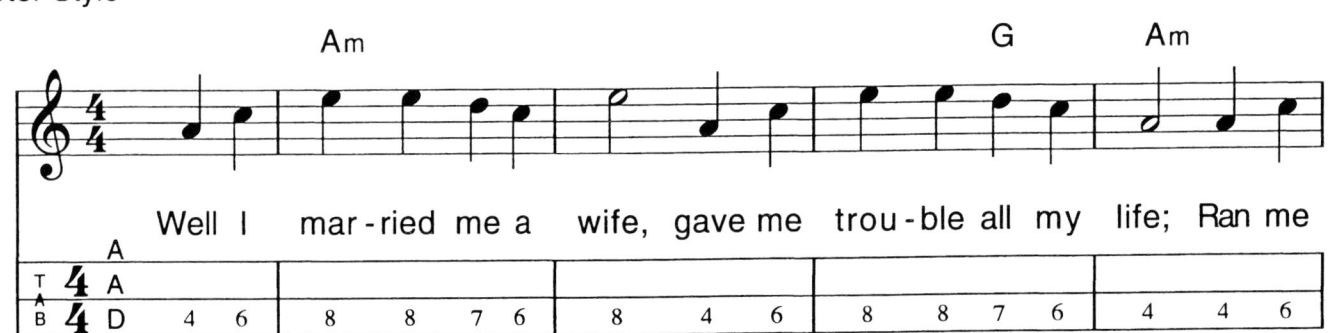

Well, I married me a wife,
Gave me trouble all my life;
Ran me out in the cold rain and snow.
Rain and snow,
Oh, Lord;
Ran me out in the cold rain and snow.

She came running all down the stairs,
Combing back her long yellow hair;
I'm so broke and I'm hungry, too.
Hungry, too,
Oh, Lord,
I'm so broke and I'm hungry, too.

Well, I ain't got no use,
For your red apple juice,
And I ain't gonna be treated this a-way.
This a-way,
Oh, Lord;
I ain't gonna be treated this a-way.

She came running all in the room,
Where she met her fatal doom,
And I ain't gonna be treated this a-way.
This a-way,
Oh, Lord;
I ain't gonna be treated this a-way.

*Although it is hard to sing songs such as this these days without a shudder,
they do represent a powerful stream in American folklore.
A quick spin of the radio dial will demonstrate that these themes are still very much alive.*

Cindy

I wish I was an apple
A-hanging on a tree,
And every time my Cindy passed by
She'd take a bite of me.

> CH
> Get along home, Cindy, Cindy;
> Get along home, Cindy, Cindy;
> Get along home, Cindy, Cindy;
> I'll marry you some day.

You ought to see my Cindy,
She lives away down south;
She is so sweet the honey bees
Buzz around her mouth.

I wish I had a needle,
As fine as I could sew,
I'd sew that gal to my coattails
And down the road I'd go.

The higher grows the berry tree
The sweeter grows the berry,
The more you hug and kiss the girls
The more they want to marry.

She took me to her parlor
She cooled me with her fan,
She said that she would be my wife
If I would be her man.

One of those great songs that once was sung everywhere from the parlor to the classroom to the stage but now seems to have momentarily fallen out of favor. Feel free to insert any verses you want – words to dance tunes and play-party songs tend to be pretty much interchangeable.

Cripple Creek

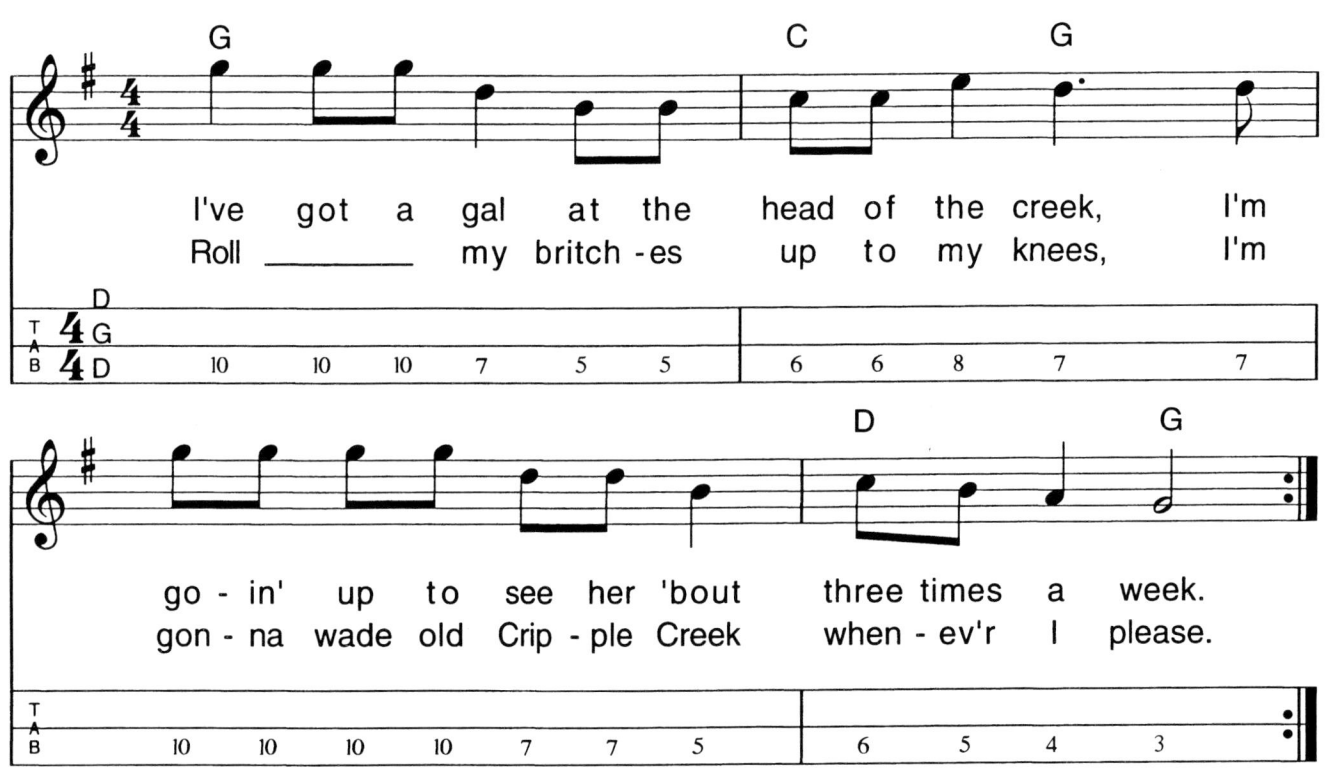
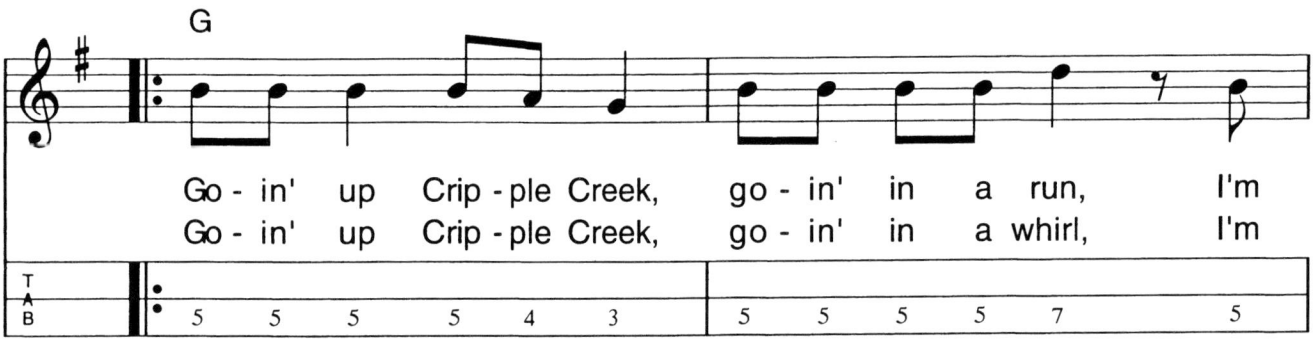
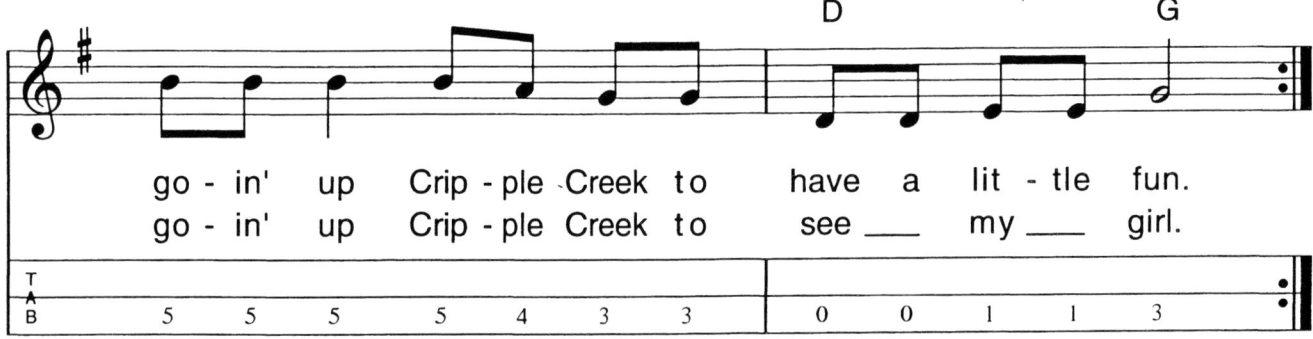

I've got a gal at the head of the creek,
I'm goin' up to see her 'bout three times a week.
Roll my britches up to my knees,
I'm gonna wade old Cripple Creek whenev'r I please.

   CH
   Goin' up Cripple Creek, goin' in a run,
   I'm goin' up Cripple Creek to have a little fun.
   Goin' up Cripple Creek, goin' in a whirl,
   I'm goin' up Cripple Creek to see my girl.

Gals up Cripple Creek about half grown,
Jump on a boy like a dog on a bone,
Hills are steep and the roads are muddy,
And I'm so drunk that I can't stand steady.

She's so doggone pretty, wish she was mine,
Wrap herself around me like a sweet potato vine.
The higher up the mountain, the sweeter grows the cherry,
The younger that you court 'em, the sooner that they marry.

Although it is of unmistakable Appalachian origin, the Rocky Mountain town of Cripple Creek, Colorado has claimed this ditty as its own. Makes a good hoedown, regardless. Old time fiddle players play it in either the key of G, as given here, or in A.

Oh Death

What is this that I can see
With icy fingers taking hold of me?
I am death that none can excel,
I'll open the gates to Heav'n or Hell.

> CH
> Oh Death, Oh Death
> Won't you spare me over for another year.

Oh Death, consider my age,
Please don't take me at this stage.
My wealth is all at your command
If you will stay your icy hand.

The rich and the poor, the young and the old;
None can escape my icy hold.
No wealth, no land, no silver, no gold
None can escape my icy hold.

I'll lock your legs so you can't walk,
Lock your jaws so you can't talk;
Drop the flesh from off your frame,
The earth and the worms both have a claim.

I first heard this haunting song in the early 1960's. Although it sounds Medieval, Oh Death *has become a pop radio crossover hit at least twice that I can think of. Different verses turn up from time to time.*

Old Joe Clark

Noter Style

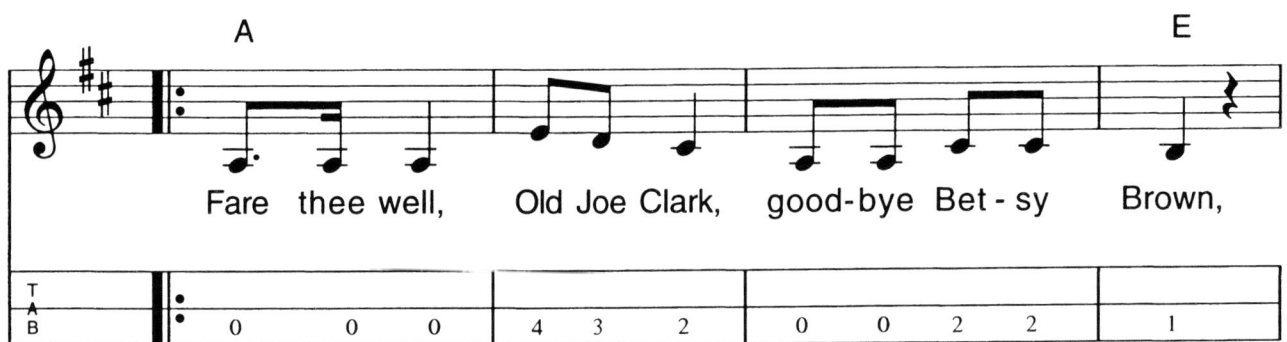
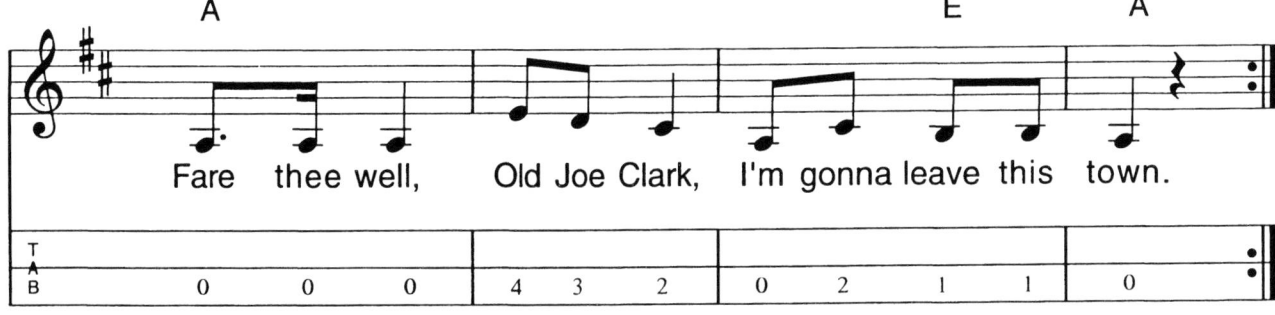

Old Joe Clark he's got a house
Fifteen stories high,
And every story of that house
Is filled with chicken pie.

   CH
   Fare thee well, Old Joe Clark;
   Good-bye Betsy Brown.
   Fare thee well Old Joe Clark;
   I'm gonna leave this town.

I went down to Old Joe Clark's,
I did not go to stay;
I got stuck on a yellow haired girl
And stayed for half a day.

Old Joe Clark is a dirty old dog,
Old Joe Clark will steal;
Old Joe Clark is a dirty old dog
And he can't go 'crost my field.

I went down to Old Joe Clark's,
I'd never been there before,
He slept on a feather bed
And I slept on the floor.

I wouldn't marry a widow gal,
Summer, spring, or fall;
She keeps her teeth right by her bed,
Wooden leg out in the hall.

   CH
   'Round and around, Old Joe Clark;
   'Round and around, I say.
   'Round and around, Old Joe Clark,
   I'm gonna go away.

I wouldn't marry an old school teacher,
I'll tell you the reason why,
She blows her nose in a piece of corn bread
And calls it custard pie.

Old Joe Clark he had a cat,
It would neither sing nor pray;
It stuck it's head in a butter milk jar
And it washed it's sins away.

I wish I had a thousand bricks
To build my chimney higher;
Keep my neighbors dogs and cats
From running through my fire.

THE dulcimer tune – so much so that old timers called any tuning with a flatted seventh (Mixolydian mode) "Old Joe Clark Tuning." There must be a million verses, some are even worse than these. I've given you two of the many chorus variations. Some say Joe Clark was a real person who lived at the time of the War of 1812. He must have been one onery old coot.

Chickens are a-Crowin'

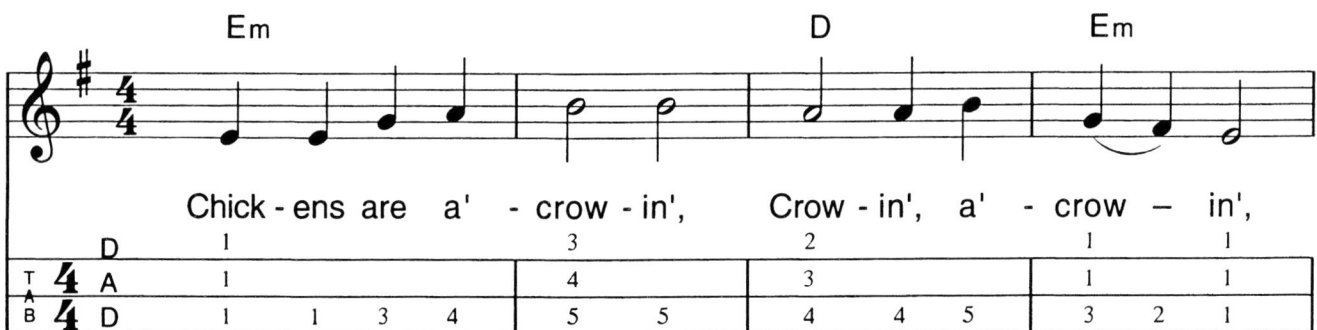

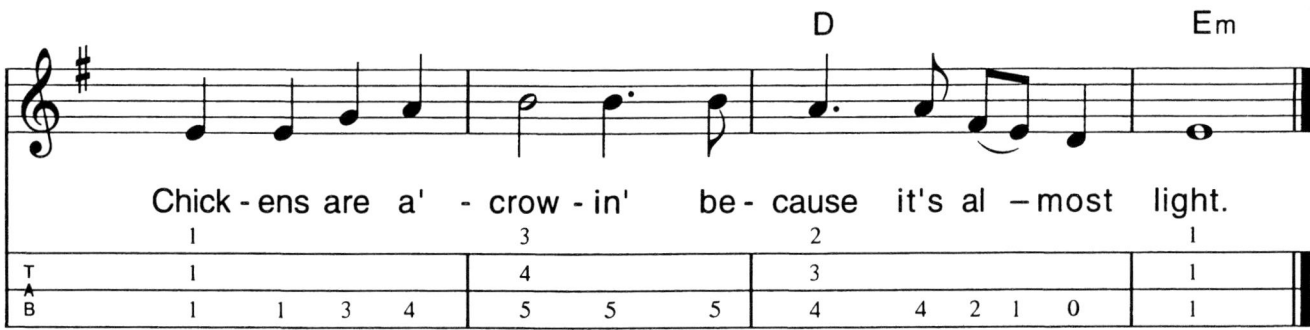

Chickens are a-crowin',
Crowin', crowin';
Chickens are a-crowin'
Because its almost light.

I won't come home till mornin',
Mornin', mornin';
I won't come home till mornin'
Stay with the girls all night.

Papa's going to scold me,
Scold me, scold me;
Papa's going to scold me
For stayin' out all night

Mama, she'll uphold me,
Uphold me, uphold me;
Mama, she'll uphold me,
Sayin' that I done just right.

Spooky tune, sweet lyrics. It beautifully captures the sense of danger one feels when first courting. Like many "Mountain Minor" tunes, the melody avoids the telltale sixth scale degree; you could just as easily play it from a Dorian modal tuning like AAD or DAG.

I am looking rather seedy now while holding down my claim…

Songs of the Frontier

When First Unto This Country

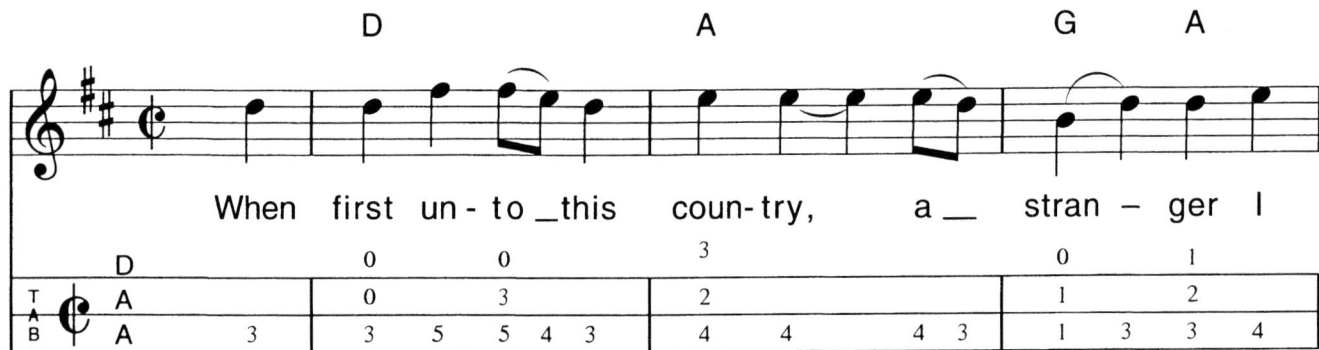
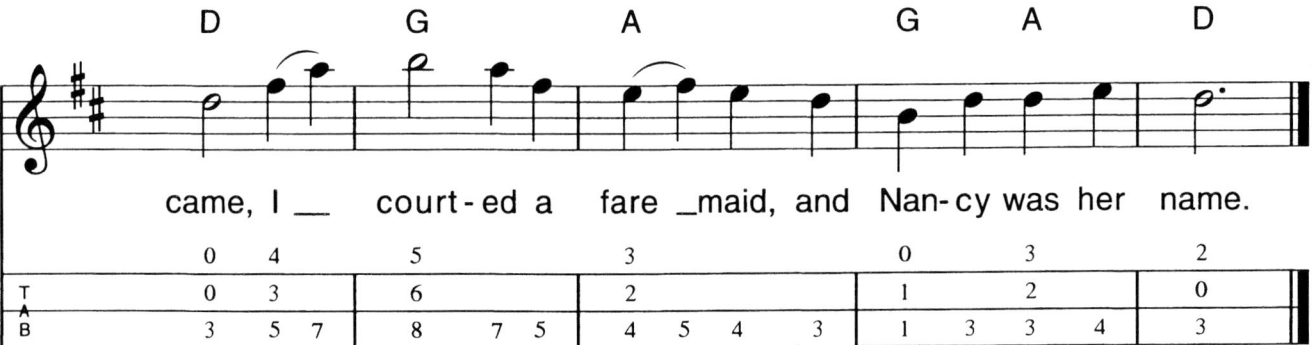

When first unto this country a stranger I came
I courted a fair maid and Nancy was her name.

I courted her for love, and her love I didn't obtain,
Do you think I've any reason or right to complain?

I rode to see my Nancy, I rode both day and night,
I courted dearest Nancy, my own heart's true delight.

I rode to see my Nancy, I rode both day and night,
Till I stole a fine grey horse from Captain William White.

The sheriff's men they followed and overtaken me,
Till they carted me away to the penitentiary.

They opened up the door, and then they took me in,
They cleared off my head, and they shaved my chin.

They beat me and they banged me and they fed me on dry beans,
Till I wished to my soul that I'd never been a thief.

With my hands in my pockets and my cap put on so bold,
With my coat of many colors, like Jacob of old.

An old song of true love and bad judgement.
Should we blame our hero for confusing his Biblical references?

Red River Valley

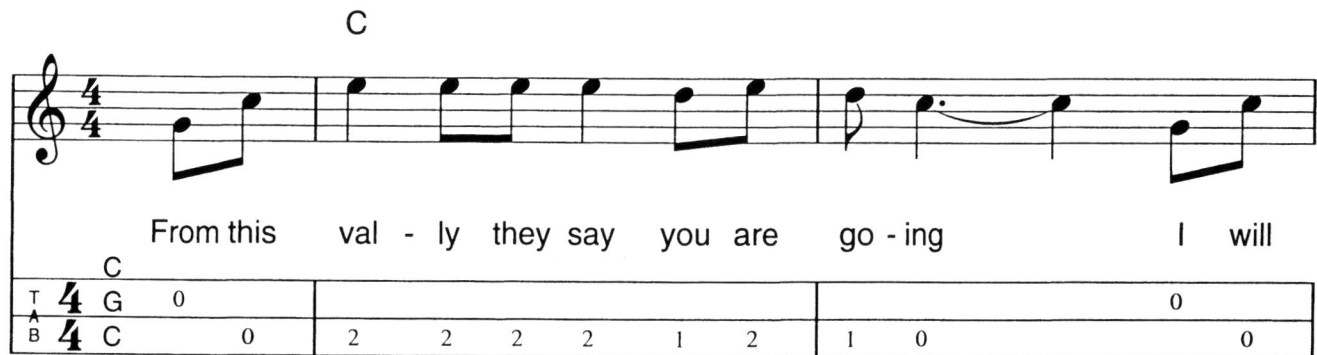

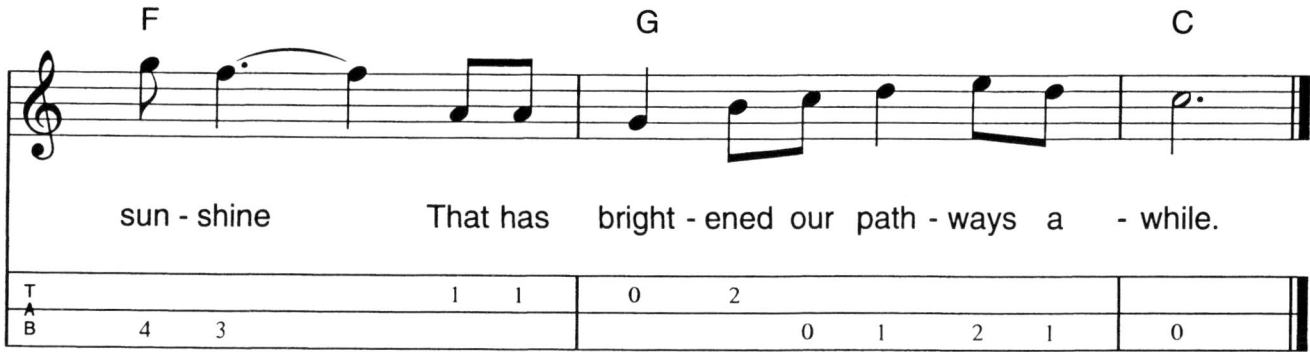

From this valley they say you are going,
I will miss your bright eyes and sweet smile,
For they say you are taking the sunshine,
That has brightened our pathways awhile.

  CH
Come and sit by my side if you love me,
Do not hasten to bid me adieu
But remember the Red River Valley
And the cowboy that loves you so true.

I have promised, my darling, that never
Will a word from my lips cause you pain;
And my life, it will be yours forever
If only you love me again.

When you go to your home by the ocean
May you never forget those sweet hours
That we spent in the Red River Valley
And the love that was ours midst the flowers.

At least three separate locations in the U.S. and Canada claim this lovely cowboy song.
Whatever its origins, it remains a sentimental favorite to any lover of the West.

In the Good Good Old Colony Times

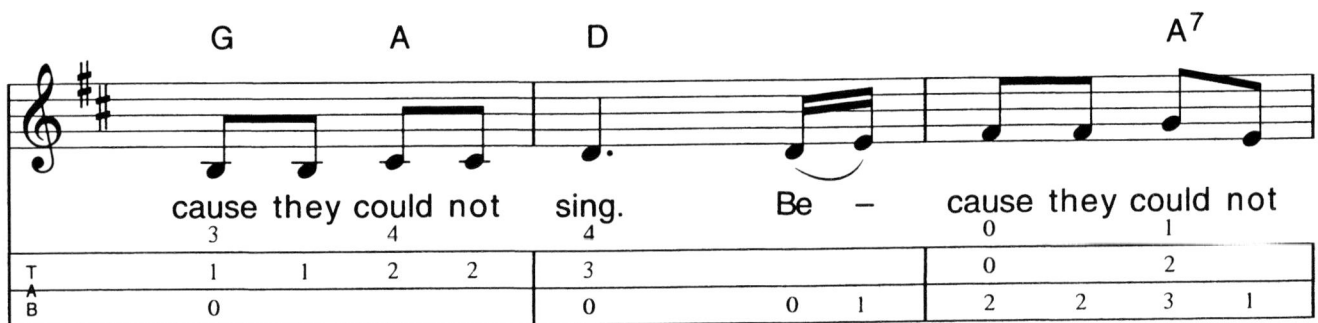

In the good old colony days,
When we lived under the king,
Three roguish chaps fell into mishaps
Because they could not sing.
Because they could not sing,
Because they could not sing,
Three roguish chaps fell into mishaps
Because they could not sing.

Oh, the first he was a miller,
And the second he was weaver.
And the third he was a little tailor,
Three roguish chaps together.
Three roguish chaps together,
Three roguish chaps together.
And the third he was a little tailor,
Three roguish chaps together.

Oh, the miller he stole corn,
And the weaver, he stole yarn,
And the little tailor he ran away
With the broadcloth under his arm.
With the broadcloth under his arm,
With the broadcloth under his arm.
And the little tailor he ran away
With the broadcloth under his arm.

The miller was drowned in his dam,
And the weaver was hanged with his yarn,
And the devil clapped his claws on the little tailor
With the broad cloth under his arm.
With the broad cloth under his arm,
With the broad cloth under his arm.
And the devil clapped his claws on the little tailor
With the broad cloth under his arm.

One of our oldest folksongs, this New England gem displays the usual country disdain for corrupt tradesman.

The Young Man Who Wouldn't Hoe Corn

I'll sing you a song and it's not very long.
It's about a young man who wouldn't hoe corn.
The reason why, I can't tell,
This young man was always well.

He planted his corn in the month of July,
And by September it was so high.
Suddenly there came a frost,
And all this young man's corn was lost.

He went to his fence and he peeped therein,
The weeds and grass grew up to his chin.
The jimson weed it grew so high,
Enough to make this young man sigh.

In the winter, as I was told,
He went courtin' very bold.
When his courtship first begun,
"Tell me, sir, did you make any corn?"

"No, kind miss," was his reply,
"Long ago I laid it by.
It wasn't worth while to strive in vain
For I didn't expect to make one grain."

"Well, here you are, a-wanting to wed
And you cannot make your own cornbread.
Single I am and will remain,
For a lazy man I'll not maintain."

No one is more worthless than the lazy man without cunning.

The Sow Took the Measles

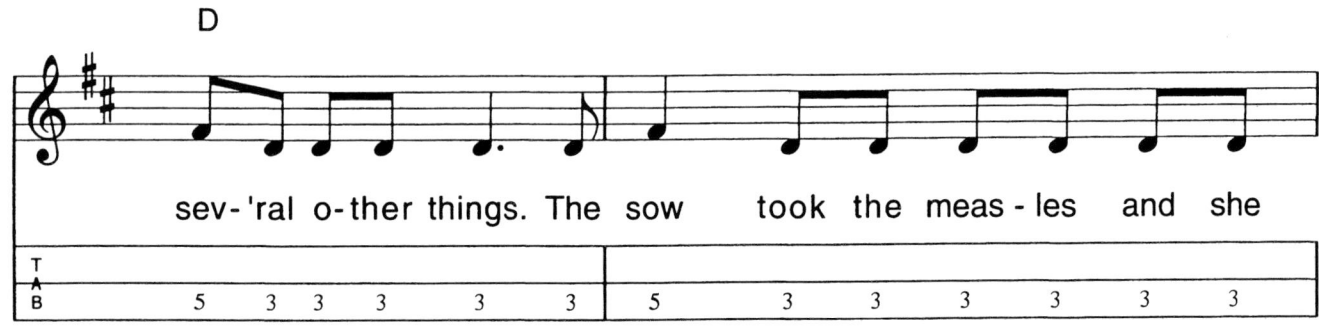

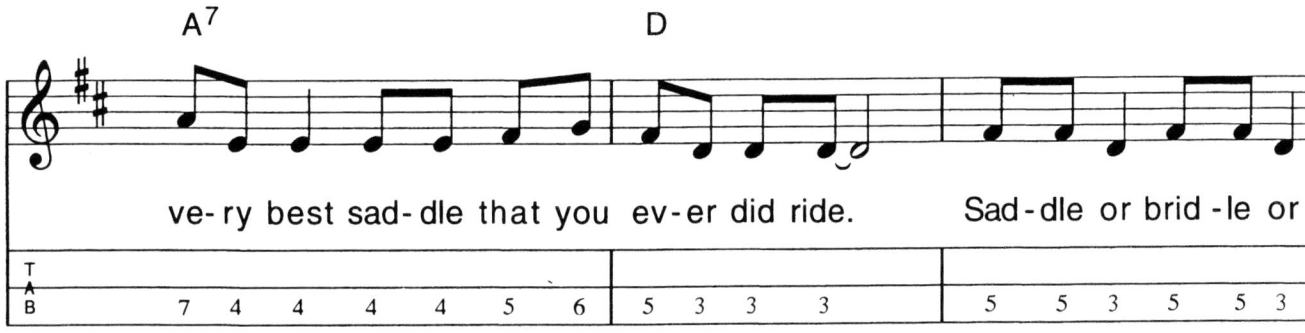

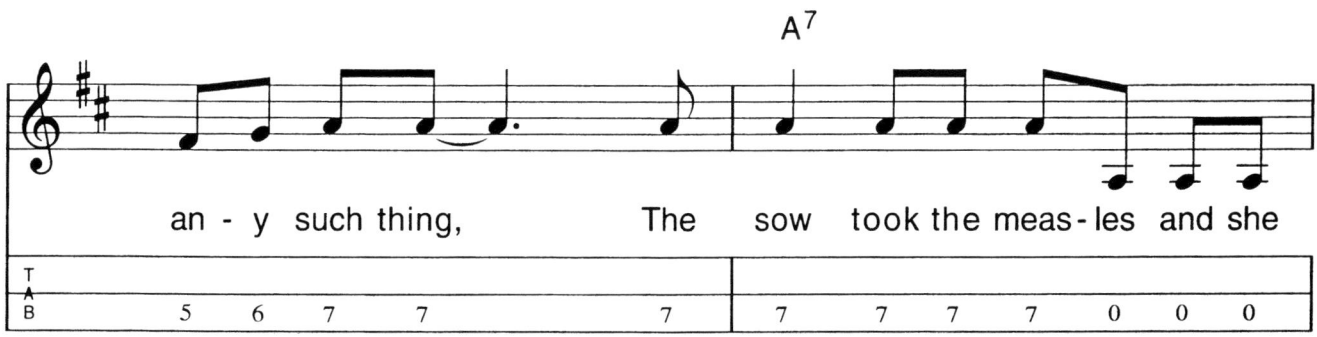

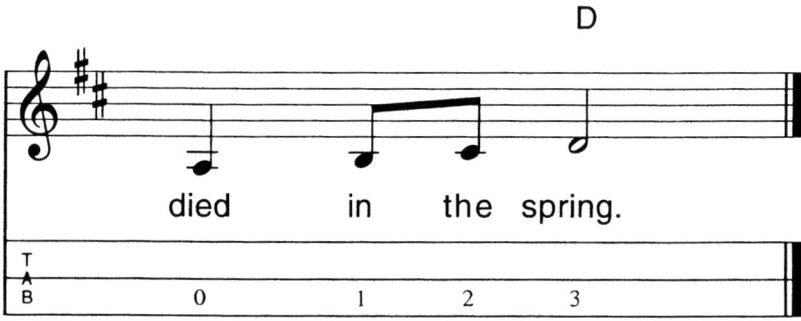

How do you think I began in this world?
I got me a sow and sev'ral other things.
The sow took the measles and she died in the spring.

What do you think I made of her hide?
The very best saddle that you ever did ride.
Saddle or bridle or any such thing,
The sow took the measles and she died in the spring.

What do you think I made of her nose?
The very best thimble that ever sewed clothes,
Thimble or thread or any such thing,
The sow took the measles and she died in the spring.

What do you think I made of her tail?
The very best whip that ever set sail.
Whip or whip socket or any such thing,
The sow took the measles and she died in the spring.

What do you think I made of her feet?
The very best pickles you ever did eat.
Pickles or glue, or any such thing,
The sow took the measles and she died in the spring.

Quite a contrast to the young dodger who wouldn't how corn.
I've heard versions that go on and on; it seems no part of the pig went unused.

Kansas Boys

Come along girls and listen to my noise.
Don't you marry the Kansas boys.
For if you do, your fortune it will be,
Cold johnny cake and hominy is all you'll see.

When they come a courtin' they bring along a chair,
And the first things they ask, "Has your daddy shot a bear?"
The next thing they say, when they sit down,
"Madam, your johnny cake is too durn brown."

When they come a courtin', let me tell you what they wear,
An old frock coat all picked and bare,
An old straw hat more brim than crown,
And a pair of dirty socks they've worn the winter round.

It seems that every territory, state, county, or two-bit town in the west has a version of this one.

Alsea Girls

(Sung to the tune of *Kansas Boys*)

Come you Alsea girls and listen to my noise,
Don't you marry the Oregon boys.
If you do your fortune it will be,
Cold johnny cake and venison is all you'll see.

They'll take you to side-hewed wall
Without any windows in it at all.
Sandstone chimney and a puncheon floor,
A clapboard roof and a button door.

Ev'ry night before you go to bed
They'll build up a fire as high as your head,
Rake away the ashes and in they'll throw
A great big chunk of old sourdough.

When they go a milkin' they milk in a gourd,
Stand it in a corner and hide it with a board,
Some gets little and some gets none,
And that's the way things in Oregon run.

Same sentiment, different locale.

Home on the Range

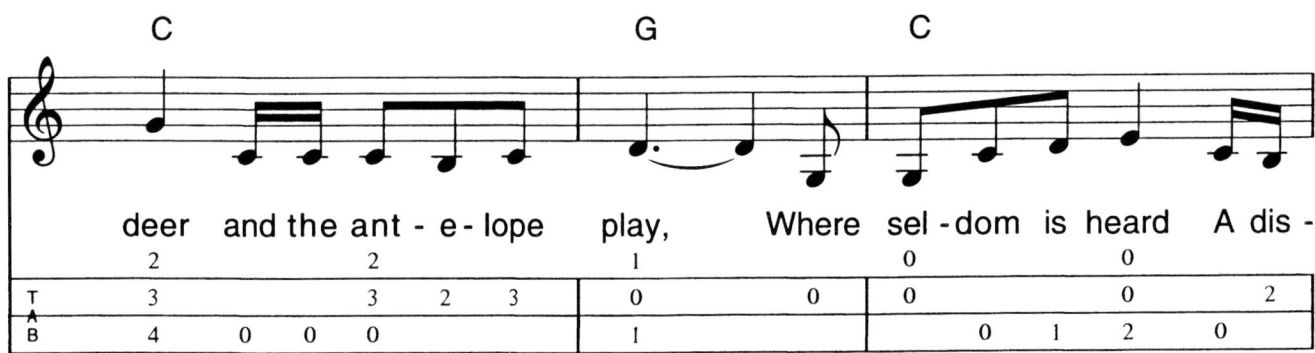

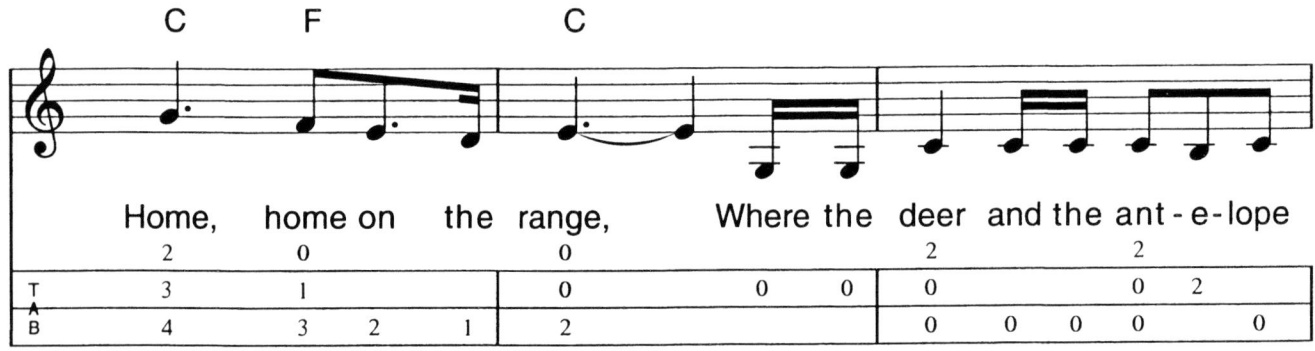

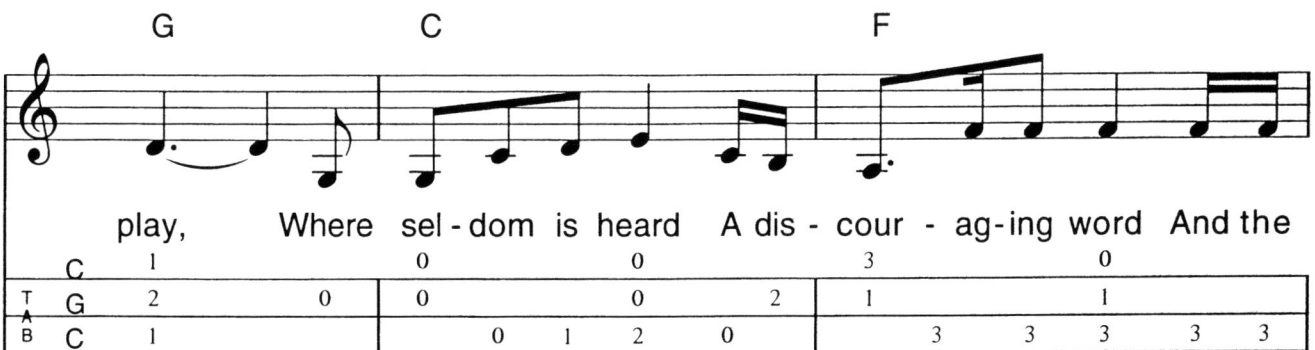

Oh, give me a home where the buffalo roam,
Where the deer and the antelope play.
Where seldom is heard a discouraging word,
And the skies are not cloudy all day.

> CH
> Home, home on the range,
> Where the deer and the antelope play.
> Where seldom is heard a discouraging word,
> And the skies are not cloudy all day.

How oft times at night, when the heavens are bright
With the light from the glittering stars,
Have I stood there amazed and I asked as I gazed
If their glory exceeds that of ours.

The air is so pure, the zephyrs to free,
The breezes so balmy and light,
That I would not exchange my home on the range
For all of your cities so bright.

Oh, give me a land where the bright diamond sand
Flows leisurely down to the stream,
Where the graceful white swan flows drifting along
Like a maid in a heavenly dream.

The finest "sense of place" song of them all. Though no one is really sure where, or when, this was written, it has become the official state song of Kansas.

Acres of Clams

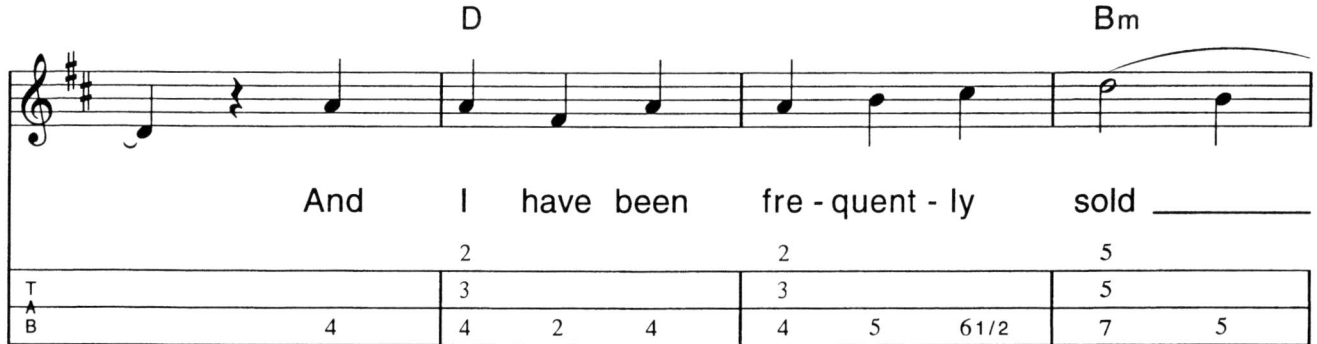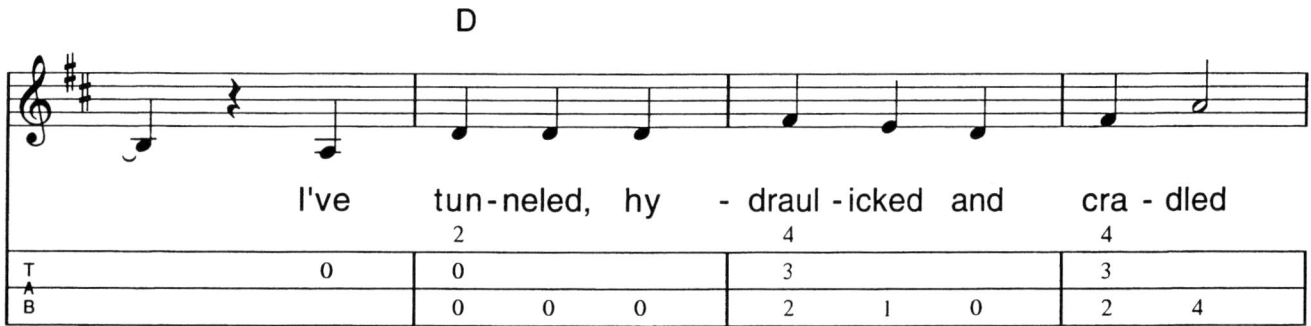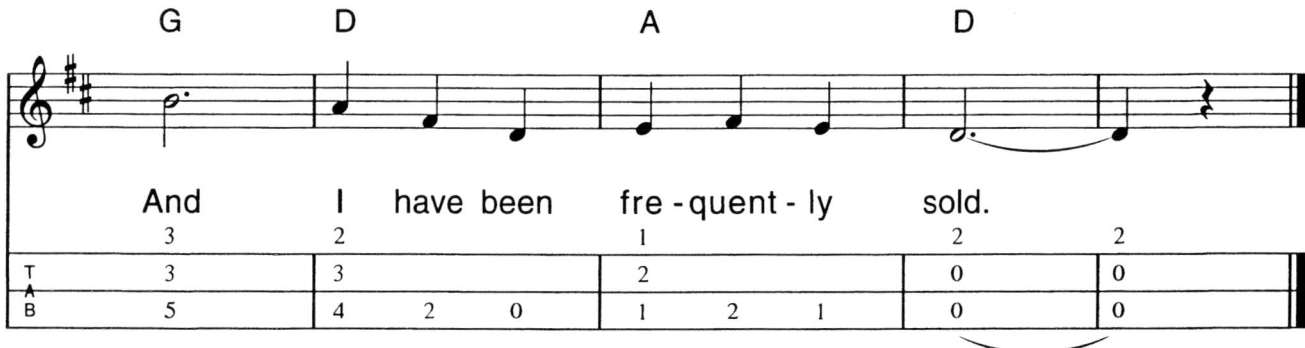

I've traveled all over this country, prospecting and digging for gold
I've tunneled, hydraulicked and cradled, and I have been frequently sold.

   CH
   And I have been frequently sold, and I have been frequently sold,
   I've tunneled, hydraulicked and cradled, and I have been frequently sold.

For one who got rich by mining, I saw there were hundreds grow poor,
So I made up my mind to try farming, the only pursuit that is sure.
   (CH—repeat final line two times, as before)

I rolled all my kit in a blanket, and left all my tools on the ground,
I started one morning to shank it for the country they called Puget Sound.

Arriving flat broke in midwinter, I found it enveloped in fog,
And covered all over with timber, as thick as the hair on a dog.

As I looked on the prospect so gloomy, the tears trickled over my face,
For I felt that my travels had brought me, to the edge of the jumping-off place.

I took up a claim in the forest, and sat myself down to hard toil,
For two years I chopped and I labored, but I never got down to the soil.

I tried to get out of the country, but poverty forced me to stay,
Until I became an old settler, now nothing can drive me away.

And now that I'm used to the climate, I think that if man ever found,
A spot to live easy and happy, that Eden is on Puget Sound.

No longer the slave to ambition, I laugh at the world and it's shams,
And I think of my happy condition, surrounded by acres of clams.

Originally entitled The Old Settler, *this poem by Francis Henry was written sometime around 1874. The tune comes from Ireland and has been the setting many different songs, including Abraham Lincoln's campaign theme.*

Bury Me Not on the Lone Prairie

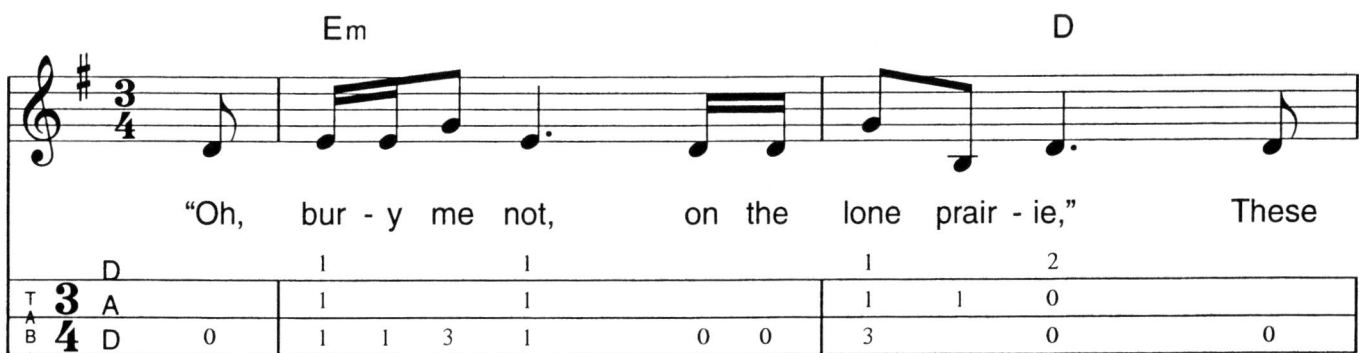

"Oh, bury me not on the lone prairie,"
These words came low and mournfully
From the pallid lips of a youth who lay
On his dying bed at the close of day.

"It matters not, I've oft been told,
Where the body lies when the heart grows cold;
Yet grant, oh grant, this wish to me:
Oh, bury me not on the lone prairie."

"Oh, bury me not on the lone prairie
Where the wild coyotes will howl o'er me,
Where the buzzards sail, and the winds blows free,
Oh, bury me not on the lone prairie."

"Oh, bury me not—" And his voice failed there,
But we took no heed of his dying prayer.
In a narrow grave just six by three
We buried him there on the lone prairie.

A lonely grave far from home and family, with no mourners save the wind. The song is a western version of the sailor's lament Oh Bury Me Not in the Deep Blue Sea.

Beulah Land

E. P. Stittes and J.R. Sweeny

This hymn, by Edgar Paige Stittes and J.R. Sweeny, captured the imagination of the pioneers like no other. The contrast between the wonderful riches of the Promised Land with the reality of the bare hills and dry valleys of the Great American Desert led to dozens of inspired parodies, such as the one below.

Dakota Land

We've reached the land of drought and heat,
Where nothing grows for man to eat,
The wind that blows with feverish heat
Across the plains is hard to beat.

CH
Oh, Dakota land, sweet Dakota land
As on your fiery soil I stand,
I look away across the plains
And wonder why it never rains
Till Gabriel blows his trumpet sound
And says the rain's just gone around.

Our fuel is of the cheapest kind,
Our women are all of one mind.
With bag in hand and turned up nose
They pick the chips of buffaloes.

Our horses are of bronco race,
Starvation stares them in the face
We do not live, we only stay.
We are too poor to get away.

Sweet Betsy from Pike

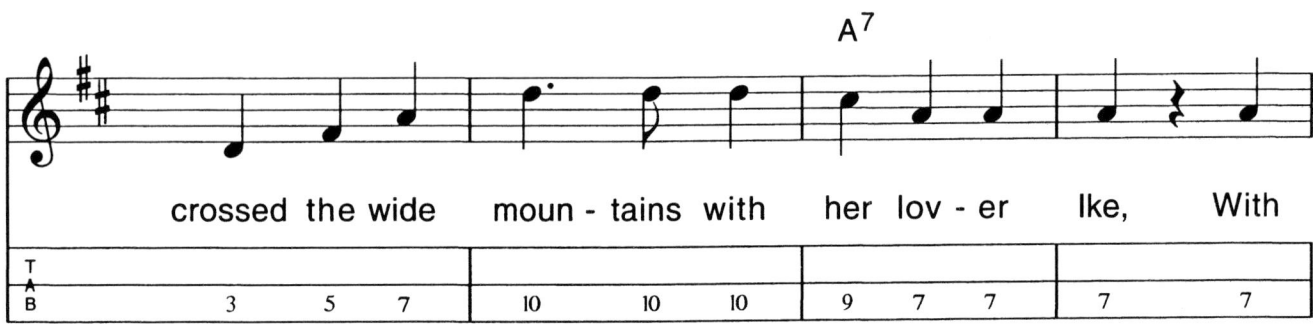

Oh do you remember sweet Betsy from Pike
Who crossed the wide mountains with her lover Ike,
With two yoke of oxen, and one spotted hog
A tall Shanghai rooster and an old yeller dog,

> CH
> Hoodle dang fol-de-di-do, hoodle dang fol-de-day.

They swam the wild rivers and climbed the tall peaks,
They camped on the prairies for weeks and for weeks.
Starvation and cholera, hard work and slaughter,
They reached California spite of hell or high water.

They camped on the prairie one bright starry night
They broke out the whiskey and Betsy got tight,
She sang and she hollered and romped 'round the plain;
And showed her bare bum to the whole wagon train.

The wagon tipped over with a terrible crash
And out on the prairie rolled all sorts of trash,
A few little baby clothes all done up with care;
It looked rather suspicious, but 'twas all on the square.

They reached the wide desert where Betsy gave out
And down on the sand she lay rolling about,
Ike looked upon her with sobs and with sighs,
"Get up, darling Betsy, you'll get sand in your eyes."

Sweet Betsy got up with a great deal of pain
And she swore she'd go back to Pike County again,
Then Ike heaved a sigh and they fondly embraced,
And they travelled along with his arm 'round her waist.

The oxen ran off and the Shanghai it died,
The last piece of bacon that morning was fried;
Ike got discouraged, and Betsy got mad,
The dog hung his head and looked wond'rfully sad.

They passed the Sierras through mountains of snow,
Til old California was sighted below.
Sweet Betsy she hollered and Ike gave a cheer,
Saying, "Betsy, my darling, I'm a made millionaire."

Betsy and Ike attended a dance,
Ike wore a pair of his Pike County pants,
Betsy was dressed up in ribbons and rings.
Quoth Ike, "You're an angel, but where are your wings?"

A miner said, "Betsy, will you dance with me?"
"I will, you old hoss, if you don't make too free.
Don't dance me too hard, do you want to know why?
Doggone you, I'm chock full of strong alkali!"

Ike and Sweet Betsy got married, of course.
But Ike became jealous and obtained a divorce,
Betsy, well satisfied, said with a smile,
"I've six good men waiting within half a mile."

The all-time favorite song of the '49ers. If all the verses made up along the trail were printed out and laid end to end, they'd stretch all the way back from the gold fields to Pike County. And that's just the polite ones!

Little Old Sod Shanty

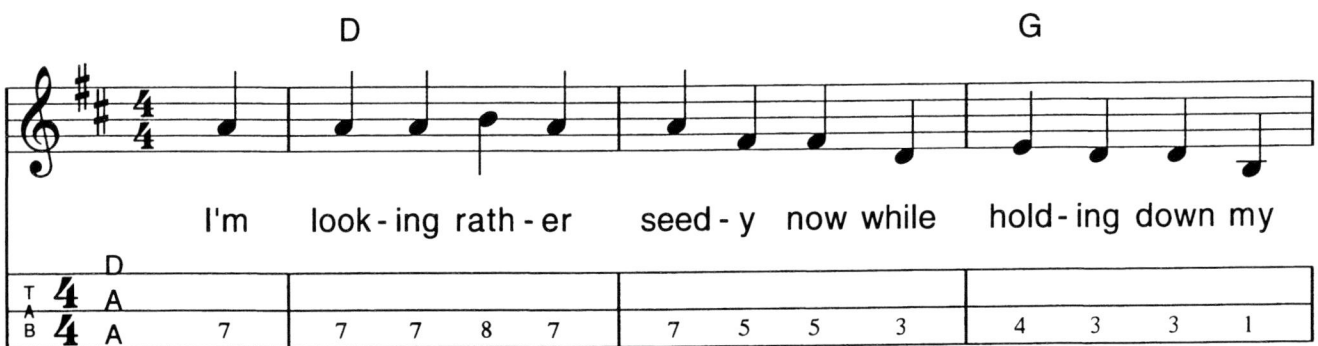
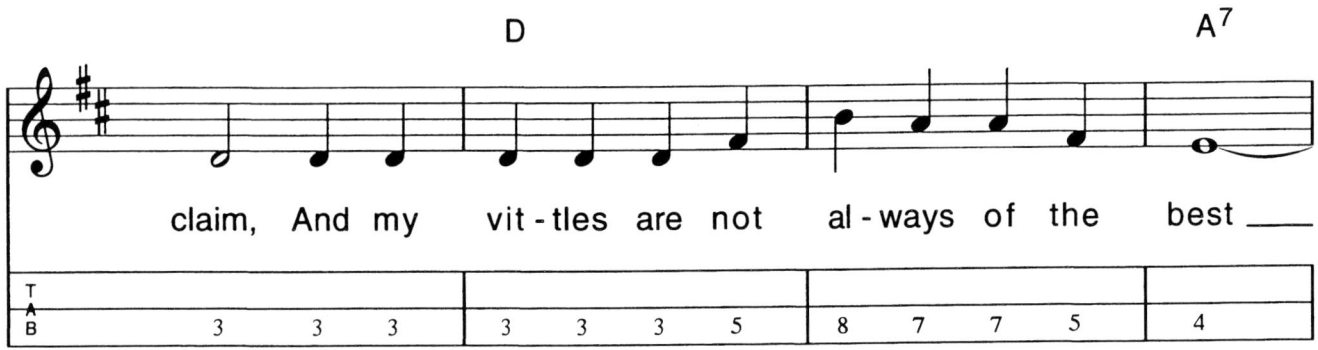

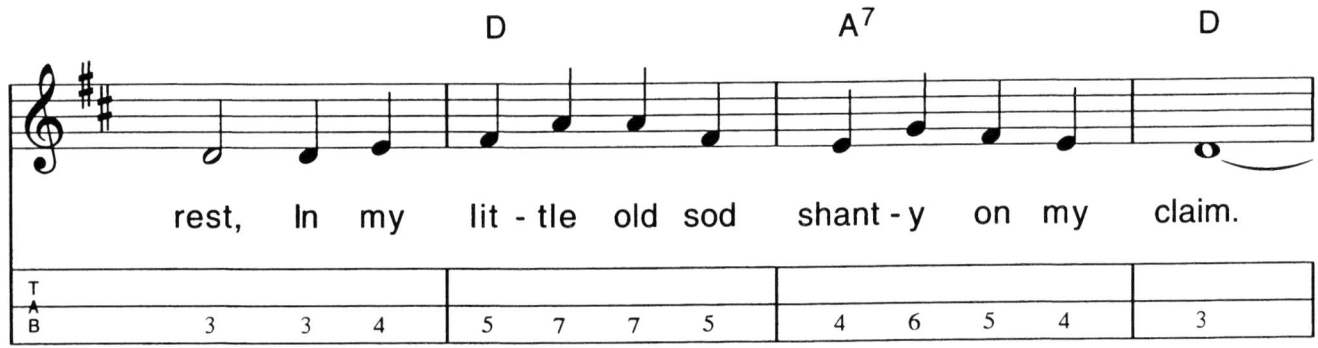

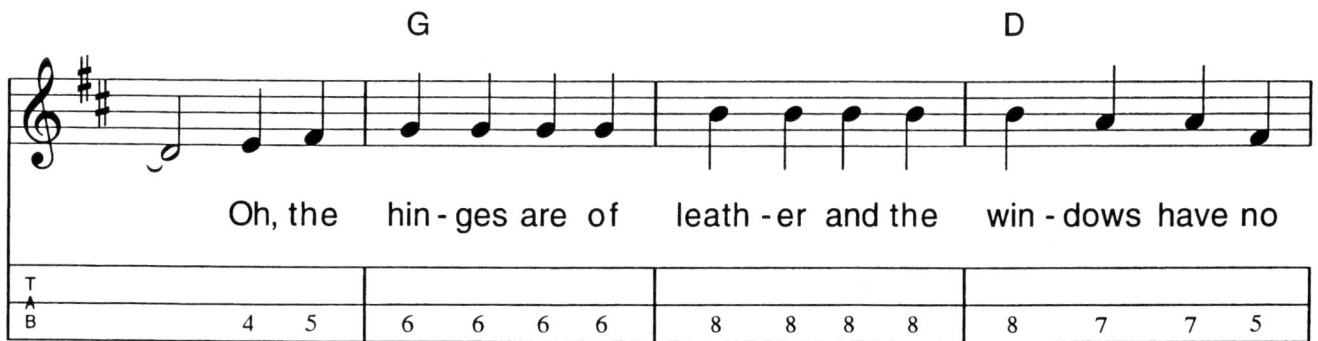
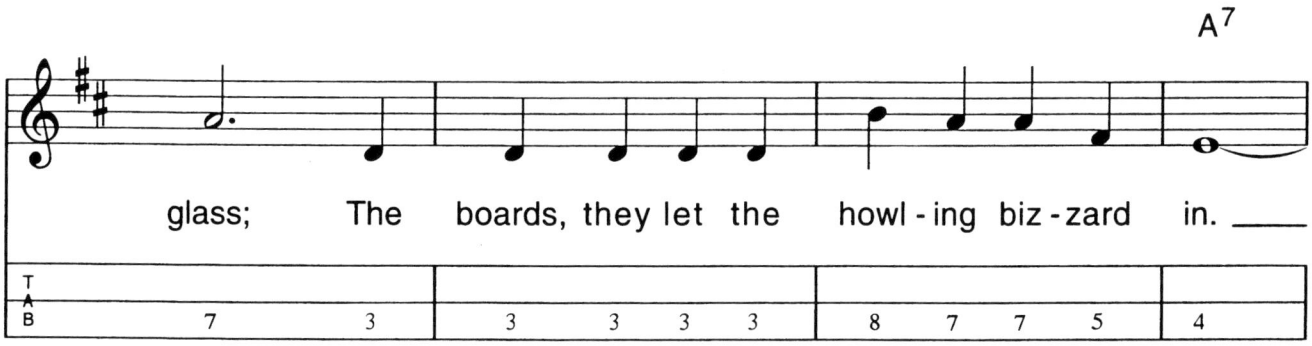

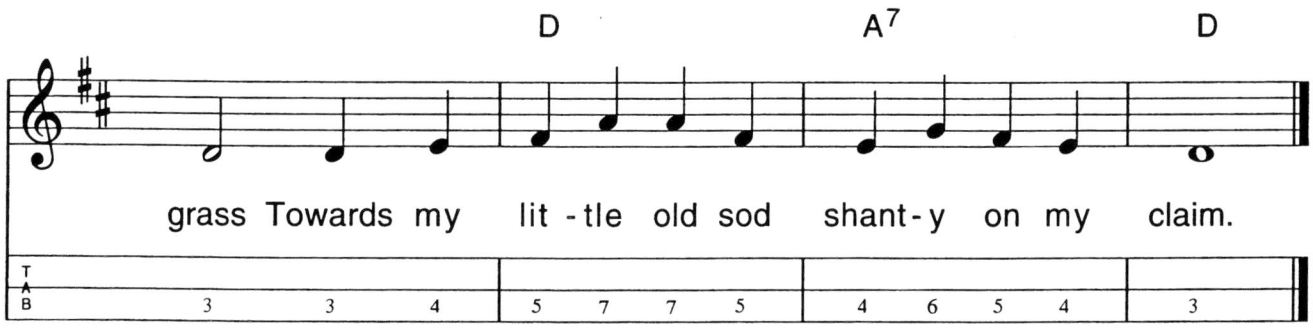

I'm looking rather seedy now while holding down my claim
And my vittles are not always of the best
And the mice play gayly 'round me as I nestle down to rest,
In my little old sod shanty on my claim.
Oh, the hinges are of leather and the windows have no glass;
The boards, they let the howling blizzards in.
I can see the hungry coyote as he sneaks up through the grass
Towards my little old sod shanty on my claim.

When I left my Eastern home, a bachelor so gay,
To try to win my way to wealth and fame,
I little thought I'd come down to burning twisted hay,
In my little old sod shanty on my claim.
Yet I rather like the novelty of living in this way,
Though my bill of fare is always rather tame;
But I'm happy as a clam on the land of Uncle Sam
In my little old sod shanty on my claim.

Still I wish some kindhearted Miss would pity on me take
And relieve me from the mess that I am in;
The angel, how I'd bless her if this her home would make,
In my little old sod shanty on my claim.
And if fate should bless us with now and then an heir
To cheer our hearts with honest pride and fame,
Oh, then we'd be contented for the toil we have spent
In the little old sod shanty on my claim.

The Homestead Act of 1862 allowed any US citizen to file a claim for 160 acres of public land – manage to live on it for five years and the land was yours. With no timber, setters built their houses from the prairie sod itself. The song is a parody of Little Old Log Cabin in the Lane *by William Shakespeare Hays.*

Oh the shantyman's life is a wearisome life
Although some think it void of care;
It's the swinging an ax from morning till night
In the forests so wild and drear.

Working on the Land and Sea

John Henry

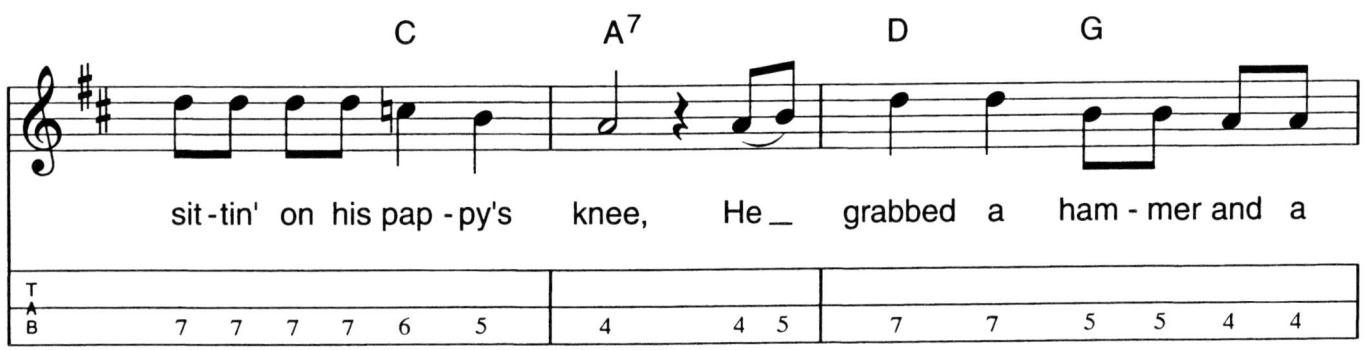

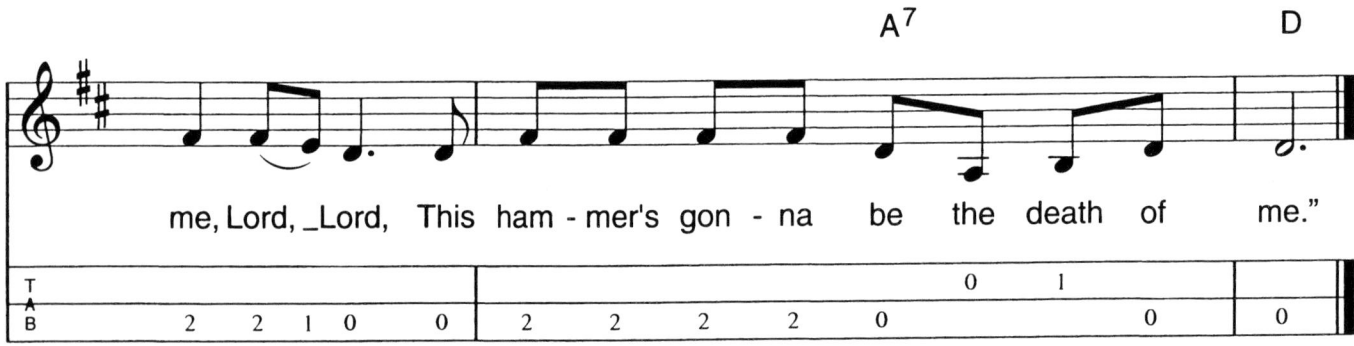

When John Henry, he was a little baby
He was sittin' on his pappy's knee;
He grabbed a hammer and a little piece of steel, said:
"This hammer's gonna be the death of me, Lord, Lord,
This hammer's gonna be the death of me."

Now the captain said to John Henry,
"I'm gonna bring that steam drill 'round,
When I take that steam drill out on the job
Gonna whup that steel on down, Lord, Lord,
Gonna whup that old steel on down."

John Henry said to that captain,
"A man ain't nothin' but a man;
But before I let that steam drill beat me down,
I'll die with that hammer in my hand, Lord, Lord,
I'll die with that hammer in my hand."

John Henry said to his shaker,
"Shaker, you'd better pray.
Cause if I miss with this nine pound maul
Tomorrow's gonna be your burying day, Lord, Lord,
Tomorrow's gonna be your burying day."

The captain said to John Henry,
"I believe this mountain's sinking in."
"Stand back, Captain, and don't be afraid,
Ain't nothin' but my hammer suckin' wind, Lord, Lord,
Ain't nothin' but my hammer suckin' wind."

The man that invented the steam drill,
He thought it was mighty fine,
But John Henry he made fourteen feet,
Steam drill only made nine, Lord, Lord,
Steam drill only made nine.

John Henry hammered on the mountain
Till his hammer was striking fire.
Hammered so hard that his poor heart broke;
He laid down his hammer and he died, Lord, Lord,
Laid down his hammer and he died.

They took John Henry to the White House
And buried him in the sand.
Every locomotive comes rolling by
Says, "There lies a steel drivin' man, Lord, Lord,
There lies a steel drivin' man."

"A man ain't nothin' but a man." The greatest of all homegrown songs. This version is a composite of several different tellings. All agree that John Henry died after besting a mechanized drill, though his grave tends to move around quite a bit from song to song.

Haul Away, Joe

When I was a little laddie, so my mother told me,
Away, haul away, we'll haul away, Joe;
That if I didn't kiss the gals my lips would all grow mouldy.
Away, haul away, we'll haul away, Joe

    Way, haul away, we're bound for better weather,
    Away, haul away, we'll haul away, Joe.

Louis was the king of France before the Rev-o-lu-ti-on.
Away, haul away, we'll haul away, Joe,
Then he got his head cut off, which spoiled his cons-ti-tu-ti-on;
Away, haul away, we'll haul away, Joe.

Singing makes the work easier. Pronounce the last two syllables of "revolution" and "constitution" to rhyme with "I am." I doubt anyone ever tried to smuggle a dulcimer on board ship to play this lovely Dorian air, but it sure sounds good!

The Little Brown Bulls

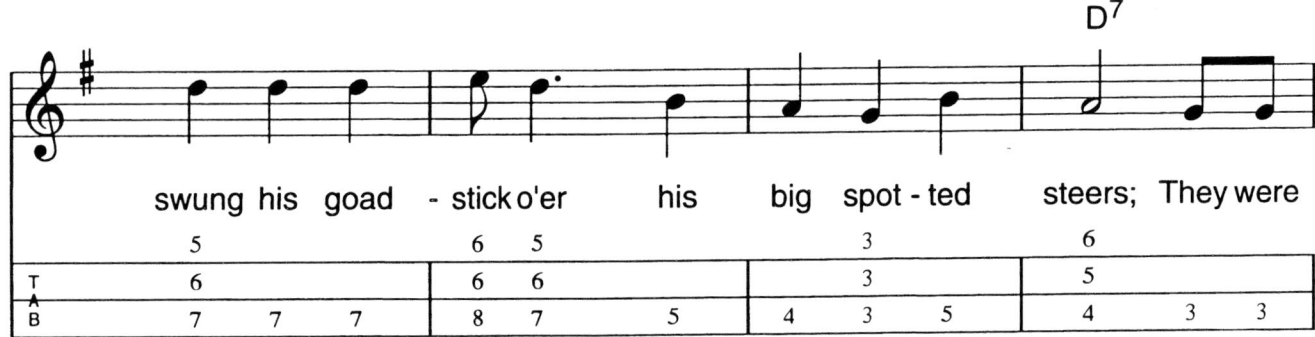
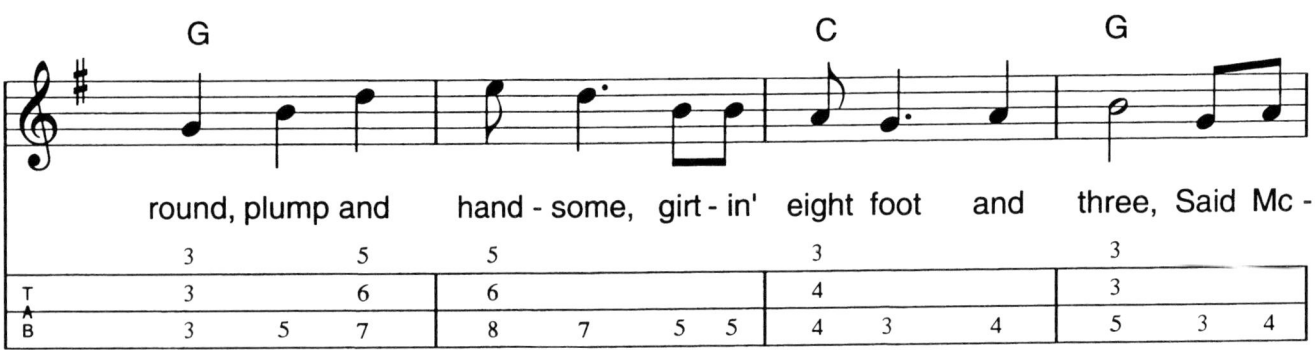

Not a thing on the river McClusky did fear,
As he swung his goadstick o'er his big spotted steers;
They were round, plump and handsome, girtin' eight foot and three,
Said McClusky, the Scotsman, "They're the laddies for me!"

Then along came bold Gordon whose skidding was full
And he hollered "Hush!" to his little brown bulls,
Short legged and shaggy, girtin' eight foot and nine,
"Too light," said McClusky, "to handle our pine,"

The day was appointed and soon did draw nigh,
For twenty-five dollars, their fortunes to try,
Both eager and anxious next morning was found
The judge and the scaler appeared on the ground.

Along came bold Gordon, his pipe in his jaw,
To his little brown bulls he hollered, "Whoa, haw!
Chew your cuds lightly, you need never fear,
For we'll easily beat them, those big spotted steers."

Says McClusky to Sandy, "We'll take off their skins,
We'll dig them a hole and we'll tumble them in,
We'll mix up a dish and feed it to them hot,
We'll learn them damn Yankees to face the bold Scot."

Then up stepped the scaler, sayin' "Hold on awhile,
Your big spotted steers are behind just one mile,
You skidded one hundred and ten, and no more,
While bold Gordon has beat you by ten and a score."

The boys then all laughed and McClusky did swear,
Then he tore out by handfuls his long yellow hair,
So it's take up your glasses and fill them up full
And we'll drink to the health of the little brown bulls.

Pride goes before a fall.
I have heard that knowing this song was a sure guarantee of a job in the North woods.

Boatman Dance

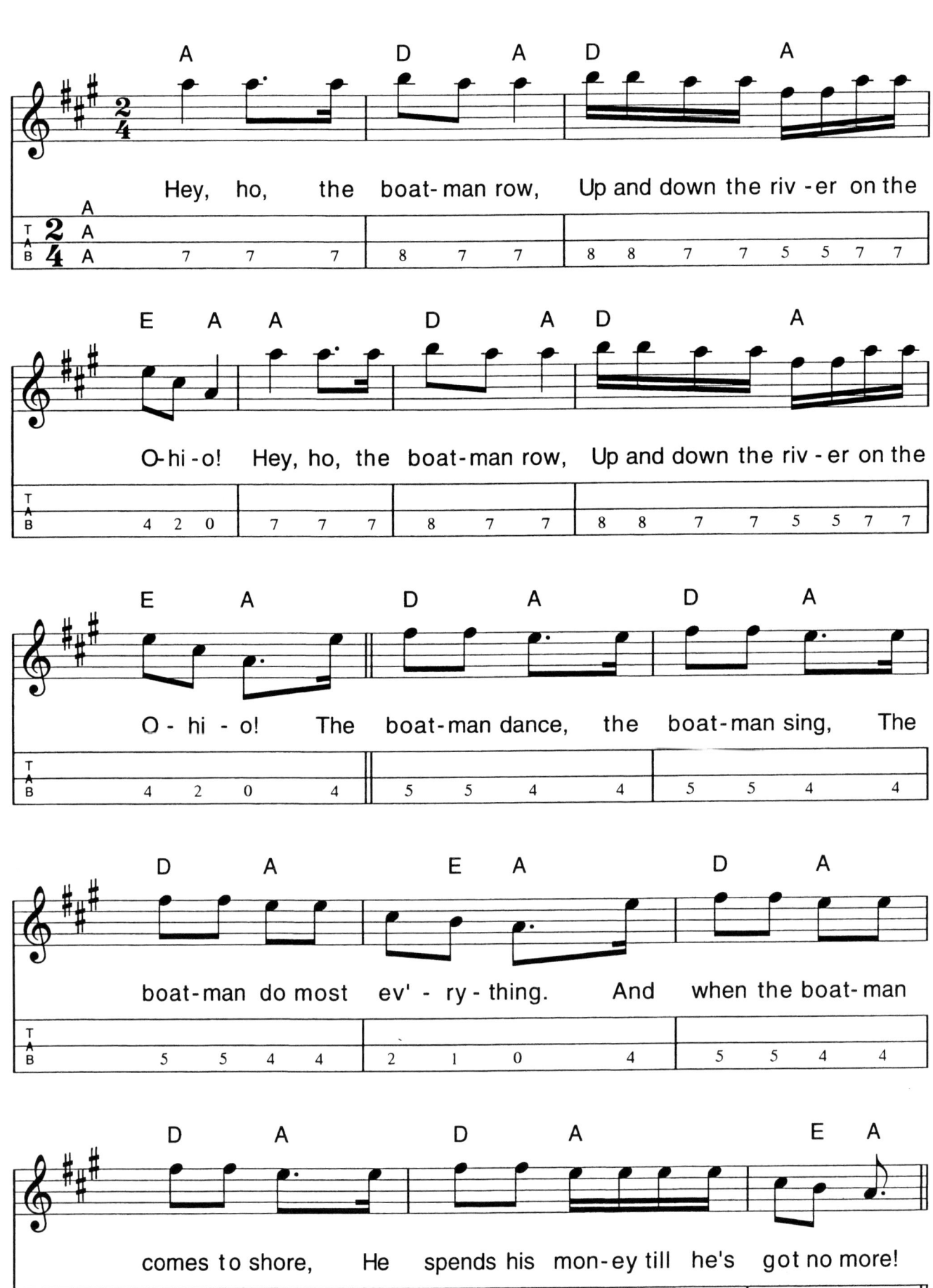

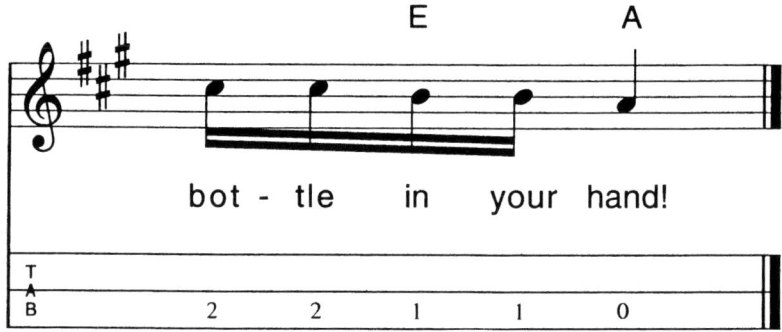

Hey ho, the boatman row,
Up and down the river on the Ohio!
Hey ho, the boatman row,
Up and down the river on the Ohio!

The boatman dance, the boatman sing,
The boatman do most ev'rything.
And when the boatman comes to shore
He spends his money till he's got no more!

Dance, boatman, dance;
Dance boatman, dance.
Dance boatman, dance;
Dance all night with a bottle in your hand.

A lively three part dance tune celebrating the carefree life of a bargeman on the Ohio.

The Glendy Burk

Stephan Foster

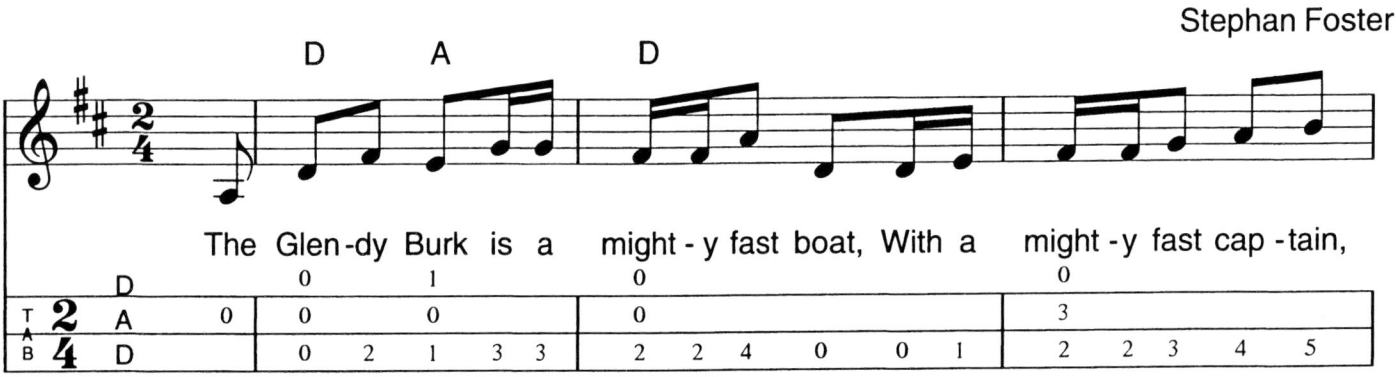

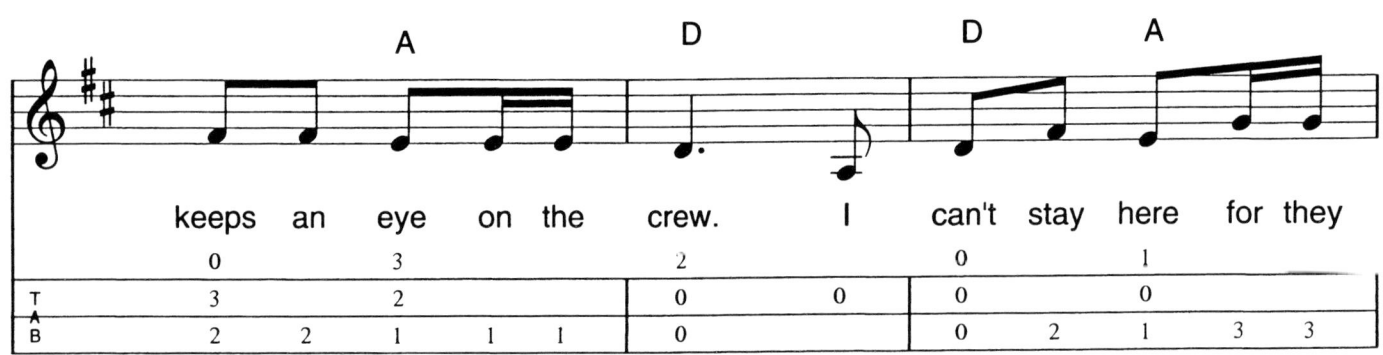

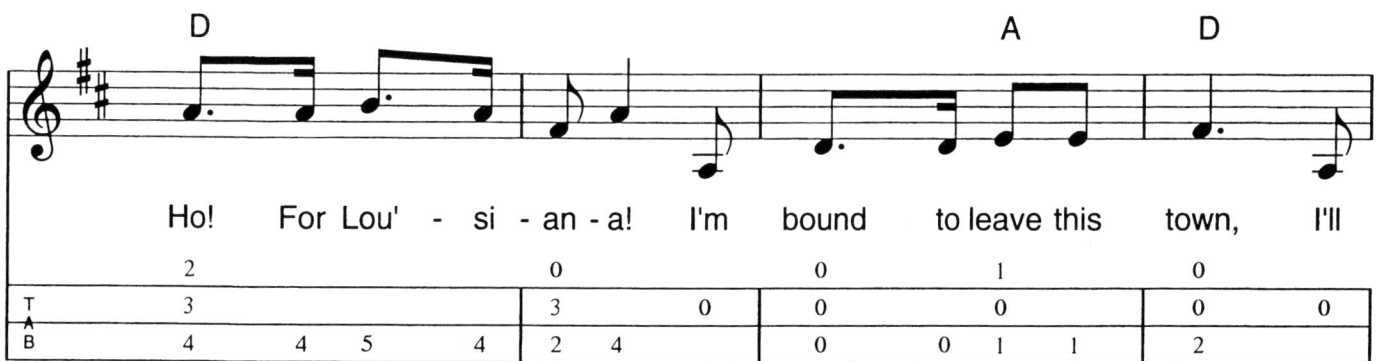

The Glendy Burk is a mighty fast boat,
With a mighty fast captain, too;
He sits up there on the hurricane roof,
And he keeps an eye on the crew.
I can't stay here for they work me too hard,
I'm bound to leave this town,
I'll take my duds and I'll tote 'em on my back,
When the Glendy Burk comes down.

    Ho! For Lou'siana!
    I'm bound to leave this town,
    I'll take my duds and tote 'em on my back
    When the Glendy Burk comes down.

The Glendy Burk has a funny old crew
And they sing the boatman's song,
They burn the pitch and the pine knot, too,
Just to move the boat along,
The smoke goes up and the engine roars
And the wheel turns 'round and 'round;
Then fare you well, for I'll take a little ride
When the Glendy Burk comes down.

Not all the hoboes rode the rods, some hopped a boat. Stephen Foster immortalized the sternwheeler Glenn D. Burke in this comic song. For some reason the name of both the craft and captain was changed to Diamond Joe *when the song came west.*

Shenandoah

O, Shenandoah, I love your daughter,
Away, you rolling river,
O, Shenadoah, I love your daughter,
Away, I'm bound away,
Across the wide Missouri.

O, Shenandoah, I long to hear you,
Away, you rolling river,
O, Shenandoah, I long to hear you
Away, I'm bound away,
Across the wide Missouri.

O, Shenandoah, I love her truly,
Away, you rolling river,
O, Shenandoah, I love her truly,
Away, I'm bound away,
Across the wide Missouri.

O, Shenandoah, I'm bound to leave you.
Away, you rolling river,
O, Shenandoah, I'll not deceive you.
Away, I'm bound away,
Across the wide Missouri.

This song started life as a ballad about a doomed love affair between a settler and a chief's daughter. Though most settings lack the strong rhythms necessary for a chantey, Shenandoah became hugely popular both on land and sea.

The Shantyman's Life

Noter Style

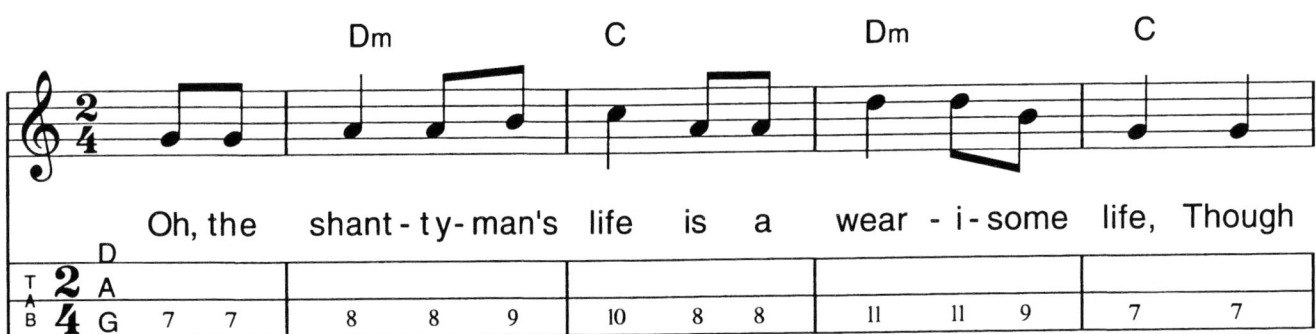

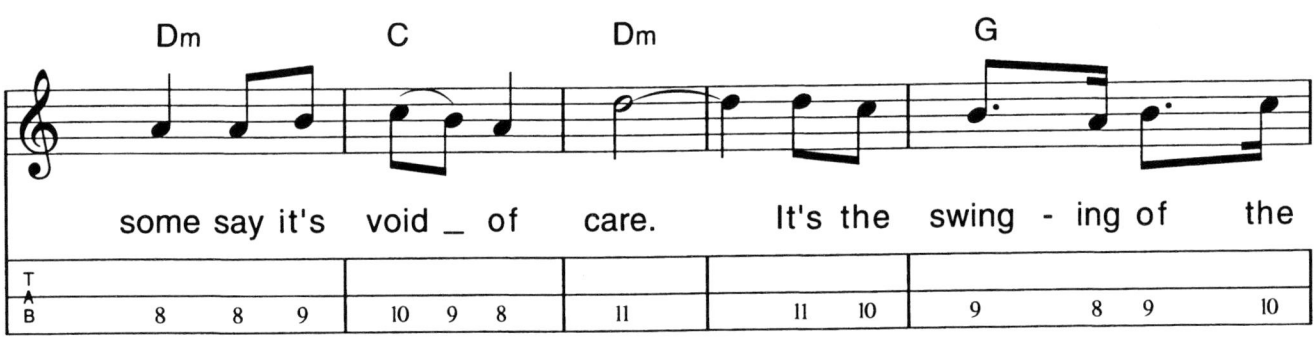

Oh the shantyman's life is a wearisome life
Although some think it void of care;
It's the swinging of the ax from morning till night
In the forests so wild and drear.

Lying in the shanty bleak and cold
While winter's stormy winds blow,
And as soon as the daylight does appear,
To the wild woods we must go.

But when the spring it does set in,
The hardships have begun.
All our clothes are dripping wet
And our fingers so numb and cold.

Yes when the spring it does set in,
Our troubles do begin;
When the waters are so icy cold
And our poles we can scarcely hold.

'Twixt rocks, shoals and sands there's employment for all hands
Our well-banded raft to steer,
And the rapids we run, oh to us seem but fun,
For we're 'void of cowardly fear.

Hard toil, scant comfort and horrid working conditions were the lot of the loggers.
Songs like this, with it's haunting Dorian mode melody, helped pass the long nights and relieved some of the misery.

The Erie Canal

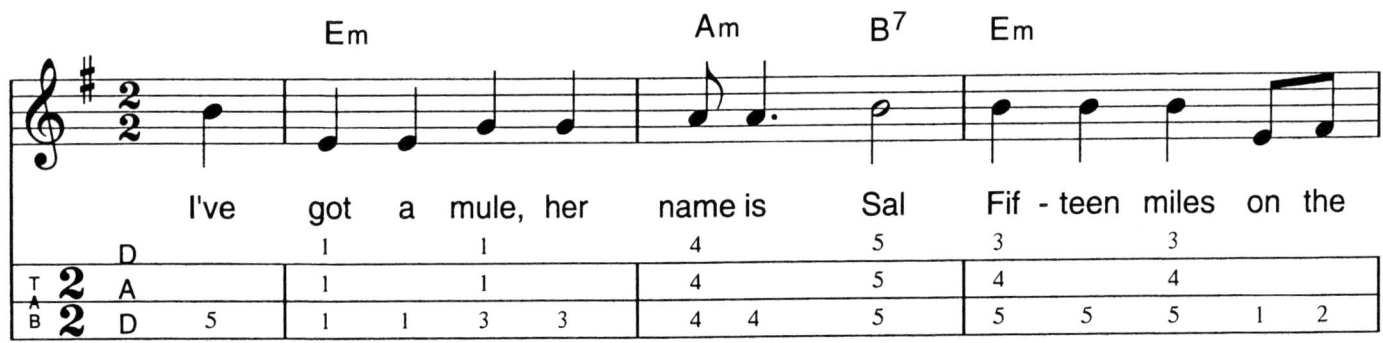

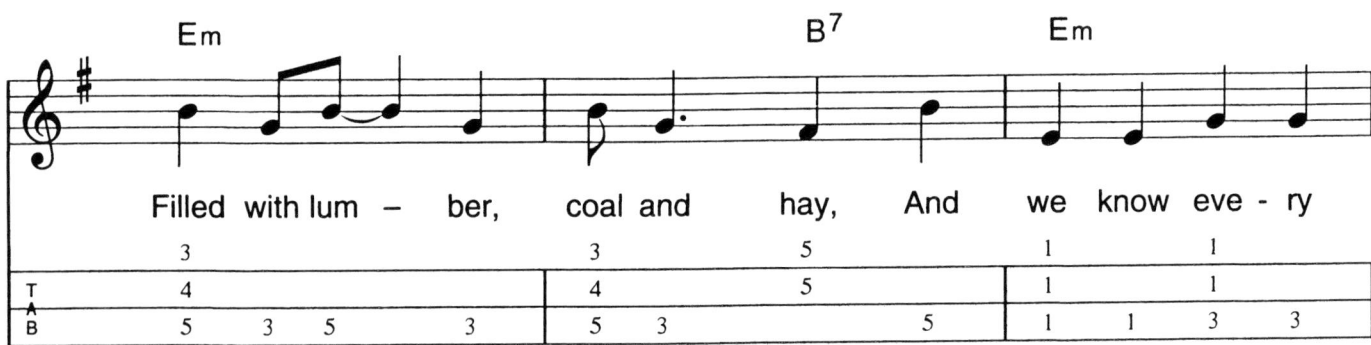
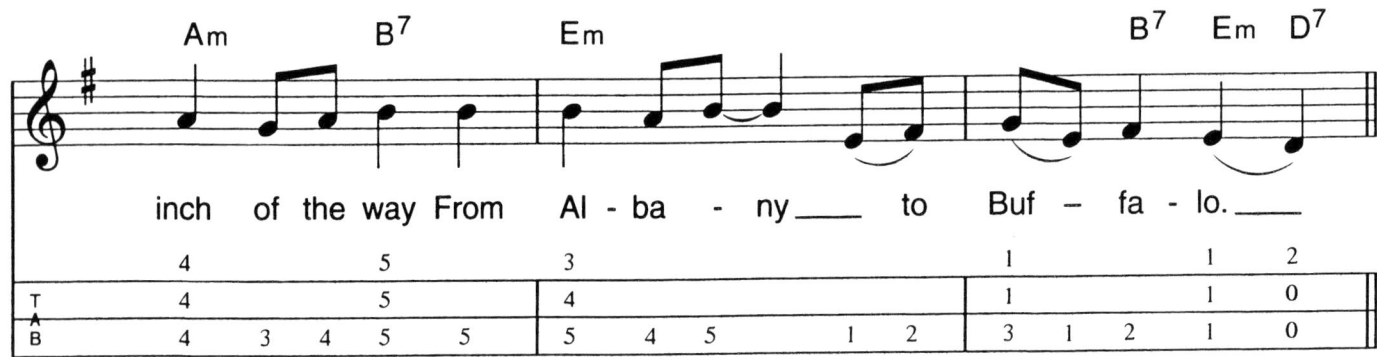

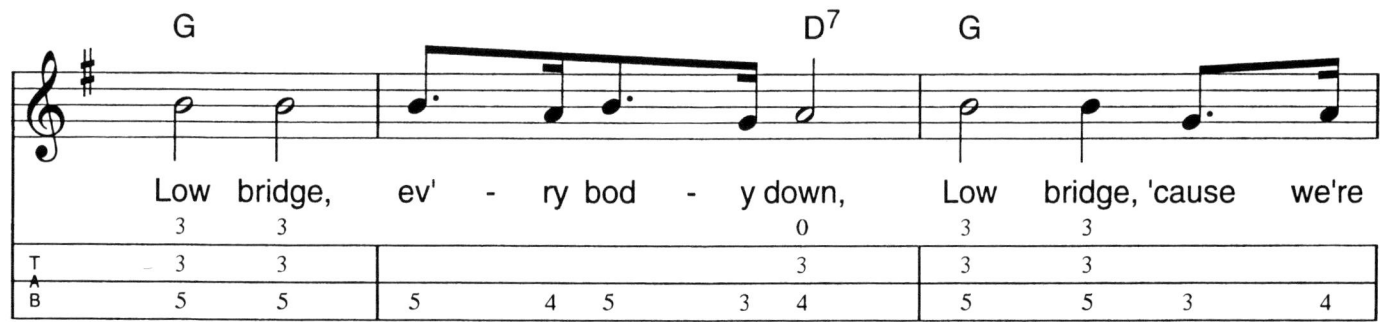

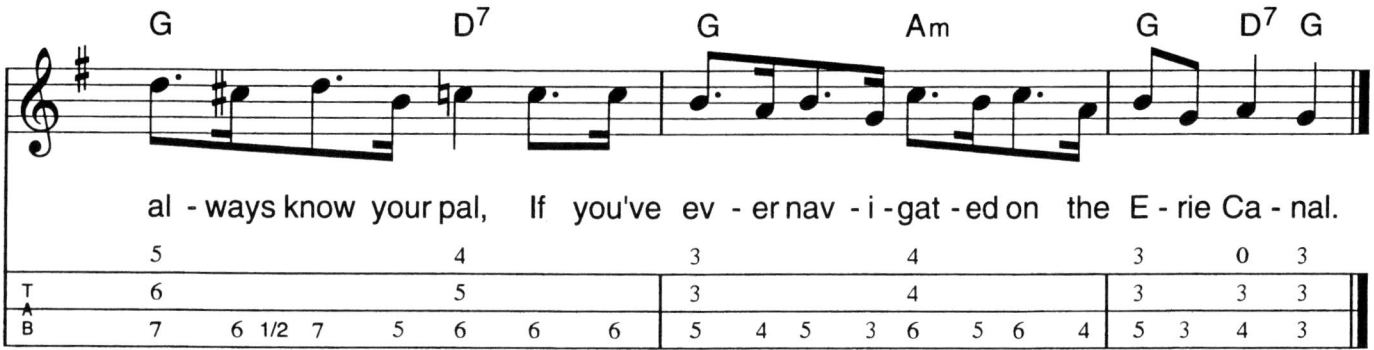

I've got a mule, her name is Sal,
Fifteen miles on the Erie Canal.
She's a good old worker and a good old pal,
Fifteen miles on the Erie Canal.
We've hauled some barges in our day,
Filled with lumber, coal and hay,
And we know every inch of the way
From Albany to Buffalo.

Better be movin' along, old pal,
Fifteen miles on the Erie Canal,
Bet your life I'll never part with Sal,
Fifteen miles on the Erie Canal.
Get up there mule, here comes a lock,
We'll make Rome by six o'clock,
One more trip and back we'll go,
Back we'll go to Buffalo.

CH
Low bridge, ev'rybody down,
Low bridge, 'cause we're comin' to a town;
And you'll always know your neighbor,
You'll always know your pal,
If you've ever navigated on the Erie Canal.

The Erie Canal, completed in 1825, totally transformed the country.

Whopee Ti Yi Yo

As I was out walking one morning for pleasure,
I spied a cowpuncher a riding along.
His hat was thrown back and his spurs were a janglin'
And as he rode by he was singin' this song:

CH
Whoopee ti yi yo git along little dogies,
It's your misfortune and none of my own;
Whoopee ti yi yo, git along little dogies,
You know that Wyoming will be your new home.

Early in the spring we round up the dogies
Rope 'em and brand 'em and bob off their tails,
Round up the horses and load the chuck wagon,
Then throw those dogies out on the trail.

Some of the boys goes out here for pleasure
But that's where they get it most awfully wrong,
They haven't the idea what trouble they give us
When we go driving them dogies along.

Your mother was raised up way down in Texas
Where the jimson weed and the sand burrs grow,
Now we'll fill you up on prickly pear and cholla
Till you are ready for the trail to Idaho.

It's whooping and yelling and driving the dogies,
It's how I wish you would go on,
Git along, git along, git along little dogies,
For you know that Chicago will be your new home.

Although it has been much romanticized, the cowboy's life was hard, the work dangerous, and the pay abysmal. The point of it all was to move cattle to the rail heads, where they'd be shipped off to the meat packing plants of Chicago.

The Drunken Sailor

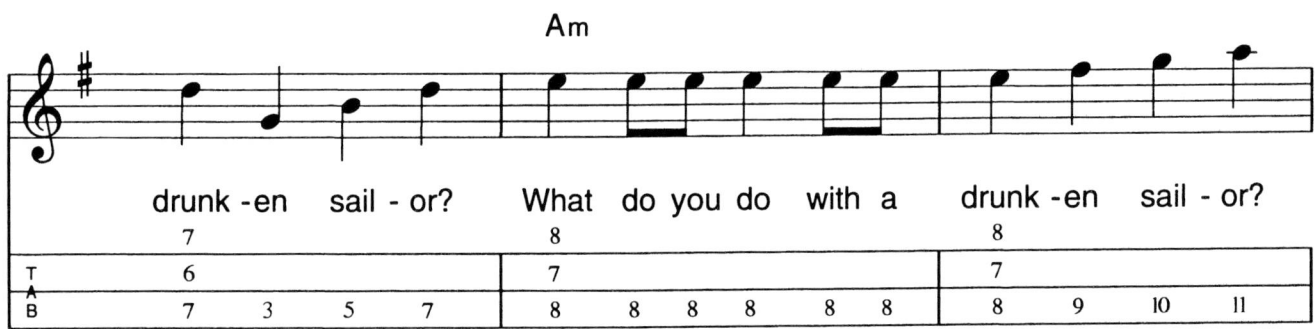
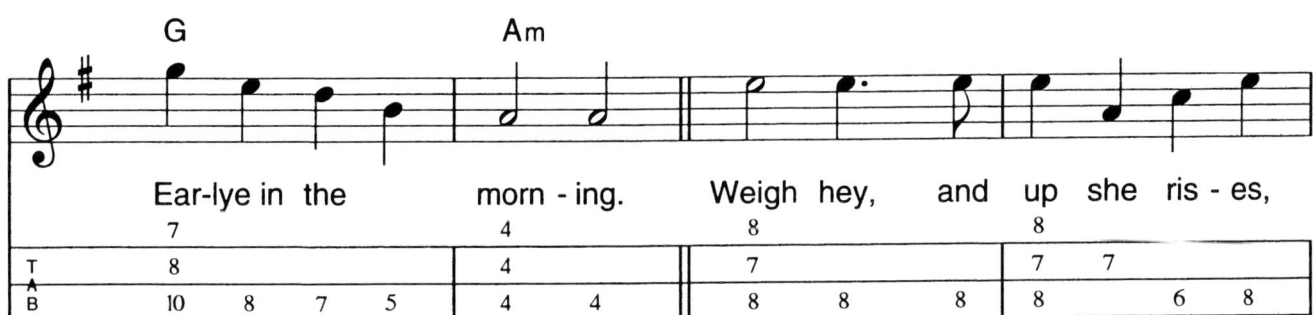

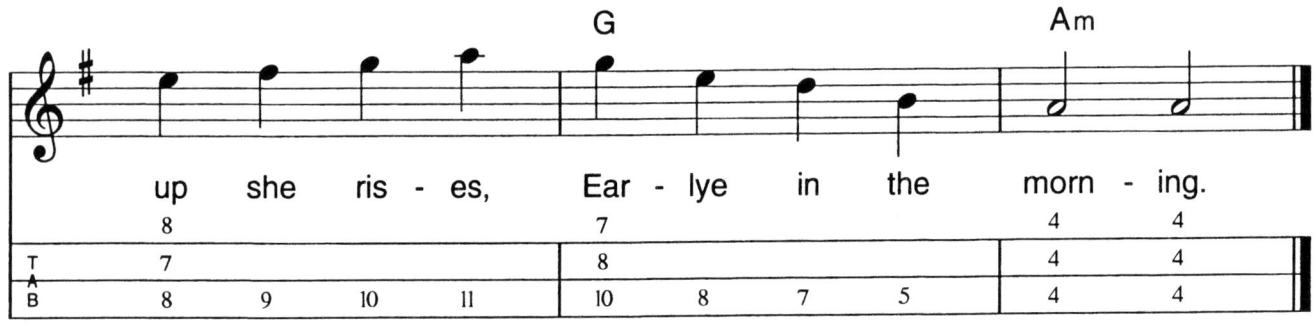

What do you do with a drunken sailor?
What do you do with a drunken sailor?
What do you do with a drunken sailor
Ear-lye in the morning?

> CH
> Weigh hey, and up she rises,
> Weigh hey, and up she rises,
> Weigh, hey, and up she rises,
> Ear-lye in the morning

Put him in the longboat till he's sober,
Put him in the longboat till he's sober,
Put him in the longboat till he's sober
Ear-lye in the morning.

Stick him in the bilge and make him drink it.

Tie him to the scuppers with the hose pipe on him.

Toss him in bed with the Captain's daughter.

Shave his belly with a rusty razor.

Tie him to the topmast when she's yardarm under.

Heave him by the leg in a running bowline.

Keel haul him till he's sober.

Considering the amount of grog, wine and beer in a ship's ration, these rustic hangover measures must have seen frequent use.

The E-RI-E

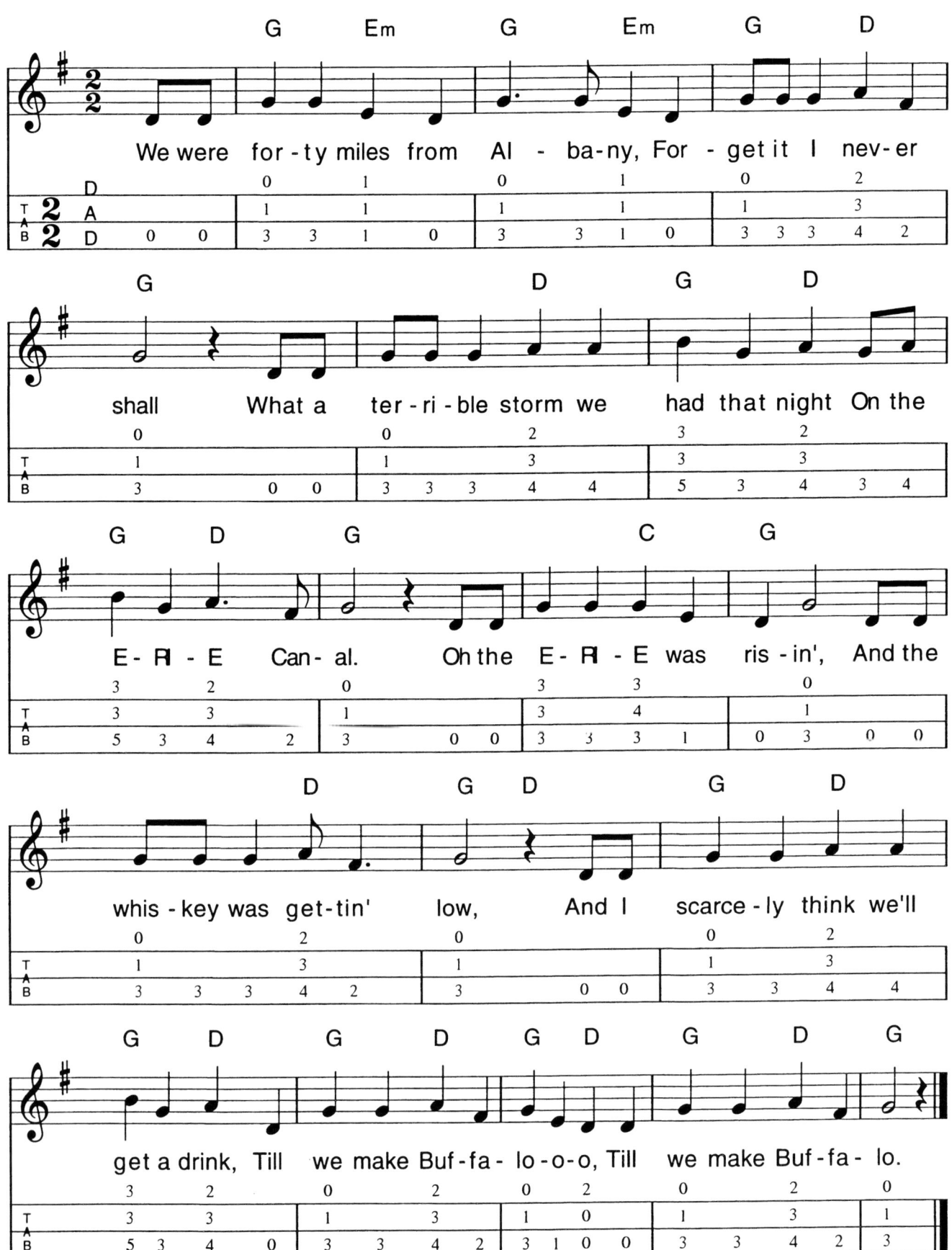

We were forty miles from Albany
Forget it I never shall.
What a terrible storm we had that night
On the E-RI-E canal.

>CH
>Oh the E-RI-E was risin' and the whiskey was gettin' low,
>And I scarcely think we'll get a drink,
>Till we make Buffalo-o-o,
>Till we make Buffalo.

Two days out from Syracuse
The vessel struck a shoal,
And we like to all have foundered
On a chunk of Lackawanna coal.

The cook she was a kind old soul,
She has a ragged dress,
So we hoisted her up on a pole
As a signal of distress.

We hollered for the captain
On the tow path treading dirt;
He jumped aboard and stanched the leak
With his brand new flannel shirt.

When we got to Syracuse,
The off mule he was dead,
The nigh mule got blind staggers
So we cracked him on the head.

The captain, he got married,
The cook, she went to jail.
And I'm the only sober man
That's left to tell this tale.

Buffalo is the terminus of the Erie Canal. We use to sing this one in elementary school even though the closest thing to a canal was a sandy channel that went dry in the summer and Albany was over 2500 miles away.

Blood Red Roses

I thought I heard the old man say,
Go down, you blood red roses, go down,
Just one more pull and then belay,
Go down, you blood red roses, go down.
Oh, you pinks and posies,
Go down, you blood red roses, go down.

Just one more pull and that'll do,
Go down, you blood red roses, go down,
And we're the boys to pull her through.
Go down, you blood red roses, go down.
Oh, you pinks and posies,
Go down, you blood red roses, go down.

Around Cape Horn in frost and snow,
Go down, you blood red roses, go down,
For that is where the whale fish blow.
Go down, you blood red roses, go down.
Oh, you pinks and posies,
Go down, you blood red roses, go down.

As I was going 'round Cape Horn,
Go down, you blood red roses, go down,
I wished to my soul I'd never been born
Go down, you blood red roses, go down.
Oh, you pinks and posies,
Go down, you blood red roses, go down.

In the early 1960's, dulcimer pioneer Richard Farina wrote some new lyrics to this venerable chantey, changing the line "Oh you pinks and posies" to "Hold your boots and poses" in the process. Pity, because I've always liked the idea of the sailors bawling about blossoms on the bounding main.

Pie in the Sky

Joe Hill

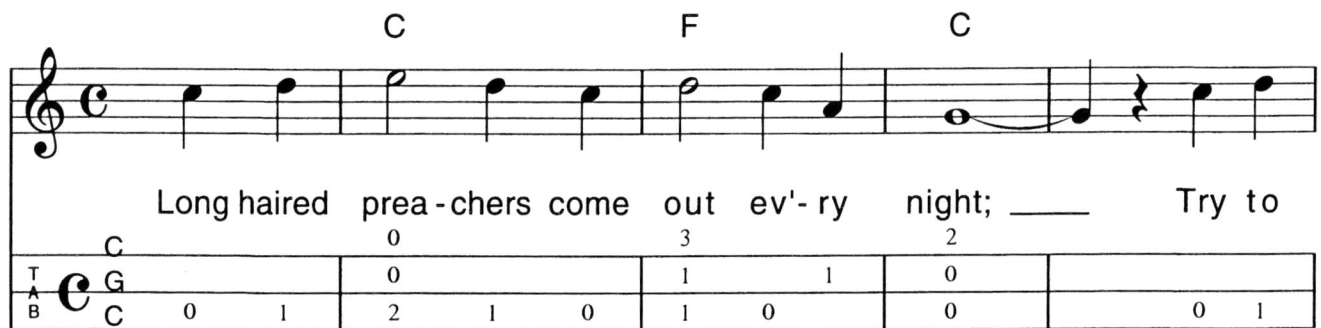
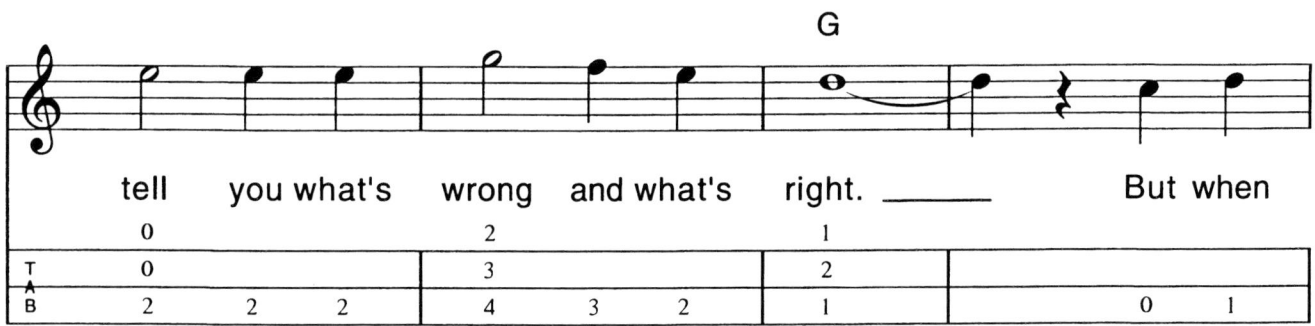
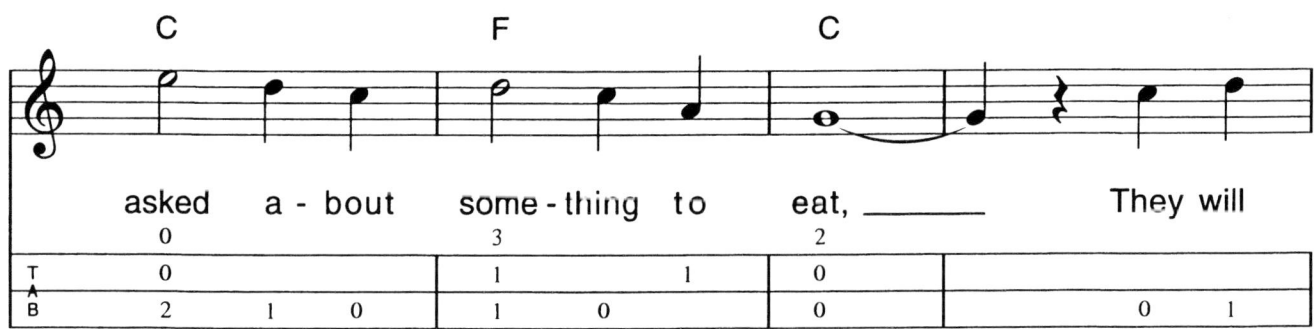
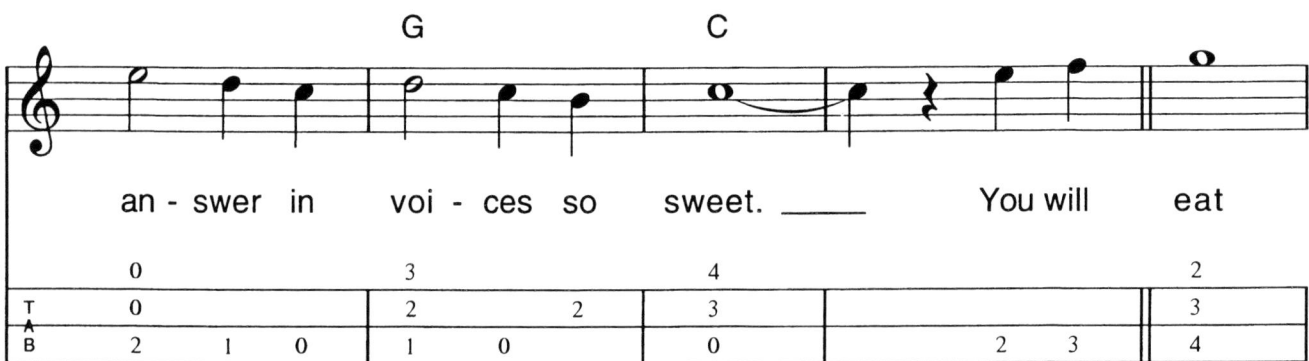

Long haired preachers come out ev'ry night,
Try to tell you what's wrong and what's right;
But when asked about something to eat,
They will answer with voices so sweet:

   CH
   "You will eat, bye and bye
   In that glorious land in the sky.
   Work and pray, live on hay,
   You'll eat pie in the sky when you die."

Oh, the Starvation Army they play,
And they sing and they clap and they pray,
Till they get all your coins on the drum,
Then they tell you when you're on the bum:

If you fight hard for children and wife,
Try to get something good in this life,
You're a sinner and bad man they tell,
When you die you will sure go to Hell.

Working men of all countries unite,
Side by side we for freedom will fight,
When the world and it's wealth we have gained,
To the grafter we'll sing this refrain:

   Last Chorus
   "You will eat, bye and bye,
   When you've learned how to cook and to fry,
   Chop some wood, 'twill do you good,
   And you'll eat in the sweet bye and bye."

Although work songs may boast of a happy life of toil, in reality things weren't so great.
Labor organizer Joe Hill was killed for his trouble in 1914.

The Greenland Whale Fishery

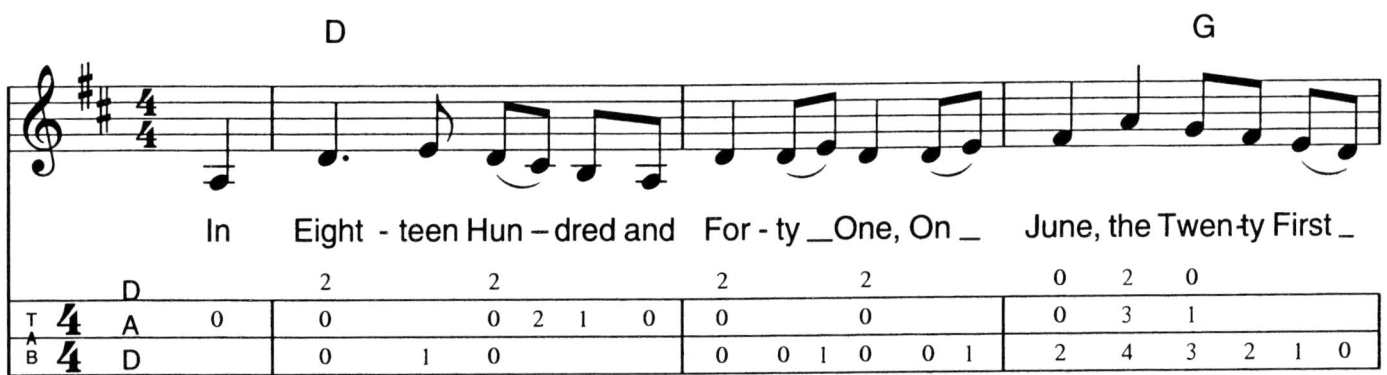

In Eighteen Hundred and Forty One,
On June, the Twenty First day;
We hoisted our colors to the top of the mast
And for Greenland bore away,
Brave boys,
And for Greenland bore away.

The lookout stood on the top mast tree,
The glass was in his hand,
"There's a whale, there's a whale, there's a whale fish," he cried,
"And she blows on ev'ry span,"
Brave boys,
"She blows on ev'ry span."

The captain stood on the quarter deck,
The ice was in his eye.
"Over haul, over haul, let your davit tackles fall,
And put your boats to sea."

We lowered the boats with the men on board,
The whale was in full view,
Resolved, resolved was each whaler lad bold,
To steer where the whale fish blew.

The harpoon struck and the line played out,
But she gave such a flourish with her tale
She capsized the boat and we lost five men,
And we did not catch that whale.

Oh the lossin' of the sperm whale fish
Did grieve our captain sore,
But the lossin' of those five jolly tars,
It did grieve him ten times more.

"A-bank her now," the captain cried,
"The winter star doth appear.
It's time to leave this cold, cold place,
And so homeward we will steer."

Oh Greenland is a cold, cold place,
A land that's never green.
Where there's ice and snow and the whalefishes blow,
And the daylight's seldom seen.

A vivid description of the dangers of whaling. Though today many abhor the practice, we can still appreciate the skill displayed and hardships suffered by the Yankee whalermen.

I'm a rambler, I'm a gambler,
I'm a long way from home,
And them that don't like me,
They can leave me alone.

Songs of Good Times and Bad Whiskey

Darlin' Cory

Wake up, wake up Darlin' Cory!
Why do you sleep so sound?
The revenue man is comin';
Gonna tear your still house down.

Last time I see Darlin' Cory,
She was standing by the sea.
Forty-five 'round her bosom
And a shotgun on her knee.

Go on, go on, Darlin' Cory;
Quit your hangin' 'round my bed.
Whiskey's ruint my body
Pretty women's gone to my head.

A great old time banjo tune that lends itself nicely to the dulcimer. I've always hoped this was true story.

Frankie And Johnnie

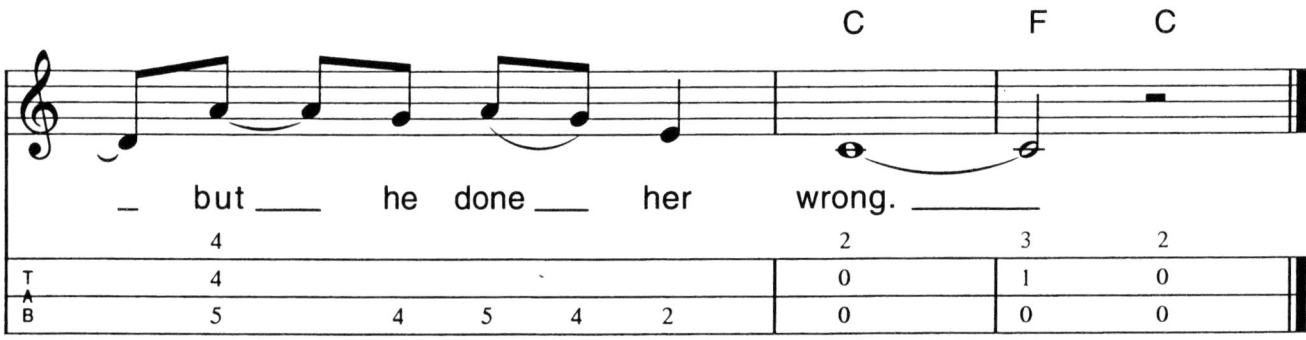

Frankie and Johnnie were lovers,
Oh, lordy how they could love,
They swore to be true to each other,
Just as true as the stars above,
He was her man, but he done her wrong!

Johnnie took Frankie out walkin'
Wearin' his brand new suit
Frankie said: "Oh, Johnnie,
Honey, you sure look cute!"
He was her man, but he done her wrong!

Johnnie said: "Frankie, I'm leavin'
But I won't be too long.
Don't you wait up for me, Frankie
Or worry while I'm gone."
He was her man, but he done her wrong!

Frankie went down to the corner,
To get her a bucket of beer,
She said to the fat bartender;
"Has my lover-man been here?"
He was her man, but he done her wrong!

"I don't want to tell you a story,
I don't want to tell you a lie,
I saw your man about an hour ago
With a gal named Alice Bly,
If he's your man, he's doin' you wrong!"

Frankie went down to the hotel;
Rang up the hotel bell.
"Get out of my way, all you floozies,
Or I'll blow you straight to hell,
Where is my man, 'cause he's doin' me wrong?"

Frankie walked down to the hotel,
Peeped over the transom so high;
There sat her Johnnie,
Just lovin' that Alice Bly,
He was her man, and he was doin' her wrong!

Frankie pulled back her kimono,
Took out a little forty-four,
She shot Alice Bly so hard
She shot through the hotel floor,
He was her man, but he done her wrong!

Johnnie took off his Stetson;
"Frankie, honey, please don't shoot!"
Frankie pulled out her revolver
And the gun went rooty toot toot,
He was her man, but he done her wrong!

"Roll out your rubber tired hearses,
Roll out your rubber tired hacks;
There's twelve men goin' to the graveyard,
Just eleven of them comin' back,
He was my man, but he done me wrong!"

"Get me a thousand policemen;
Go and lock me in your cell.
'Cause I shot my Johnnie so dead
That I know I'm going to hell!"
He was her man, but he done her wrong!

Frankie and Johnnie were lovers,
Oh, lordy how they could love,
They swore to be true to each other,
Just as true as the stars above,
He was her man, but he done her wrong!

*A truly great song from the African-American ballad tradition.
There are as many versions and verses as waves in the sea.*

Bonnie Black Bess

When Fortune's blind goddess had fled my abode
And friends proved unfaithful, I took to the road
To plunder the wealthy and relieve my distress.
I brought you to aid me, my Bonnie Black Bess.

No vile whip nor spur did your sides ever gall,
For none did you need, you would bound at my call;
And for each act of kindness, you would me caress.
Thou art never unfaithful, my Bonnie Black Bess.

When dark able midnight her mantle had thrown
O'er the bright face of nature, how oft we have gone
To the famed Hounslow heath, though an unwelcome guest
To the minions of fortune, my Bonnie Black Bess.

How silent you stood when the carriage I stopped.
The gold and the jewels it's inmates would drop.
No poor man I plundered nor e'er did oppress
The widows and orphans, my Bonnie Black Bess.

When auger-eyed justice did me hot pursue,
From Yorktown to London like lightening we flew.
No toll bars could stop you, deep waters you'd breast,
And in twelve hours we made it, my Bonnie Black Bess.

But hate darkens o'er me, despair is my lot,
And the law does pursue me for the many I've shot;
To save me, dumb friend, you have done your best,
You are worn out and weary, my Bonnie Black Bess.

Hark, hear the hounds-but they never shall have
A beast like thee, so noble and brave.
You must die, my dumb friend, though it does me distress.
There, there, I have shot you, my Bonnie Black Bess.

In after years, when I am dead and gone,
This story will be handed from father to son;
My fate some will pity, and some will confess,
'Twas through kindness I killed her, my Bonnie Black Bess.

Although not as well known as it deserves to be, this superb ballad about the English highwayman Ben Turpin served as a model for many songs celebrating famous American outlaws. No doubt because of Turpin's obvious love for his horse, the song was popular among cowboys.

Camptown Races

The Camptown ladies sing this song,
Doo Dah, Doo Dah
The Camptown racetrack five miles long,
All the Doo Dah Day.

> CH
> Going to run all night, going to run all day.
> I'll bet my money on the bob-tailed nag,
> Somebody bet on the bay.

The long tailed filly and the big black horse,
Doo Dah, Doo Dah
They flew the track and they both cut across.
All the Doo Dah Day.

Blind horse stickin' in a big mud hole.
Couldn't touch bottom with a ten foot pole.

Old muley cow came on the track,
The bob-tail threw her on her back.

They flew around like a railroad car
Running a race with a shooting star.

I went downtown with my hat caved in,
Came back home with a pocket full of tin.

Foster wrote this in 1850 as part of a review; it quickly became the most popular song in the country. When I was a very little kid I used to worry about that poor blind horse. Why would anyone have allowed it on the racetrack? As for the muley cow, well...

I'm a Rambler, I'm a Gambler

I'm a rambler, I'm a gambler, I'm a long way from home;
And if people don't like me, they can leave me alone.

I had me a sweetheart, her age was sixteen,
She was the flower of Bolton, the rose of Sharleen.

But her parents didn't like me, now she feels the same,
If I'm writ in your book, love, you can blot out my name.

I'll tune up my fiddle and rosin my bow
And I'll make myself welcome werever I go.

You may boast of your knowledge and brag of your sense
It'll all be forgotten a hundred years hence.

This lovely piece is related to a whole slew of "broken-hearted I'll wander" songs. It sometimes shares verses with songs like Oh, Can't You Hear That Turtle Dove, Jack of Diamonds, The Wagoner's Lad, *and many others.*

Handsome Molly

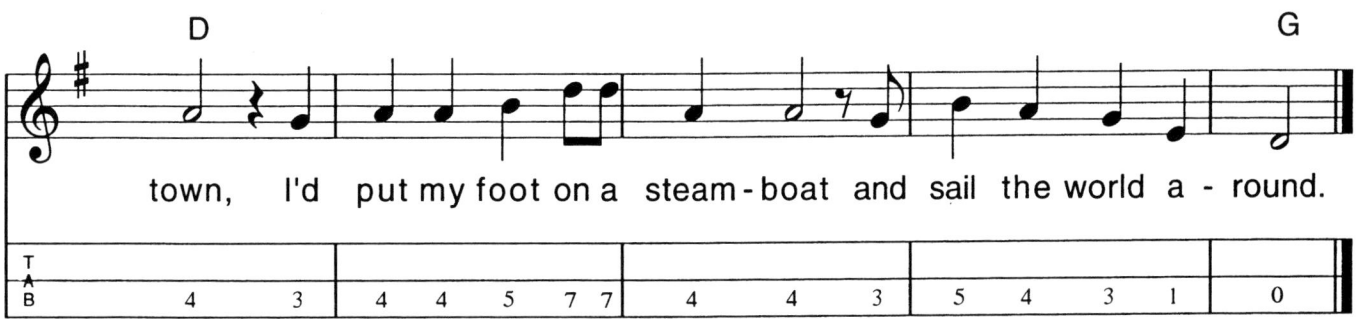

I wish I was in London or some other seaport town;
I'd put my foot on a steamboat and sail the world around.

While sailing 'round the ocean, while sailing 'round the sea,
I'd think of handsome Molly wherever she may be.

She rode to church one Sunday, she passed me right on by,
I could tell her mind was changin' from the roving of her eye.

Do you remember, Molly, you gave me your right hand?
You said that if you'd marry that I would be the man.

Now you've broke your promise, go home with who you please,
While I'm out on the ocean, you're lying at your ease.

They say that every sailor's story starts with a broken heart.

Jack o' Diamonds

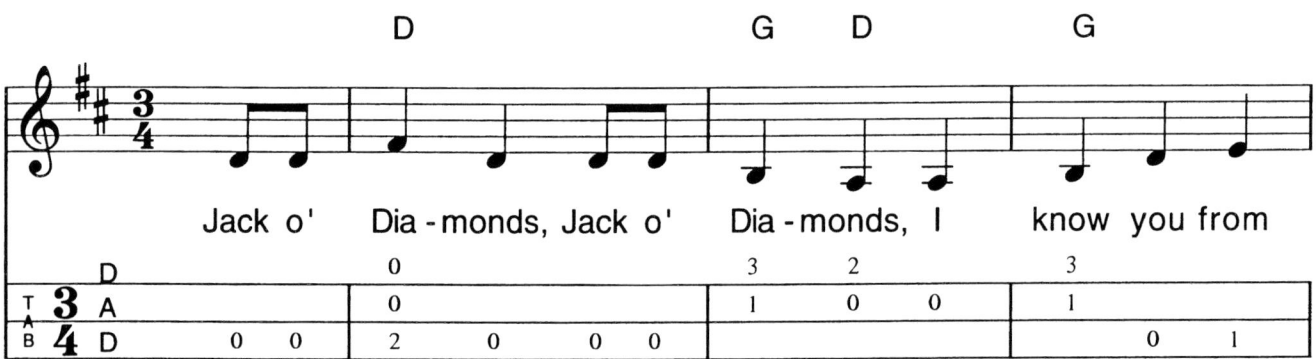
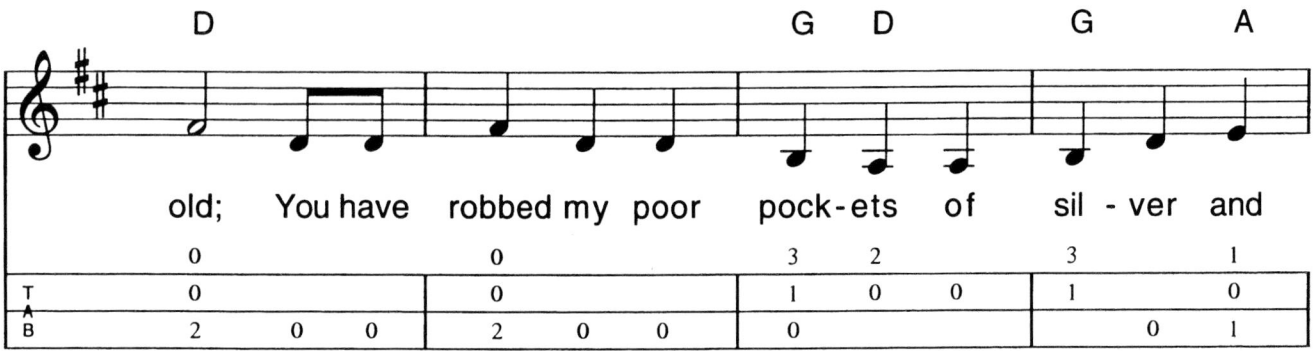
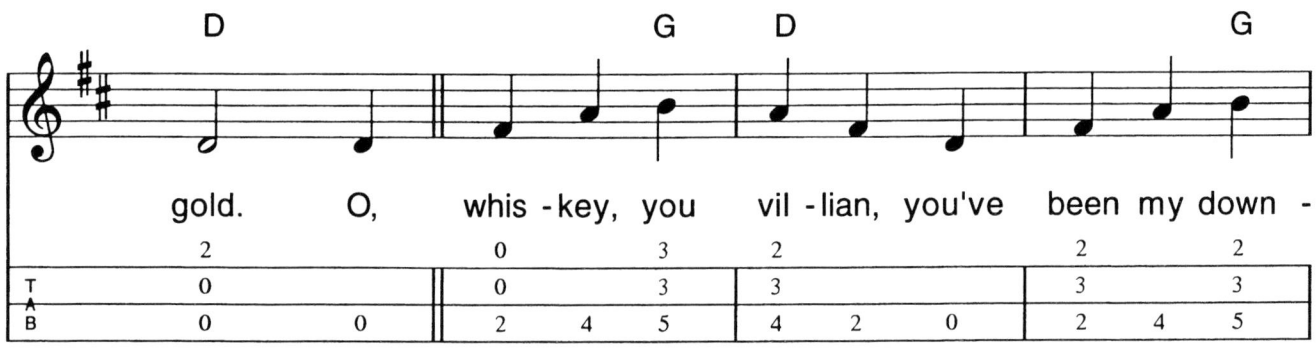

Jack o' Diamonds, Jack o' Diamonds, I know you from old;
You have robbed my poor pockets of silver and gold.
O, whiskey, you villain, you've been my downfall,
You've kicked me, you've cussed me, but I love you for all.

O Molly, O Molly, it's for your sake alone,
That I've left my old parents, my house and my home.
I'll drink and I'll gamble, my money's my own,
And them that don't like me can leave me alone.

Rye whiskey, rye whiskey, rye whiskey I cry,
If I don't get rye whiskey I surely will die.
It's beefsteak when I'm hungry, whisky when I'm dry
Greenbacks when I'm hard up and heaven when I die.

If the river was whiskey and I was a duck,
I'd dive to the bottom and never come up.
But the river ain't whisky, and I ain't a duck,
I'll play Jack o' Diamonds and trust to my luck.

I've play cards in England, I've played cards in Spain,
I'll bet you five dollars I'll beat you this game.
O Molly, O Molly, I've told you before,
Make me a pallet, I'll lie on the floor.

Jack o' Diamonds, Rye Whiskey, The Rebel Soldier, Drunken Hiccoughs; *this one's got almost as many names as it has verses. Old time fiddlers sometimes add a pull-off section to simulate the hics.*

Jimmy Crack Corn

Dan Emmett

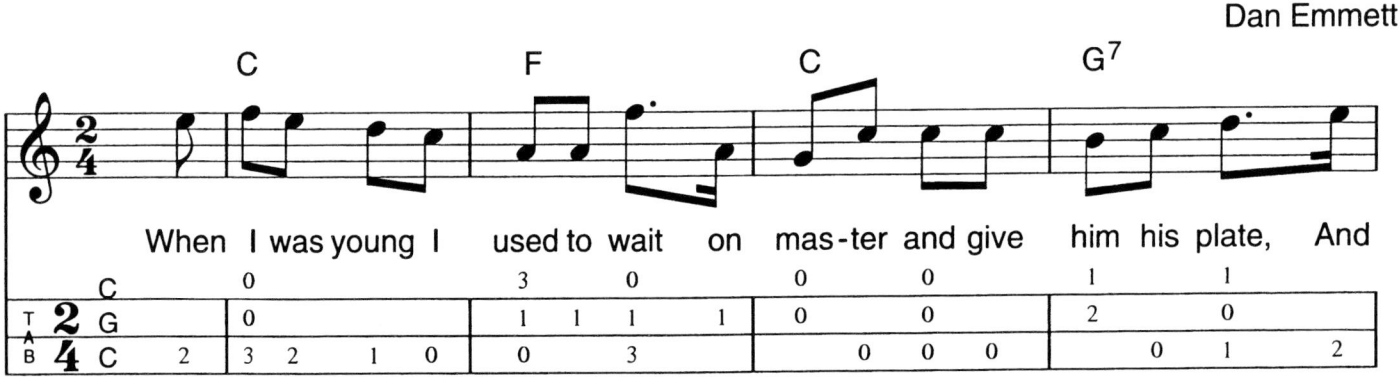

When I was young I used to wait
On master, and bring him his plate,
And pass the bottle when he got dry,
And brush away the blue-tail fly.

   CH
   Jimmy crack corn, and I don't care,
   Jimmy crack corn, and I don't care,
   Jimmy crack corn, and I don't care,
   My master's gone away.

When he would ride in the afternoon
I'd follow with my hickory broom,
The pony being rather shy
When bitten by the blue-tail fly.

Once when he rode 'round the farm
The flies around him thick did swarm;
The pony which was very shy
Was bitten by the blue-tail fly.

The pony run, he jump, he pitch,
He threw my master in a ditch,
He died, the jury wondered why;
The verdict was, "The blue-tail fly."

They laid him under a 'simmon tree,
His epitaph for all to see,
"Beneath this stone I'm forced to lie,
A victim of the blue-tail fly."

*A popular 1840's minstrel song that entered the folk tradition as a children's song.
I used to sing it in grade school – given that cracking corn refers to the process of distilling whiskey,
maybe this wasn't such a good idea.*

Hallelujah, I'm a Bum

"Haywire Mac" McClintock

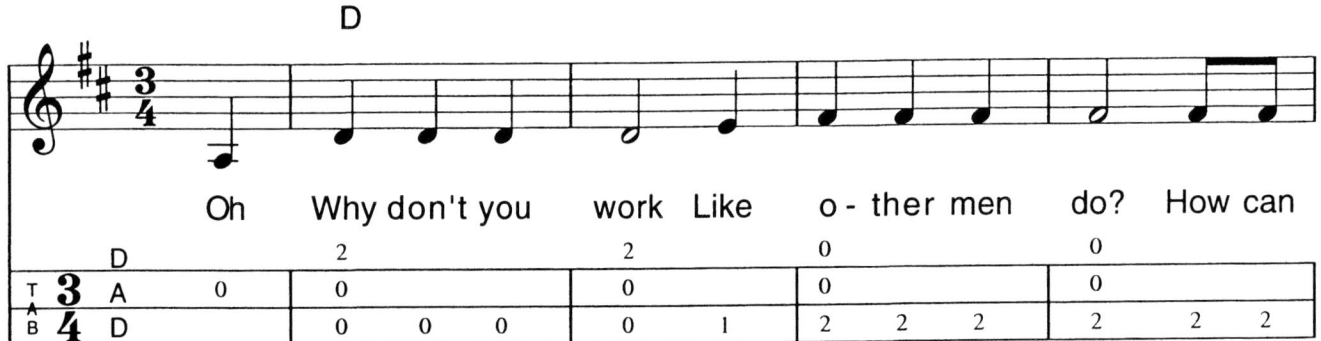

Oh, why don't you work like other men do?
How can I get a job when there's no work to do?

> CH
> Hallelujah! I'm a bum;
> Hallelujah! Bum again;
> Hallelujah, give us a handout
> To revive us again.

When springtime rolls around, oh won't we have fun?
We'll get out of jail and we'll go on the bum.

Oh, why don't you work like other men do?
How can I get a job when you're holding down two?

I went to my boss to ask for a drink,
He handed me a glass and he showed me the sink.

I went to a house and I knocked on the door,
The lady said, "Scram, bum! You've been here before."

I went to a house to beg for some bread,
A man there said "Poor bum, the baker is dead."

I like my boss, he's a good friend of mine,
That's why I starving out on the bread line.

I like my boss, he's a good friend of mine,
That's why I walking down Joe Hill's main line.

It seems there's always a depression on for a certain percentage of the population. It was true at the turn of the Twentieth Century when the Wobblies were active; it was true in the Thirties when breadlines filled the streets; and it is still true today for the homeless and the working poor.

Don't Let Your Deal Go Down

Noter Style

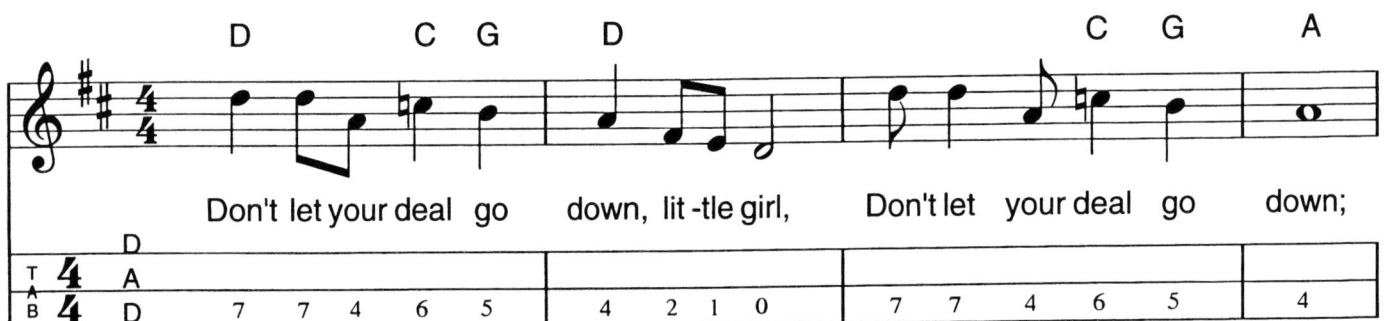

Don't let your deal go down, little girl,
Don't let your deal go down.
Don't let your deal go down, little girl,
Till your last gold dollar is gone.

Where did you get those shoes that you wear,
And that dress so fine?
I got my shoes from an old engineer,
Got my dress from a driver in the mine.

Who's gonna shoe your pretty little foot;
And who's gonna glove your hand?
And who's gonna kiss your red ruby lips
Tell me, who's gonna be your man?

My mama will shoe my pretty little foot;
And Papa's gonna glove my hand.
Sister will kiss my red ruby lips
'Cause I don't need no man!

This great old time song shares verses with at least a dozen other songs.
Though it may be a recent addition, I've always liked the defiance in the heroine's answer to the question
"Who's gonna kiss your red ruby lips?"

What wondous love is this;
O my soul, O my soul?

Songs of Faith and Hope

Wondrous Love

Noter Style

What wondrous love is this,
O my soul, O my soul;
What wondrous love is this,
O my soul.
What wondrous love is this
That caused the Lord of bliss
To send this blessed gift
For my soul, for my soul;
To send this blessed gift
For my soul.

When I was sinking down,
Sinking down, sinking down;
When I was sinking down, sinking down.
When I was sinking down beneath God's righteous frown,
Christ laid aside his crown
For my soul, for my soul,
Christ laid aside his crown for my soul.

And when from death I'm free,
I'll sing on, I'll sing on;
And when from death I'm free,
I'll sing on.
And when from death I'm free,
I'll sing and joyful be,
And through eternity
I'll sing on, I'll sing on.
And through eternity I'll sing on

The Dorian melody is a perfect fit for this plaintive Appalachian hymn. Surprisingly, the same air has been used to extol the dubious virtues of Captain Kidd, a notorious pirate, and the western outlaw Sam Bass.

Little David, Play on Your Harp

Little David play on your harp
Hallelu', Hallelu'
Little David play on your harp
Hallelu'!

Little David was a shepherd boy,
He killed Goliath and shouted for joy.

Little David dance, little David sing,
Little David do most anything.

Little David pray, little David bow,
But God loved David anyhow.

Joshua was the son of Nunn;
He never quit till the work was done.

I don't know but I've been told,
Streets of Heav'n are paved with gold.

You better listen to my advice,
Quit drinkin' that gin and shootin' dice.

*Since mouth organs are commonly called "harps" almost every harmonica player I know plays this.
I'd like to think little David blew a mean blues.*

He's Got The Whole World In His Hands

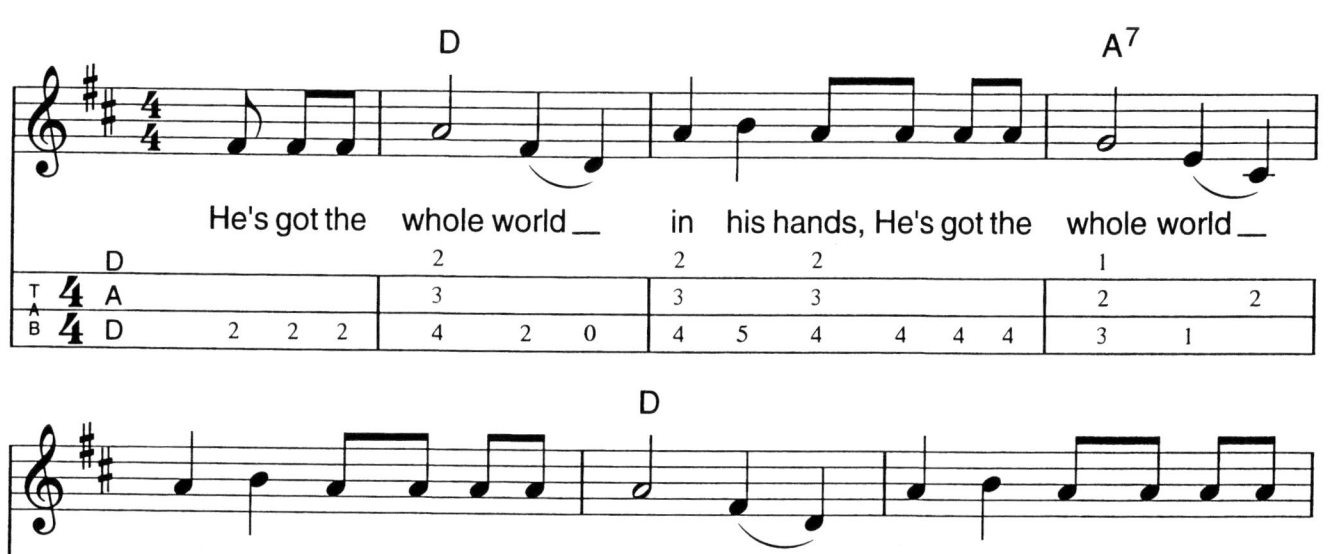

He's got the whole world in His hands,
He's got the whole world in His hands,
He's got the whole world in His hands,
He's got the whole world in His hands.

He's got you and me, brother, in His hands, etc.

He's got you and me, sister, in His hands, etc.

He's got the little bitty babies in His hands, etc.

This fine old gospel sing-a-long is a favorite of little bitty babies everywhere.

Amazing Grace

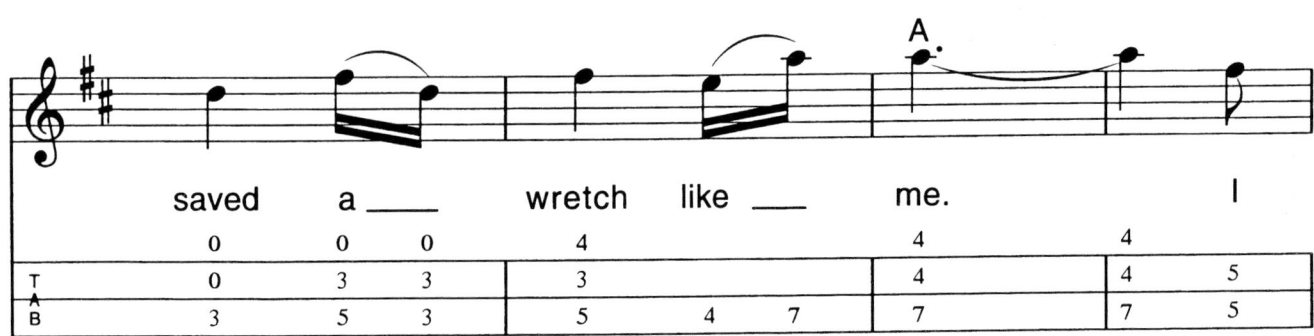
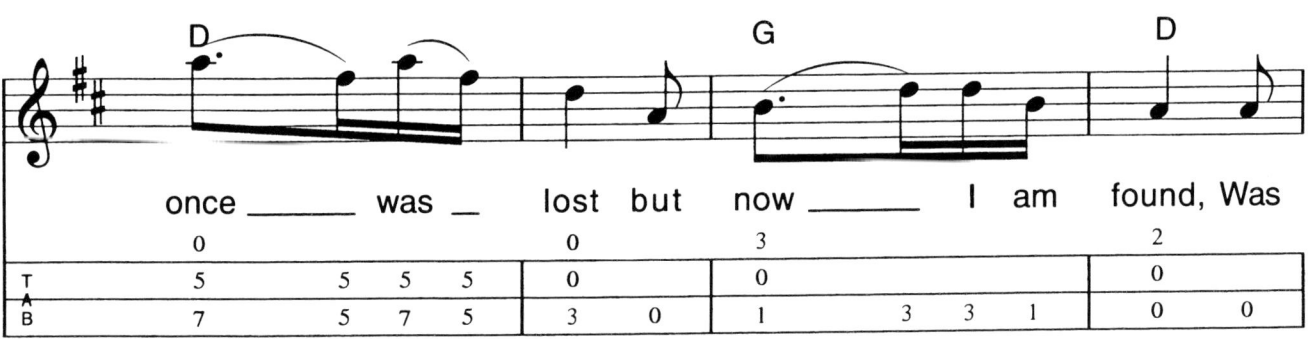

Amazing grace, how sweet the sound
That saved a wretch like me.
I once was lost but now I'm found,
Was blind but now I see.

It was grace that taught my heart to fear
And grace my fears relieved,
How precious did that grace appear
The hour I first believed.

Through many dangers, toils and snares,
I have already come.
It was grace that brought me safe thus far,
And grace will lead me home.

The Lord has promised good to me,
His word my hope secures.
He will my shield and portion be
As long as life endures.

And when this heart and flesh shall fail
And mortal life shall cease,
I shall possess within the veil
A life of health and peace.

When we've been there ten thousand years
Bright shining as the sun;
We've no less time to sing God's praise,
Then when we've first begun.

This stunning hymn was composed by reformed slaver John Newton in 1779. The final verse, as good a description of eternity as may be found, was added some years later by an anonymous writer. A number of variant melodies exist; this one comes from the singing of a congregation in the Pacific Northwest.

Let My People Go

When Israel was in Egypt's land, let my people go.
Oppressed so hard they could not stand, let my people go.

CH
Go down Moses, 'way down in Egypt land,
Tell old Pharoah, let my people Go.

Thus said the Lord, old Moses said, let my people go.
If not I'll smite your first born dead, let my people go.

Hold On

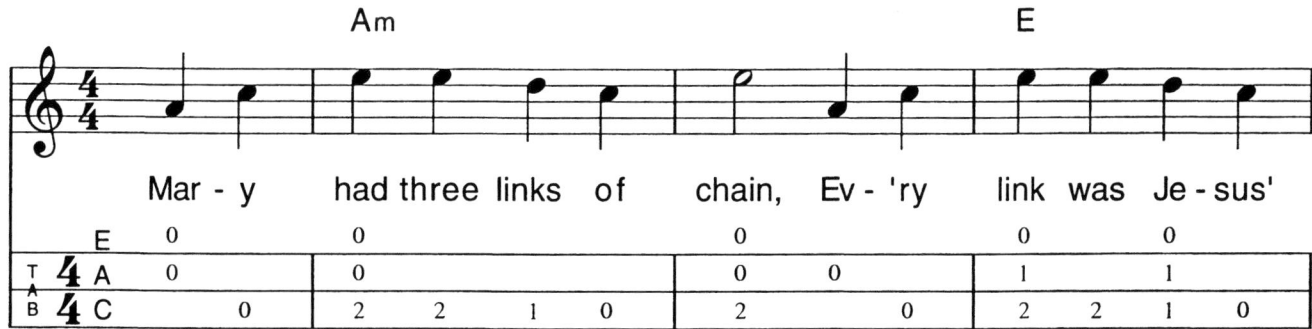
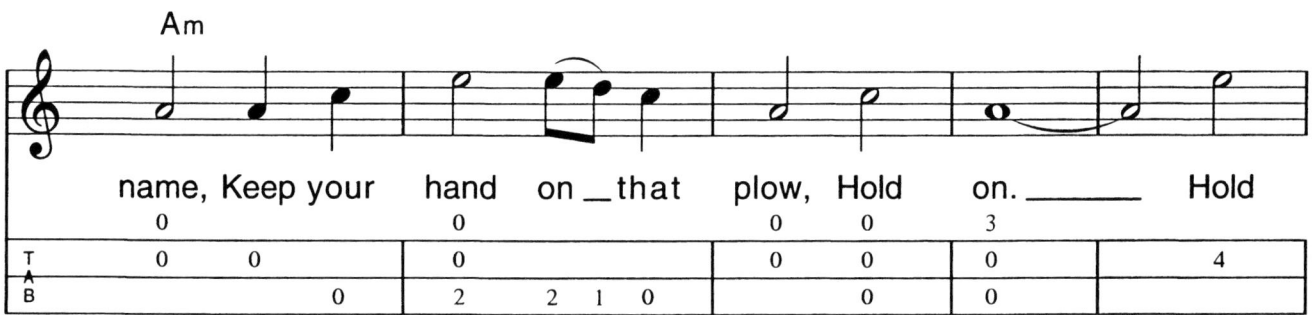
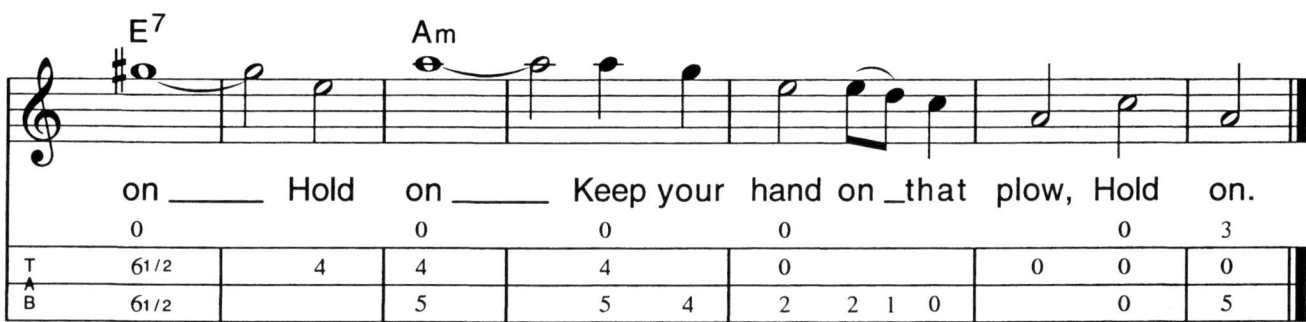

Mary wore three lengths of chain,
Every link was Jesus' name.
Keep your hand on that plough,
Hold on, Hold on.
Keep your hand on that plough, Hold on.

One of these days about four o'clock,
This old world's gonna reel and rock.

Go away Satan, let me be,
You fooled my brother but you can't fool me.

Satin wears a sinful shoe,
Look out, Brother, he'll slip it on you!

Got my hand on the gospel plough,
Wouldn't take nothin' for my journey now.

I get to heaven gonna sit right down,
Wear a white robe and a starry crown.

I don't know but I've been told
The streets of Heaven are paved with gold.

A pair of old-time favorites, both Go Down Moses *and* Hold On *use unexpected notes derived from a variation of the familiar minor scale. They present a worthwhile challenge to the dulcimer player.*

Poor Wayfaring Stranger

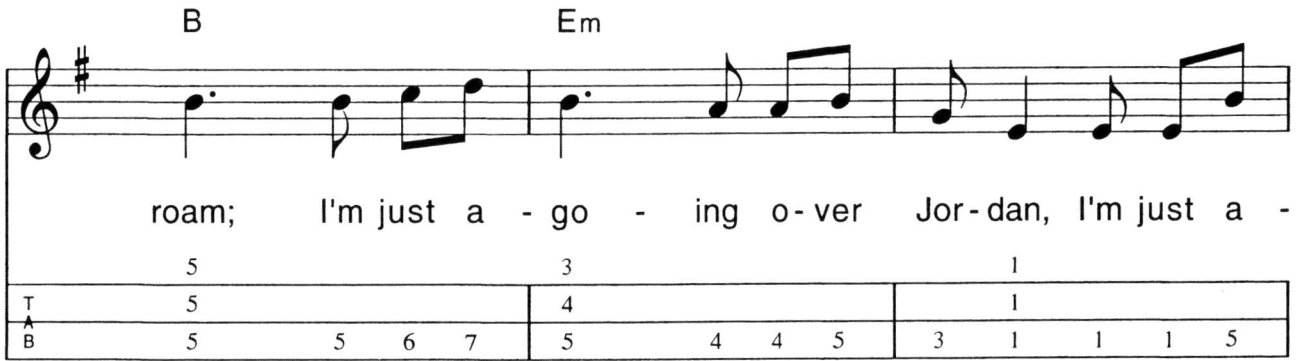

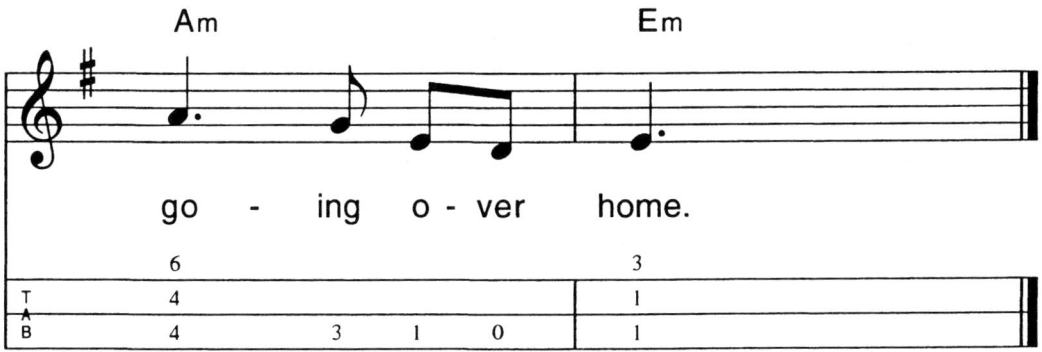

I am a poor wayfaring stranger,
A trav'ling through this world of woe;
But there's no sickness, toil or danger
In that bright world, to which I go.

I'm going there, to see my mother,
I'm going there no more to roam;
I'm just a-going over Jordan,
I'm just a- going over home.

I'm going there, to see my father,
I'm going there no more to roam;
I'm just a-going over Jordan,
I'm just a-going over home.

I'm going there, to see my sister, *etc.*

I'm going there, to see my brother, *etc.*

This beautiful old gospel hymn sounds wonderful on the dulcimer. Play it slowly to bring out its haunting quality.

Simple Gifts

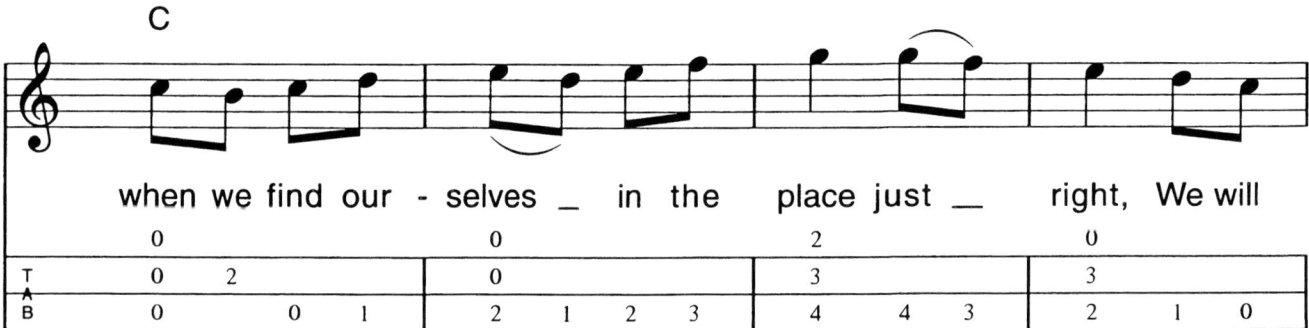

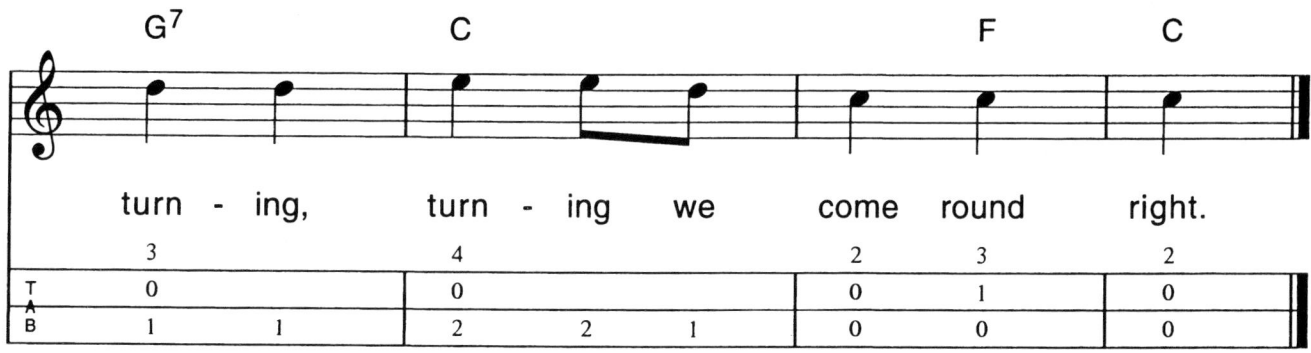

'Tis a gift to be simple, 'tis a gift to be free,
'Tis a gift to come down where we ought to be,
And when we find ourselves in the place just right,
We will be in the valley of love and delight.

When true simplicity is gained,
To bow and to bend we will not be ashamed,
To turn, turn will be our delight,
Till by turning, turning we come round right.

Composed as a dance in 1848 by Shaker Elder Joseph Brackett, Simple Gifts *has become one of the most widely recognized of all American folk songs. In 1944, Aaron Copland's* Appalachian Spring *rescued this lovely melody from certain obscurity. Since then it has been used for everything from a car commercial to Presidential inaugurations (and funerals) to a touring Irish dance extravaganza.*

Steal Away

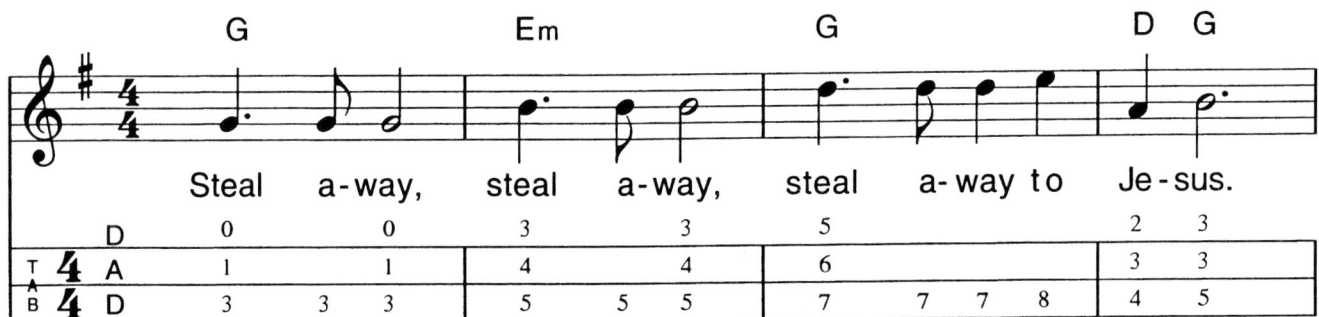

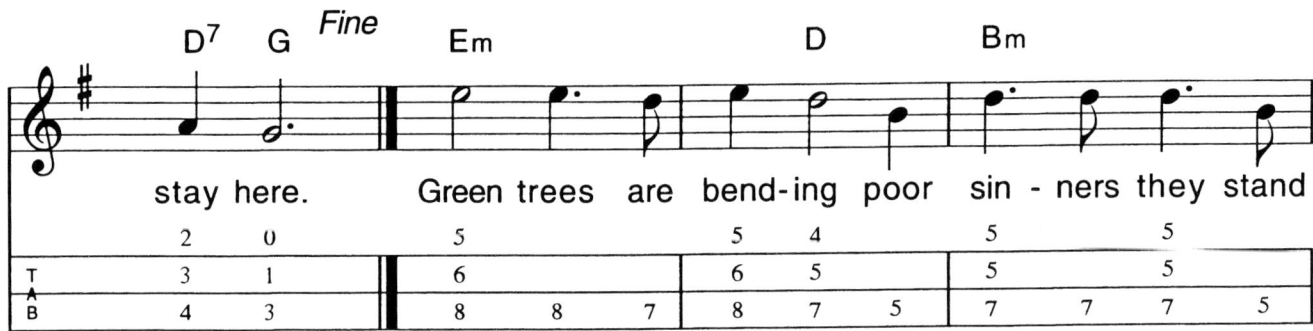

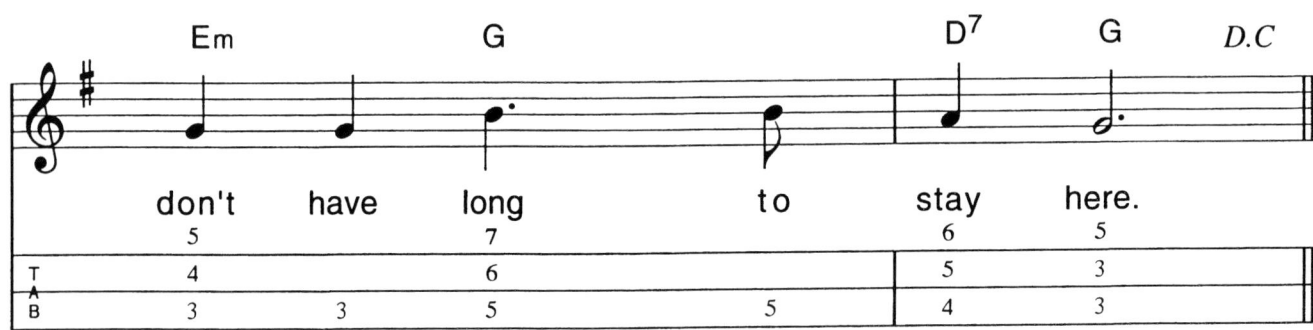

Steal Away, Steal away,
Steal away to Jesus.
Steal away, steal away home,
I ain't got long to stay here.

Green trees are bending,
Poor sinners they stand trembling,
The trumpet sounds within my soul,
I ain't got time to stay here.

Tombstones are bursting,
Poor sinners stand trembling,
The trumpet sounds within my soul,
I ain't got time to stay here.

My Lord calls me.
He calls me by lightening;
The trumpet sounds within my soul,
I ain't got time to stay here.

My Lord calls me,
He calls me by thunder,
The trumpet sounds within my soul
I ain't got time to stay here.

Information about the Underground Railroad, an escape route from slavery, was conveyed in an elaborate system of codes. Directions were hidden in songs, stories, and even quilt patterns. A slave might announce his intention to escape and say farewell to friends and family by singing this song.

Nobody Knows the Trouble I've Seen

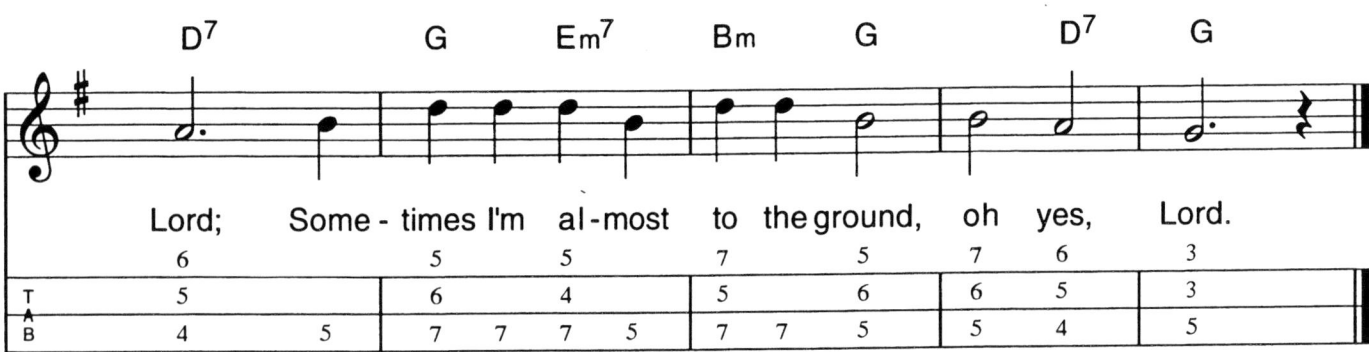

Nobody knows the trouble I've seen,
Nobody knows but Jesus,
Nobody knows the trouble I've seen,
Glory hallelujah!

Sometimes I'm up, sometimes I'm down, oh yes, Lord;
Sometimes I'm almost to the ground, oh yes Lord.

Although you see me going slow, oh yes Lord;
I have great trials here below, oh yes Lord.

One day when I was walking along, oh yes Lord;
Heav'n opened wide and love came down, oh yes Lord.

Why does old Satan hate me so? Oh yes Lord;
He had me once but let me go, oh yes Lord.

I never will forget the day, oh yes Lord;
When all my sins were washed away, oh yes Lord.

Spirituals, devotional songs arising from the African-American tradition, first came to nationwide attention through concerts and tours of the Fisk University Jubilee Singers in the late 19th Century.

I'm on my Way

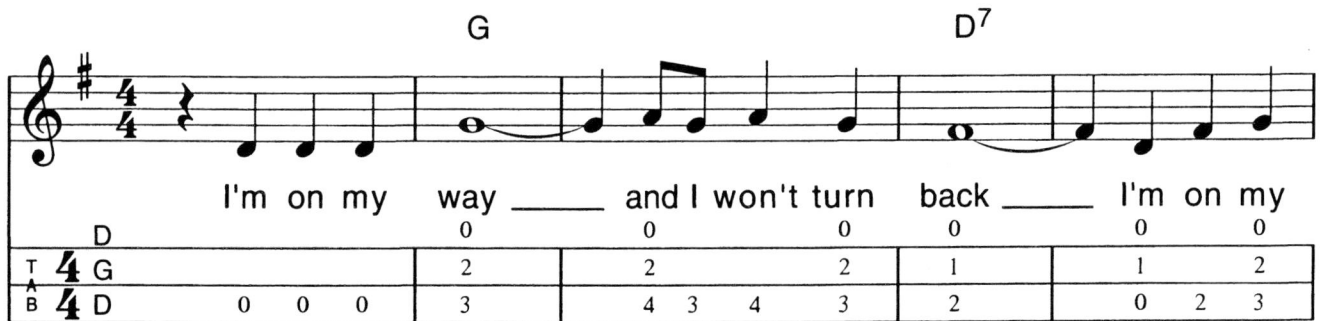
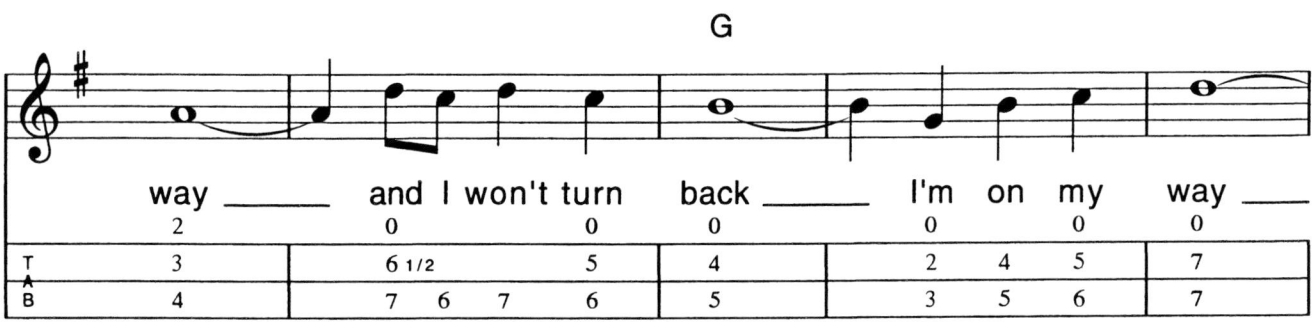

I'm on my way and I won't turn back,
I'm on my way and I won't turn back,
I'm on my way and I won't turn back;
I'm on my way, great God, I'm on my way.

I asked my brother to come with me,
I asked my brother to come with me,
I asked my brother to come with me;
I'm on my way, great God, I'm on my way.

If he won't come I'll go alone,
If he won't come I'll go alone,
If he won't come I'll go alone;
I'm on my way, great God I'm on my way.

I asked my sister to come with me,
I asked my sister to come with me,
I asked my sister to come with me;
I'm on my way, great God I'm on my way.

If she won't come I'll go alone, *etc.*

I asked my boss to let me go, *etc.*

If he says "No," I'll go anyhow, *etc.*

I'm on my way to Freedom Land, *etc.*

As with Steal Away *and* Follow the Drinkin' Gourd*, there is slightly more to this song than it seems.*

All Night, All Day

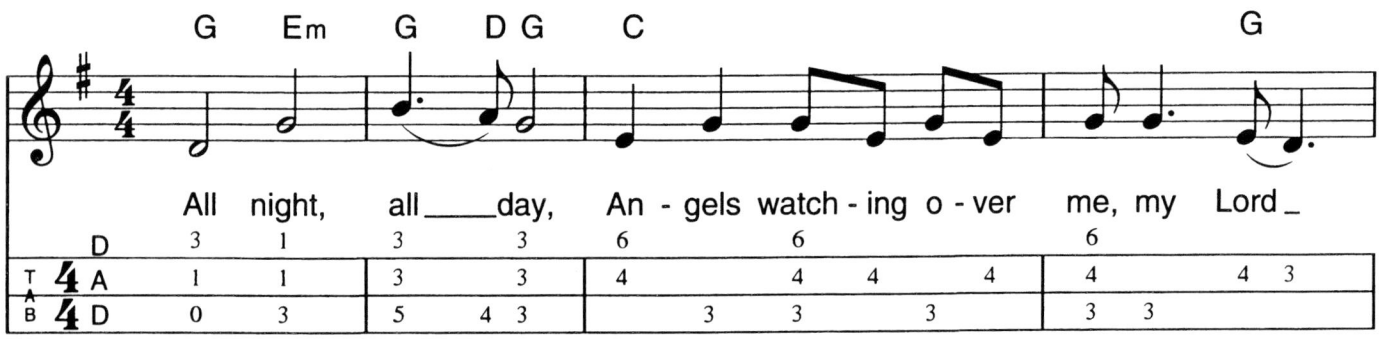
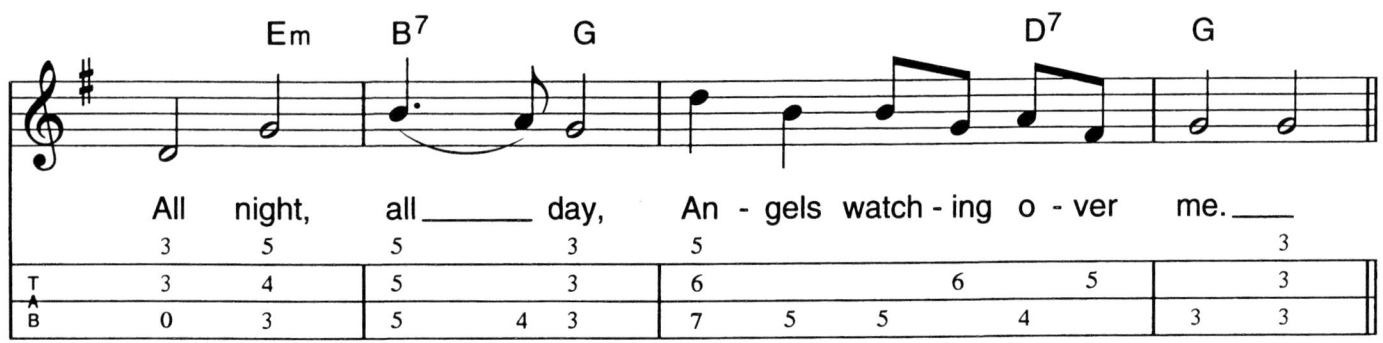
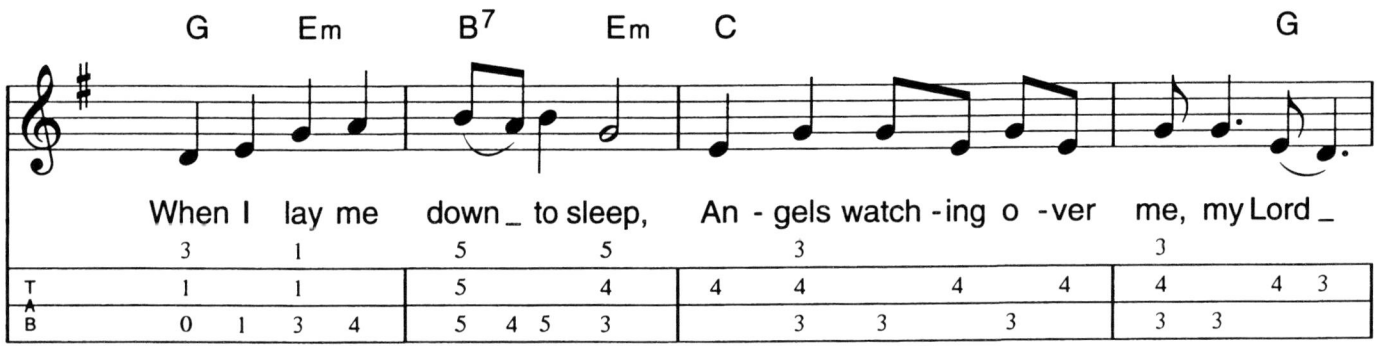

All night, all day,
Angels watching over me, my Lord,
All night, all day,
Angels watching over me.

Now I lay me down to sleep,
Angels watching over me, my Lord.
Pray the Lord my soul to keep,
Angels watching over me.

If I should die before I wake,
Angels watching over me, my Lord.
Pray the Lord my soul to take,
Angels watching over me.

This has long been a favorite lullaby, play it sweetly and see if it doesn't become one of yours, too.

Nearer, My God, To Thee

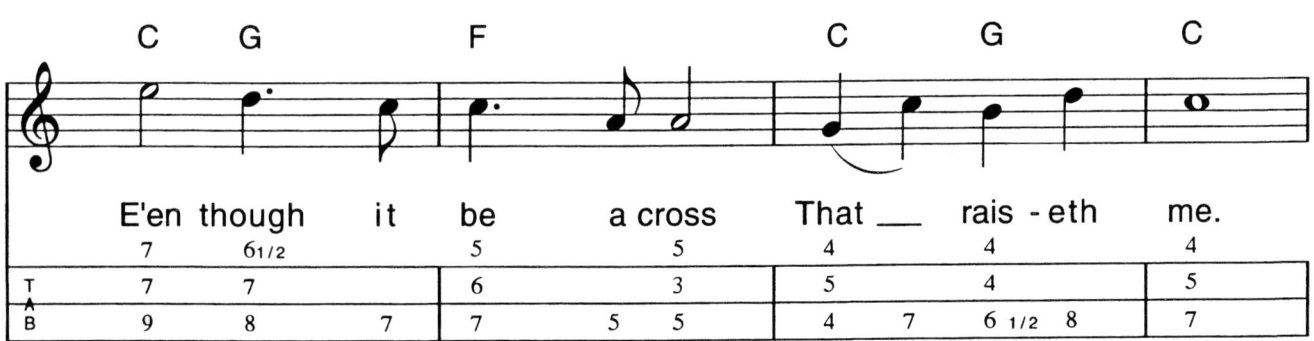

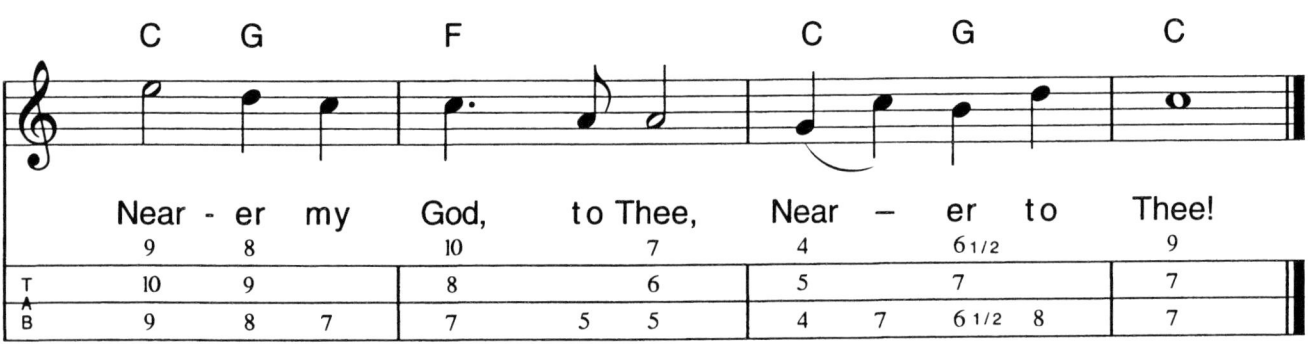

Nearer, my God, to Thee, nearer to Thee!
E'en though it be a cross that raises me;
Still all my song shall be,
Nearer, my God, to Thee,
Nearer, my God, to Thee, nearer to Thee.

Though like the wanderer, the sun gone down,
Darkness be over me,
My rest a stone, yet in my dreams I'd be,
Nearer, my God, to Thee,
Nearer, my God, to Thee, nearer to Thee.

There let the way appear,
Steps unto heaven;
All that Thou sendest me
In mercy given;
Angels to beckon me
Nearer, my God, to Thee,
Nearer, my God, to Thee, nearer to Thee.

Then with my waking thoughts
Bright with thy praise,
Out of my stony griefs,
Bethel I'll raise;
So by my woes to be,
Nearer, my God, to Thee,
Nearer, my God, to Thee, nearer to Thee.

Or if on joyful wing,
Cleaving the sky,
Sun moon and stars gorget,
Upwards I fly,
Still all my song shall be
Nearer, my God, to Thee,
Nearer, my God, to Thee, nearer to Thee.

Tradition has it that as the great liner Titanic headed to the bottom of the North Atlantic the last sound many of the doomed crew and passengers heard was the ship's band playing Nearer, My God, To Thee. *True story or not, Lowell Mason's heartfelt 1856 composition has endured.*

There's a Little Wheel a-Turnin'

There's a little wheel a-turnin' in my heart;
There's a little wheel a-turnin' in my heart;
In my heart, In my heart,
There's a little wheel a-turnin' in my heart.

There's a little song singin' in my heart,
There's a little song singin' in my heart,
In my heart, In my heart,
There's a little song singin' in my heart.

Oh I feel just like shoutin' in my heart,
Oh I feel just like shoutin' in my heart,
In my heart, In my heart,
Oh I feel just like shoutin' in my heart.

You can play this as a soothing lullaby or a rousing Gospel shout; either way its a great song for participation.

Many are the hearts that are weary tonight,
Wishing for the war to cease,
Many are the hearts that are looking for the right,
Waiting for the dawn of peace.

Songs of Freedom and Strife

The Girl I Left Behind Me

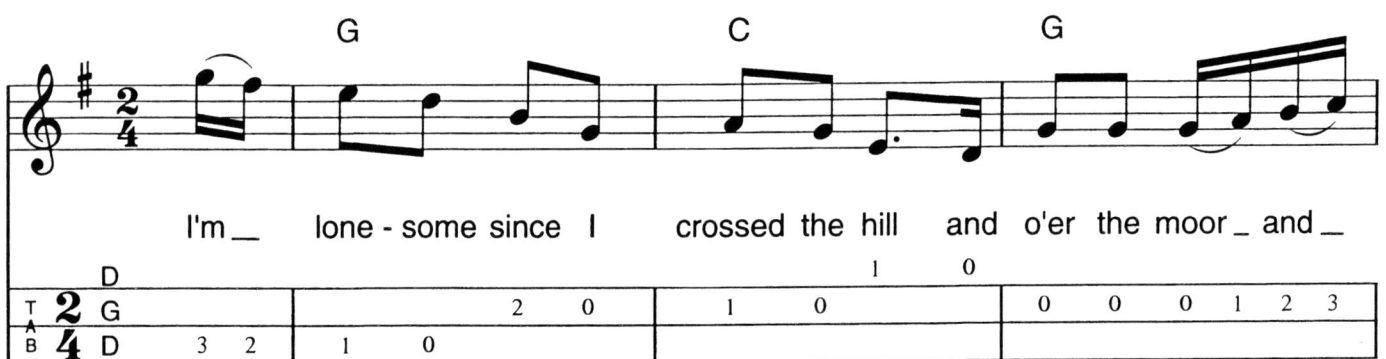

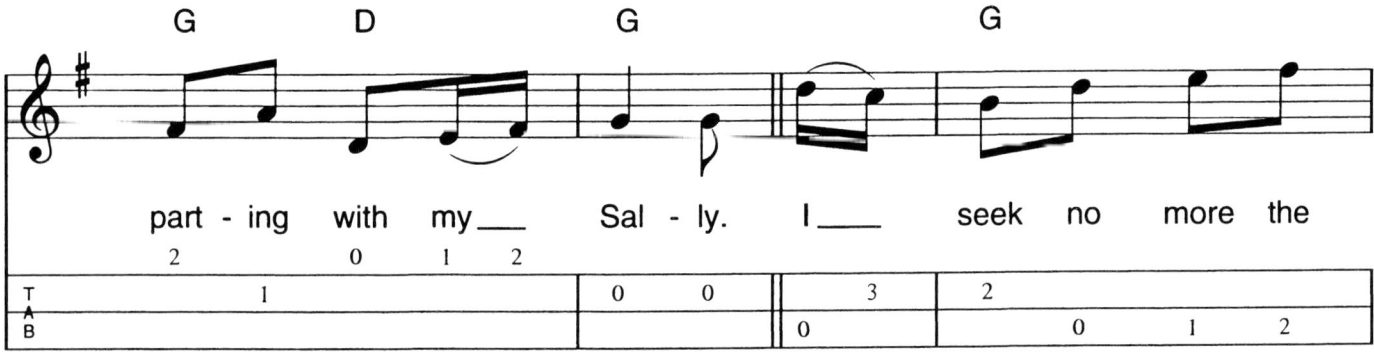

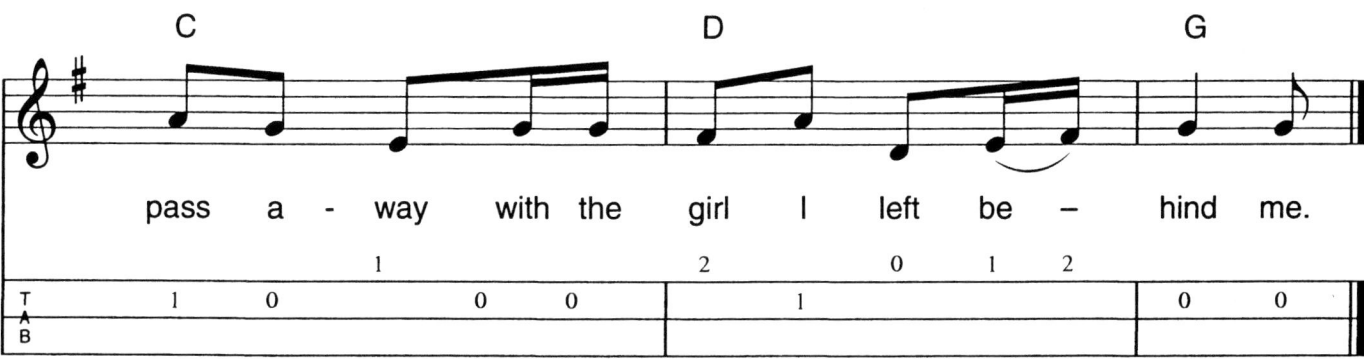

I'm lonesome since I crossed the hill and o'er the hill and valley,
Such heavy thoughts my heart do fill since parting with my Sally.
I seek no more the fine and gay, for each does but remind me,
How swift the hours did pass away with the girl I left behind me.

Oh, I never shall forget the night, the stars were bright above me,
They gently shed their silvery light when first she vowed to love me.
But now I'm off to Brighton Camp, and may good favor find me,
And send me safely back again to the girl I left behind me.

My thoughts her beauty shall retain if sleeping or if waking,
Until I see my love again, for her my heart is aching.
Whenever I return that way, if she should not decline me
I've vowed I evermore will stay with the girl I left behind me.

The bee shall honey taste no more, the dove become a ranger,
And the ocean's waves shall cease to roar if she become a stranger,
The vows we made when last we met shall never cease to bind me,
And my heart will ever more be true to the girl I left behind me.

As a rousing fife tune, The Girl I left Behind Me *(also called* Brighton Camp) *was popular with both sides during the Revolutionary War. Although parodied countless times, I find these sentimental 18th Century lyrics charming.*

When Johnny Comes Marching Home

L. Lambert

When Johnny comes marching home again,
Hurrah, hurrah!
We'll give him a hearty welcome then,
Hurrah, hurrah!
Oh the men will cheer and the boys will shout,
The ladies they will all turn out,
And we'll all feel gay when Johnny comes marching home.

The old church bell will peal with joy,
Hurrah, hurrah!
To welcome home our darling boy,
Hurrah, hurrah!
The village lads and lasses say,
With roses they will strew the way,
And we'll all feel gay when Johnny comes marching home.

    Rebel verses:

In eighteen hundred and sixty-one,
Hurrah, hurrah!
In eighteen hundred and sixty-one,
Hurrah, hurrah!
In eighteen hundred and sixty-one,
We licked the Yankees at Bull Run,
And we'll all drink stone blind,
Johnny fill up the bowl.

In eighteen hundred and sixty-five,
We all thanked God we were alive.

    Union verses:

In eighteen hundred and sixty-one,
The cruel rebellion had begun.

In eighteen hundred and sixty-three,
Abe Lincoln set the Negroes free.

When Johnny Comes Marching Home was written by an Irish soldier in the Union Army. Using the name Louis Lambert, Patrick Gilmore set patriotic words to the tune of an older Irish anti-war song. It became popular on both sides of the struggle. Lately it has resurfaced in its original guise as a protest song.

Eating Goober Peas

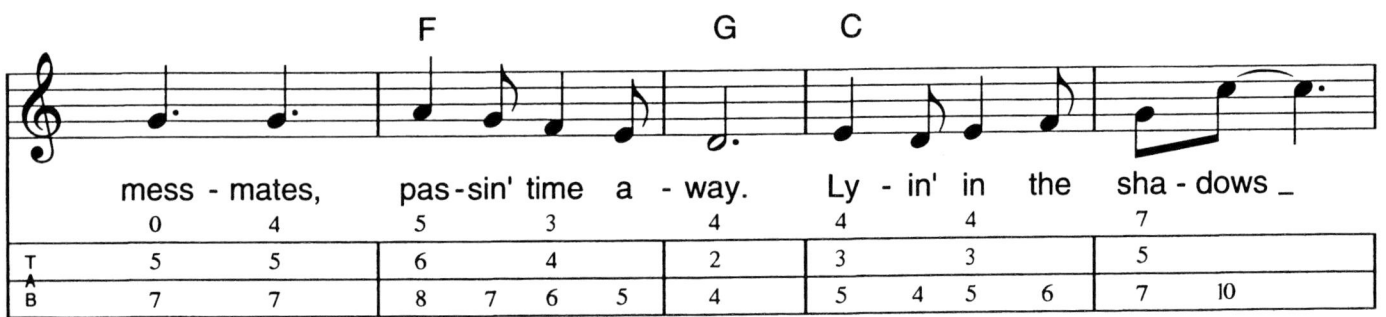

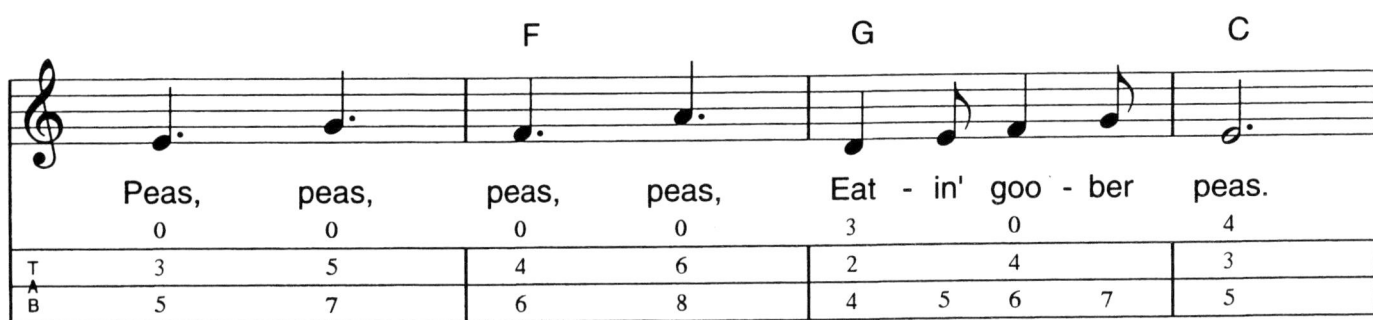
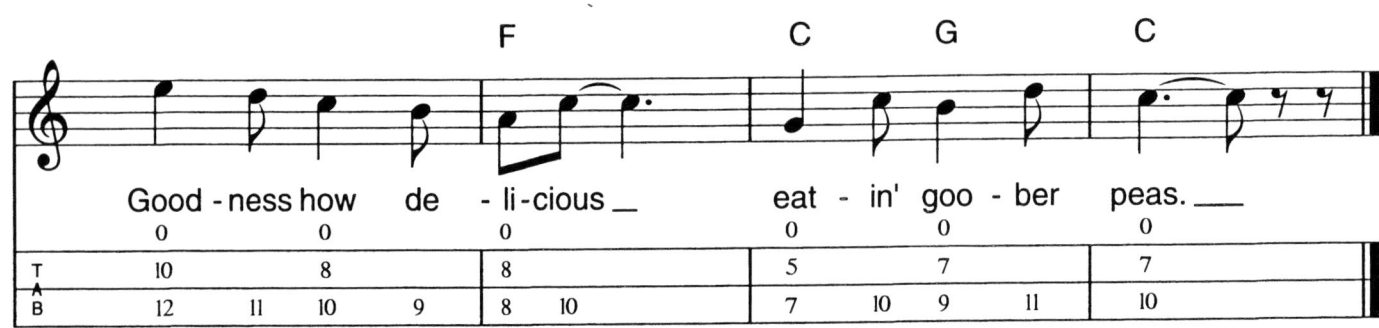

Sittin' by the roadside on a summer's day,
Chattin' with my mess mates passin' time away,
Lying in the shadows underneath the trees,
Goodness how delicious, eatin' goober peas.

Peas, peas, peas, peas, eatin' goober peas.
Goodness how delicious, eatin' goober peas.

Just before the battle, the General hears a row,
He says, "The Yanks are comin'! I hear their rifles now,"
He turns around in wonder, and what do you think he sees,
The Georgia Militia, eatin' goober peas.

When a horseman passes, the soldiers have a rule,
To cry out at their loudest, "Mister, here's your mule."
But there's another pleasure, enchantinger than these,
It's wearing out your grinders, eaten' goober peas.

I think my song has lasted almost long enough,
The subject may be int'resting but rhymes are mighty tough.
I wish this war was over; when free from rags and fleas,
We'll kiss our wives and sweethearts and gooble goober peas.

Goober peas, better known as peanuts, became a staple ration in the cash-starved Confederate Army as the Civil War ground on. Soldiers have always found a way to make light of their hardships.

Yankee Doodle

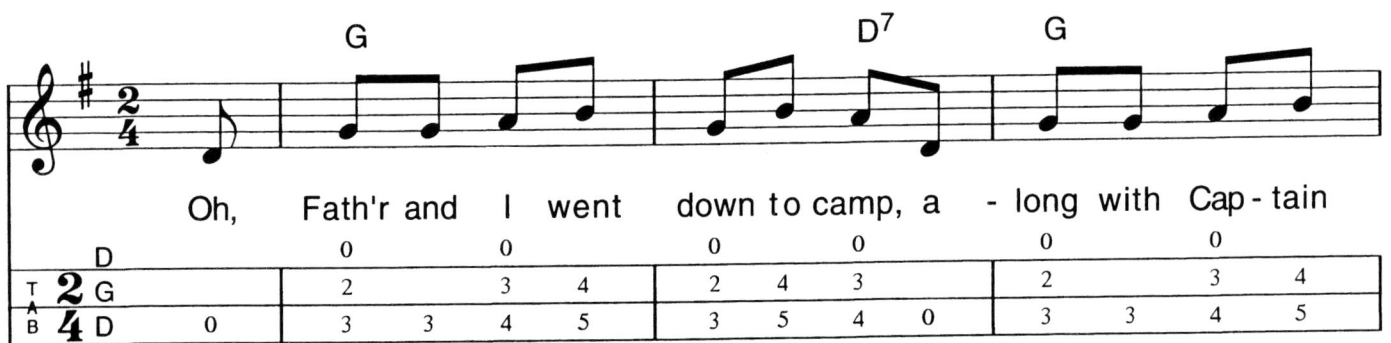
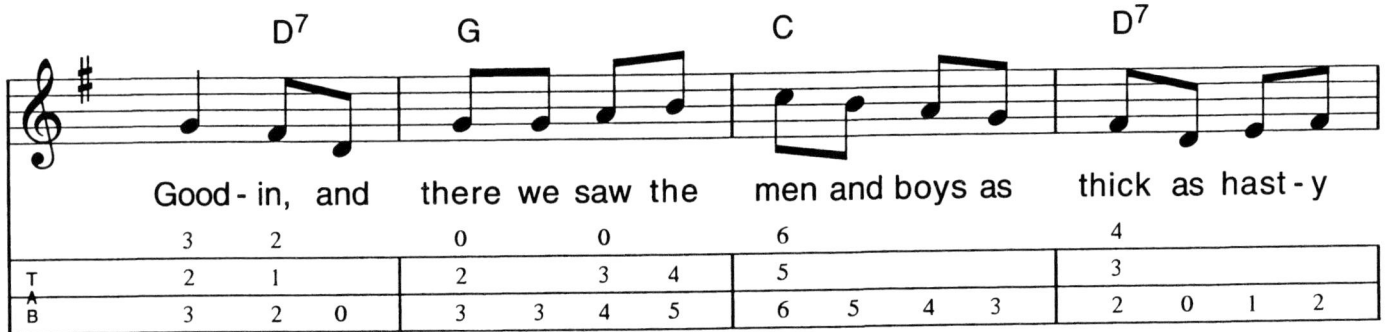

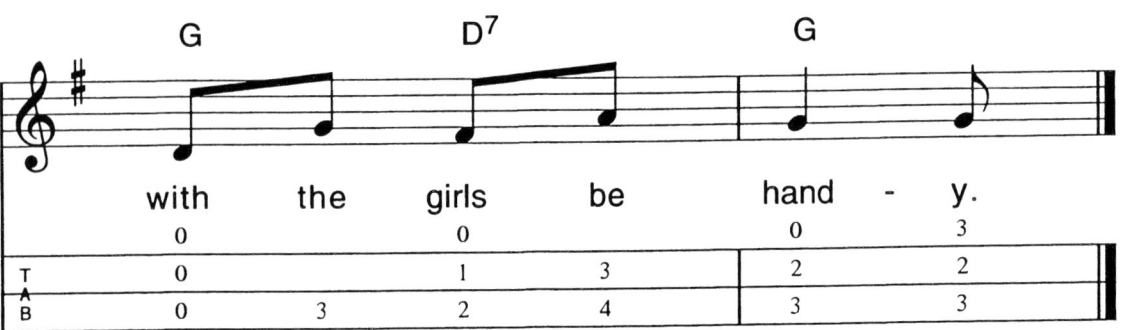

Oh Fath'r and I went down to camp,
Along with Captain Goodin'.
And there we saw the men and boys
As thick as hasty puddin'.

> CH
> Yankee Doodle keep it up,
> Yankee Doodle dandy,
> Mind the music and the step
> And with the girls be handy.

And there we saw a thousand men,
As rich as Squire David,
And what they wasted every day
I wish it could be savéd.

And there was Captain Washington
Upon a strapping stallion.
A-giving orders to his men,
There must have been a million.

The flamin' ribbons in his hat,
They looked so tarnal fine, ah;
I wanted very much to get
And give to my Jemimah.

And there I saw a swamping gun,
Large as a log of maple,
Upon a deucéd little cart,
A load for father's cattle.

And every time they fired it off
It took a horn of powder;
It made a noise like father's gun,
Only a nation louder.

Yankee Doodle went to town,
A-riding on a pony.
Stuck a feather in his cap
And called it macaroni.

It should come as no surprise that this song originated with British soldiers. They may have sung it as early as the French and Indian War of 1754-63 to mock the Colonial troops. Little did they know it would be played by the victorious American army to celebrate Cornwallis' surrender at Yorktown.

All Are Talking of Utah

Who'd ever think that Utah would stir the world so much?
Who'd ever think the Mormons were widely known as such?
I hardly dare to scribble or on such a subject touch,
For all are talking of Utah.

> CH
> Hurrah! Hurrah! We Mormons have a name;
> Hurrah! Hurrah! We're on the road to fame.
> No matter how they style us it's all about the same,
> For all are talking of Utah.

They say that Utah cannot be numbered as a state,
They want our lands divided, but left it rather late;
'Tis hard to tell of Mormons, what yet may be their fate,
For all are talking of Utah.

They say they'll send an army to put us Mormons right,
Regenerate all Utah and show us Christian light,
Release our wives and daughters and put us men to fight,
For all are talking of Utah.

I now will tell you something you haven't thought of yet,
We bees are nearly filling the hives of Deseret,
If hurt we'll sting together, and gather all we get,
For all are talking of Utah.

This song expresses defiance and indignation at the prospect of US intervention in extraterritorial affairs. Seeking religious freedom, the Mormons settled in the largely unclaimed Utah territory in 1847. Deseret is a Mormon word for honeybee.

The Yellow Rose of Texas

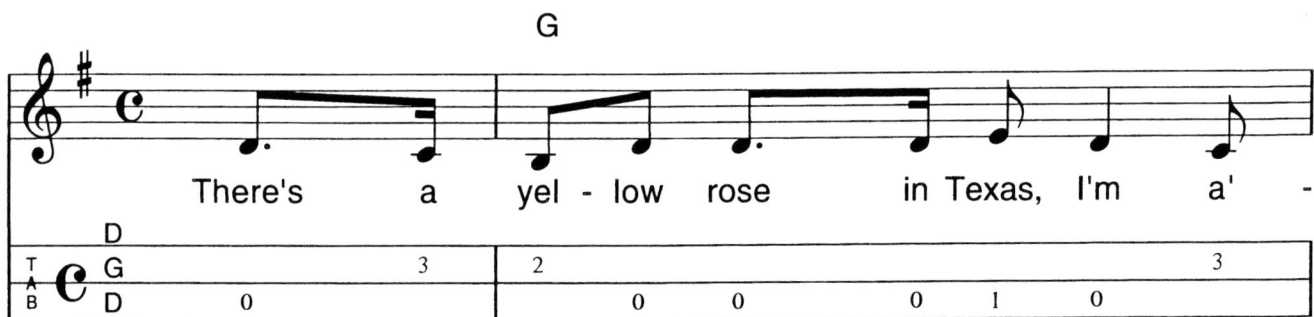

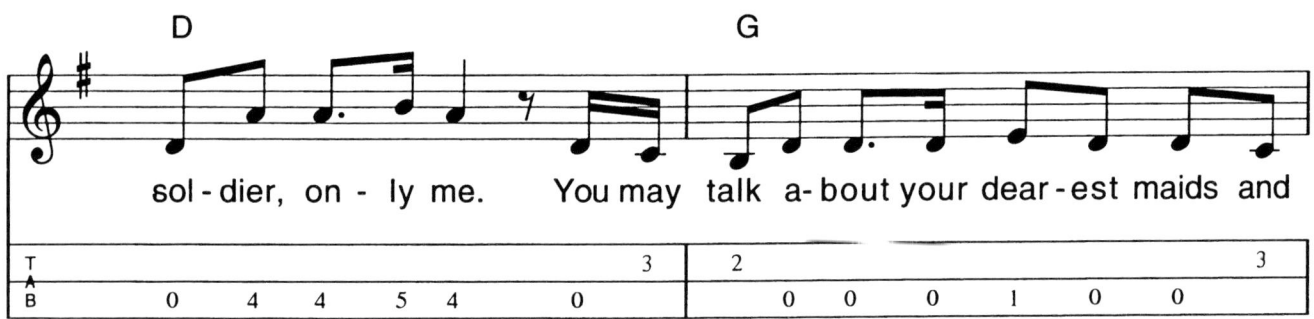
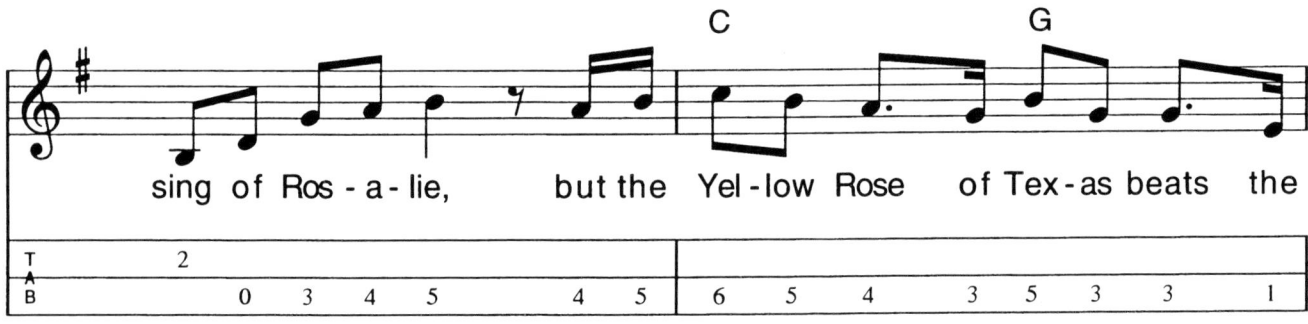

There's a Yellow Rose of Texas I'm a-goin' for to see,
No other soldier knows her, no soldier, only me;
You may talk about your dearest maids and sing of Rosalie
But the Yellow Rose of Texas beats the belles of Tennessee.

She's the sweetest rose of color this soldier ever knew,
Her eyes are bright as diamonds, they sparkle like the dew;
She cried so when I left her it almost broke my heart,
And if I ever find her, we never more will part.

Oh now I'm going to find her, my heart is full of woe,
We'll sing the songs together that we sang so long ago;
We'll play the banjo gaily and we'll sing the songs of yore,
And the Yellow Rose of Texas shall be mine forevermore.

*A sentimental favorite sung by Confederate soldiers
and later taken up on the western plains by soldiers and cowboys alike.
I've included an instrumental second part that is often played by fiddlers at dances throughout the West.*

The Texas Rangers

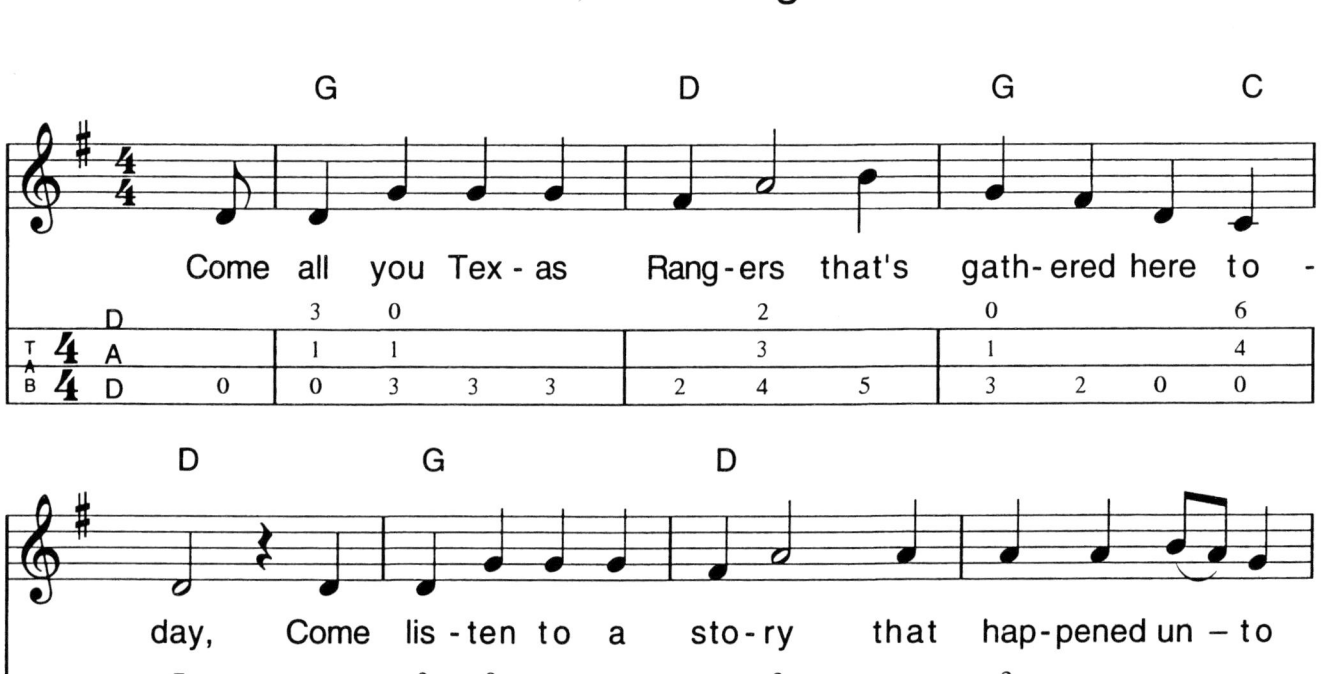
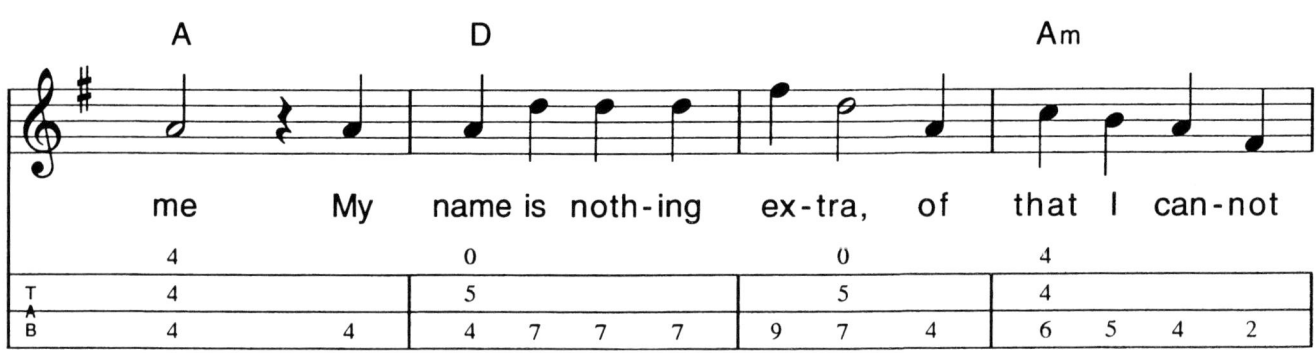
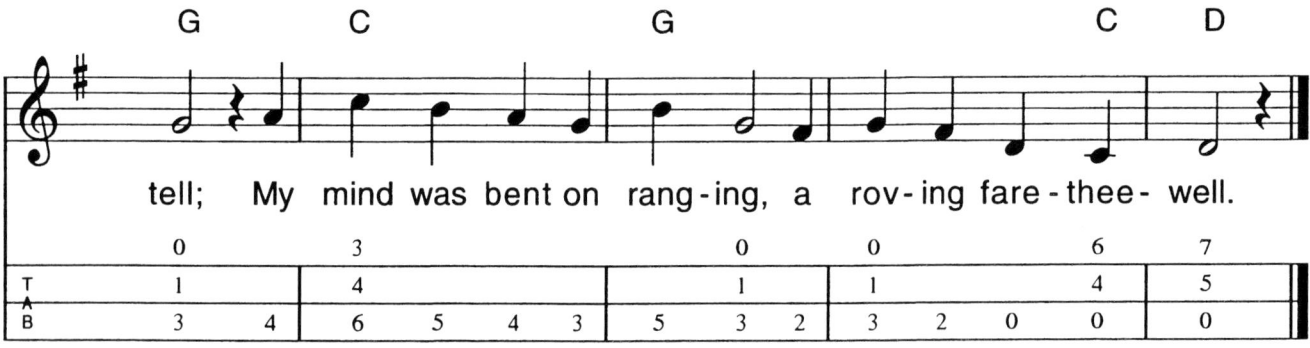

Come all you Texas Rangers that's gathered here today;
Come listen to a story that happened unto me.
My name is nothing extra, of that I cannot tell;
My mind was bent on ranging, a roving fare-thee-well.

Then up spoke my own mother, these words she said to me:
My boy, they all are strangers, I think you'd better stay.
I thought you were quite childish, and you inclined to roam,
Let me tell you by experience you'd better stay at home.

'Twas at the age of sixteen that I joined the gallant band.
We marched from San Antonio all to the Rio Grande.
The captain he gave orders, he thought it was just right:
Before you reach the station, my boys, you're going to fight.

I saw those Indians coming, I heard their fearful yell.
My feelings at that moment, no mortal words could tell.
I saw their glittering lances, their arrows round us fell;
My mind was bent on ranging, a roving fare-thee-well.

We fought for full nine hours before the fight was o'er;
The sight of dead and wounded I had never seen before.
A hundred gallant Rangers, that ever left the West,
Lay buried by their comrades and peace shall be their rest.

Come all you gallant people that's gathered here tonight;
Whatever you do for a living, for God's sake never fight!
For the enemy, they're quite careless; they'll shoot right in the crew.
They are bound to hit somebody and perhaps it might be you.

Perhaps you have a mother, likewise a sister, too;
Perhaps you have a sweetheart who will weep and mourn for you.
If that be your situation, and you inclined to roam;
I'll tell you by experience you'd better stay at home.

For much of the 19th Century the United States maintained an almost perpetual state of war against the original inhabitants of the land. Though undoubtedly fictitious, this haunting ballad nonetheless captures the fear and wastefulness of battle.

The Battle Hymn of the Republic

J. W. Howe

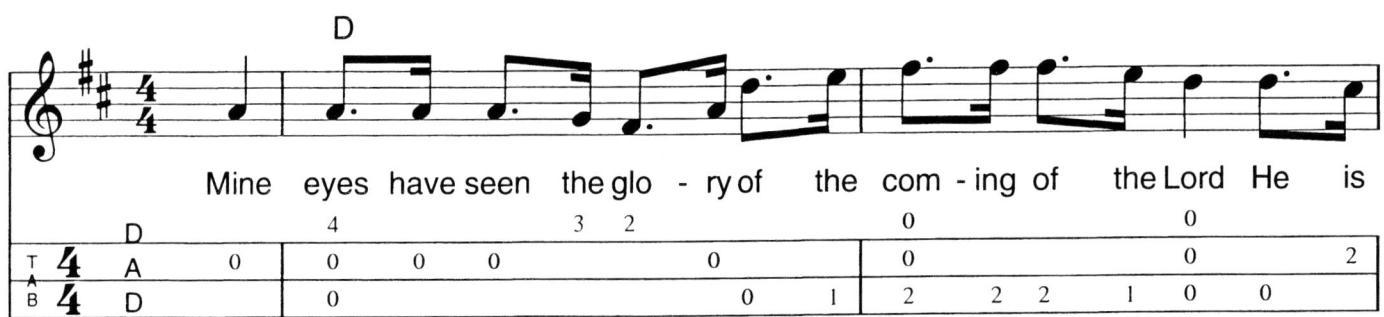
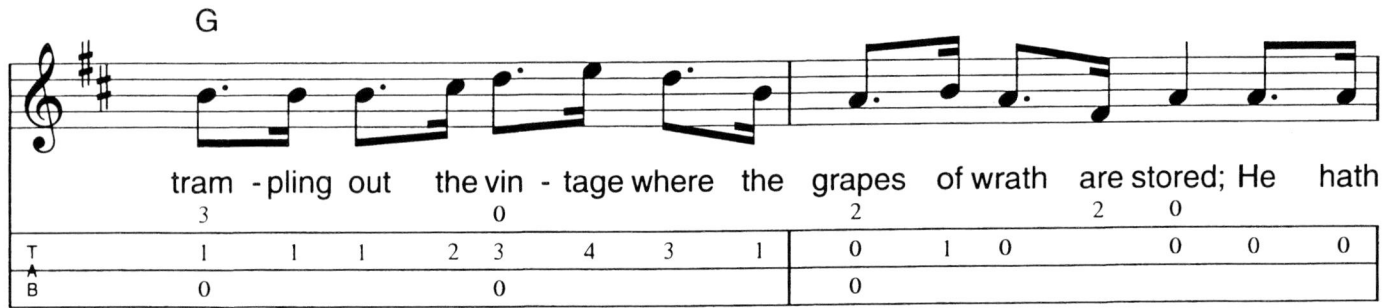
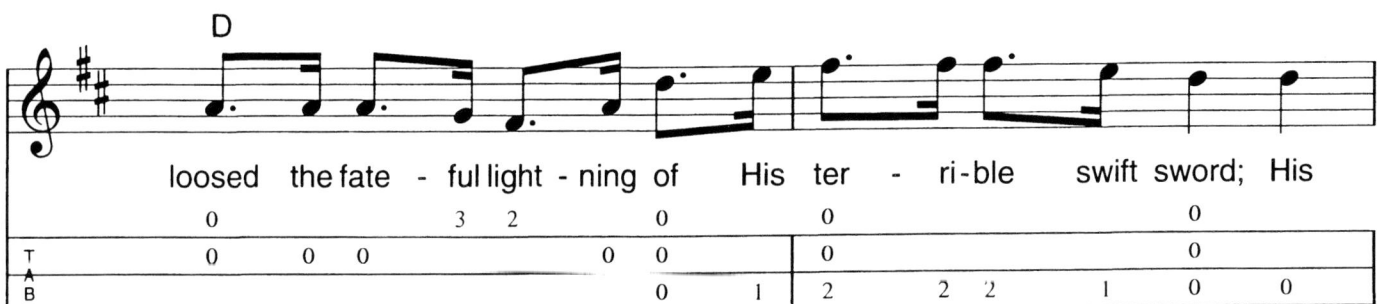

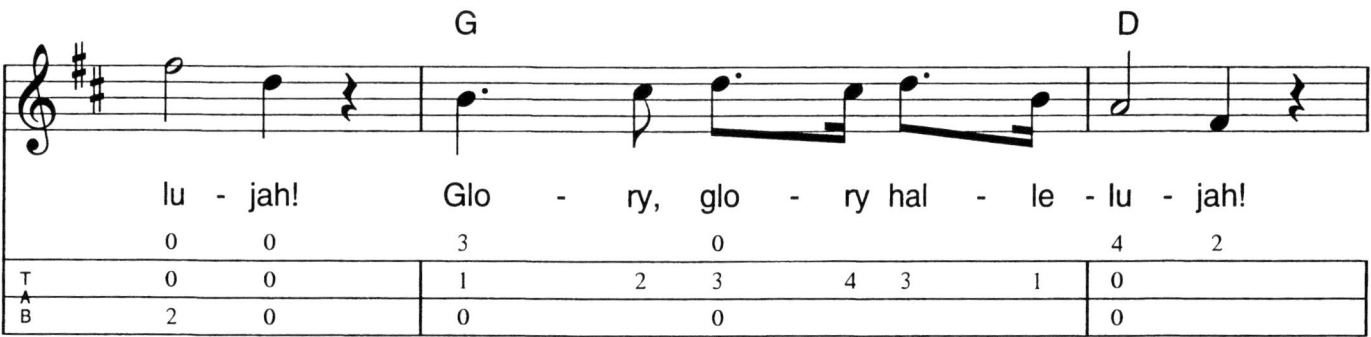

Mine eyes have seen the glory of the coming of the Lord;
He is trampling out the vintage where the grapes of wrath are stored;
He hath loosed the fateful lightning of his terrible swift sword;
His truth is marching on.

CH
Glory, glory hallelujah!
Glory, glory hallelujah!
Glory, glory hallelujah!
His truth is marching on.

I have seen him in the watch-fires of a hundred circling camps,
They have builded Him an alter in the evening dews and damps,
I can read His righteous sentence by the dim and flaring lamps,
His day is marching on.

He has sounded forth the trumpet that shall never call retreat,
He is sifting out the hearts of men before his judgment seat,
Oh, be swift, my soul, to answer Him! Be jubilant my feet,
Our God is marching on.

In the beauty of the lilies Christ was born across the sea,
With a glory in his bosom that transfigures you and me;
As he died to make men holy, let us die to make men free,
While God is marching on.

Julia Ward Howe (1819-1910) was inspired to write this poem after hearing a group of soldiers singing John Brown's Body *at a camp outside of Washington, D.C. The Battle Hymn of the Republic became the marching song of the Union Army – surely not the first time men have slaughtered their fellows assured that God was on their side.*

Dixie

Daniel Emmett

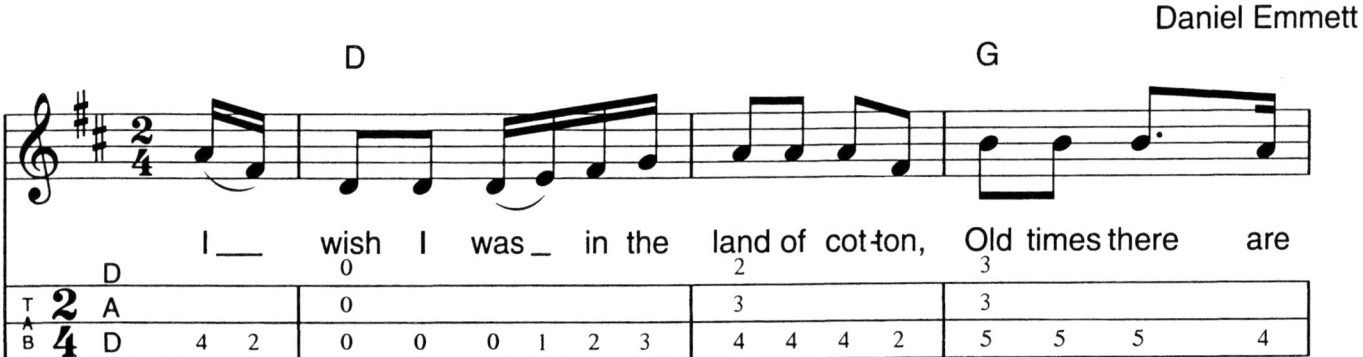

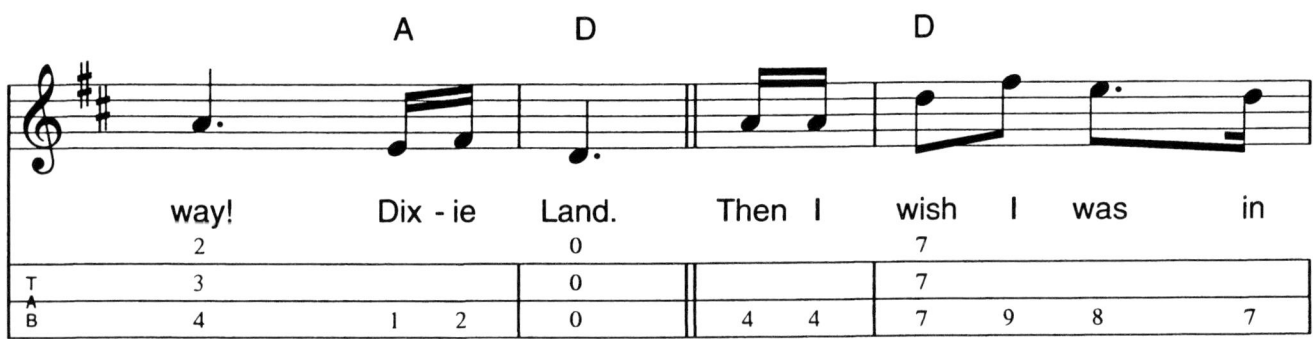

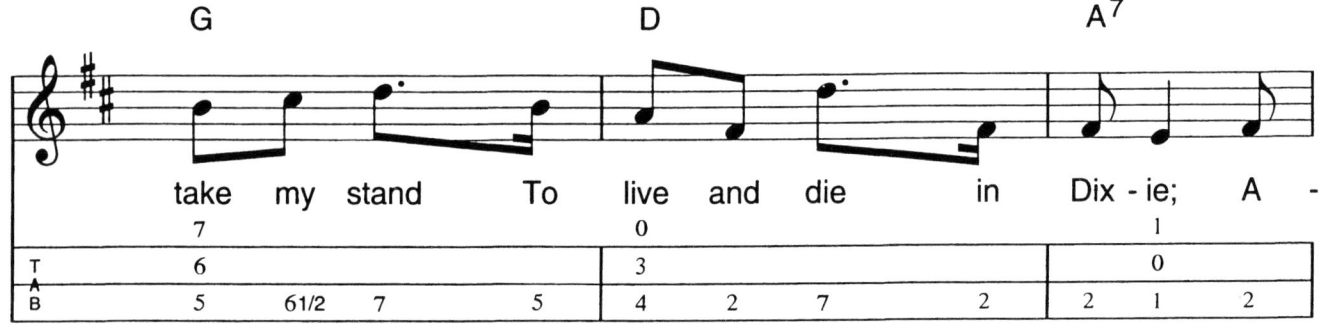

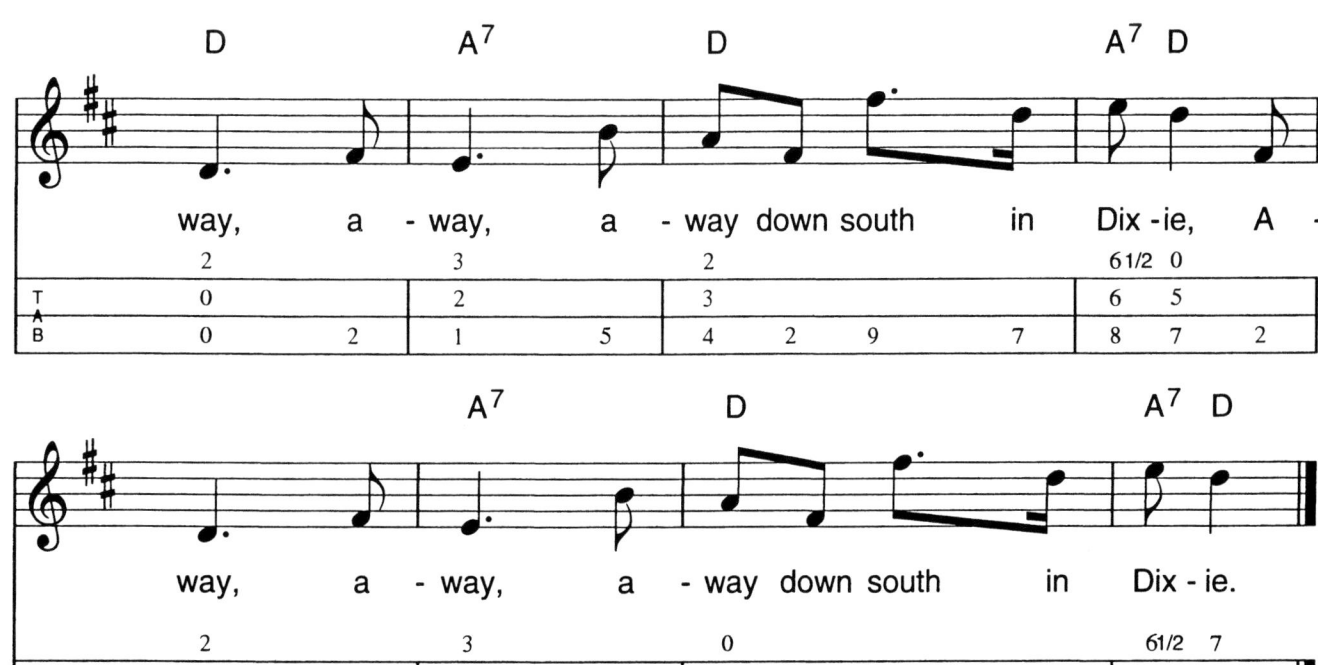

I wish I was in the land of cotton,
Old times there are not forgotten,
Look away! Look away! Look away! Dixie Land.

In Dixie Land where I was born,
Early on one frosty mornin',
Look away! Look away! Look away! Dixie Land.

    CH
Then I wish I was in Dixie, Hooray! Hooray!
In Dixie Land I'll take my stand, to live and die in Dixie;
Away, away, away down south in Dixie;
Away, away, away down south in Dixie.

There's buckwheat cakes and Indian batter,
Makes you fat or a little fatter,
Look away! Look away! Look away! Dixie Land.

Then hoe it down and scratch your gravel,
To Dixie Land I'm bound to travel,
Look away! Look away! Look away! Dixie Land.

Written by minstrel composer (and dedicated Northerner) Daniel Emmett,
Dixie became such a hit in the South that it was sung at Jefferson Davis' inauguration in 1861.

Follow the Drinking Gourd

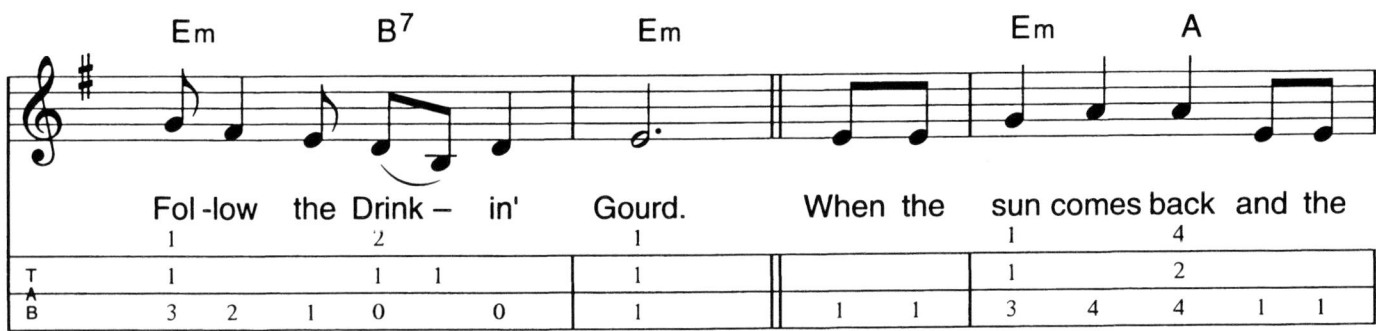

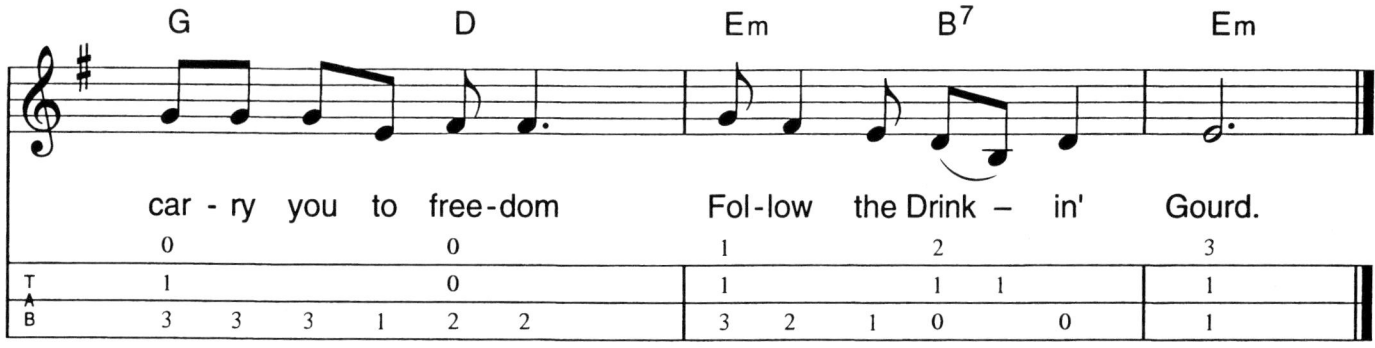

Follow the Drinkin' Gourd
Follow the Drinkin' Gourd
For the old man is a-waitin' for to carry you to freedom
Follow the Drink in' Gourd.
When the sun comes back and the first quail calls,
Follow the Drinkin Gourd
The old man is a-waitin' for to carry you to freedom
Follow the Drinkin' Gourd.

Now the river bank'll make a pretty good road,
The dead trees'll show you the way,
And left foot, peg foot, travelin' on,
Follow the Drinking Gourd.

Now the river ends between two hills;
Follow the Drinkin' Gourd,
And there's another river on the other side,
Just follow the Drinkin' Gourd.

To prevent runaways, slaves were forbidden to gather without a white person present. But many were able to escape to relative freedom in the North by relying on travelling directions hidden in this song. The Drinkin' Gourd is the constellation now called the Big Dipper, which points out the North star.

Tenting Tonight

Wm. Kittredge

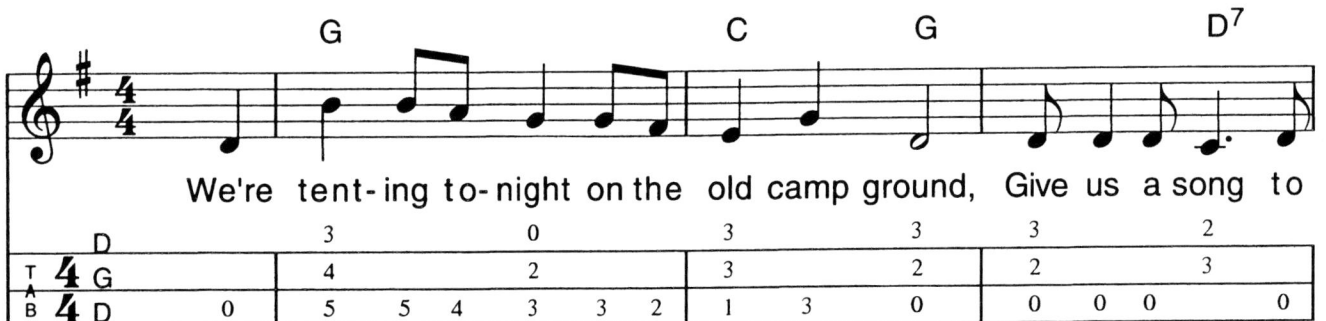

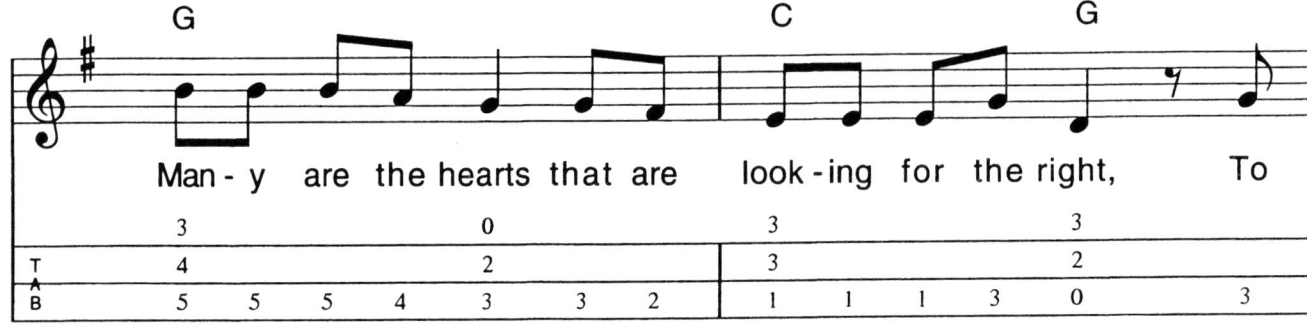

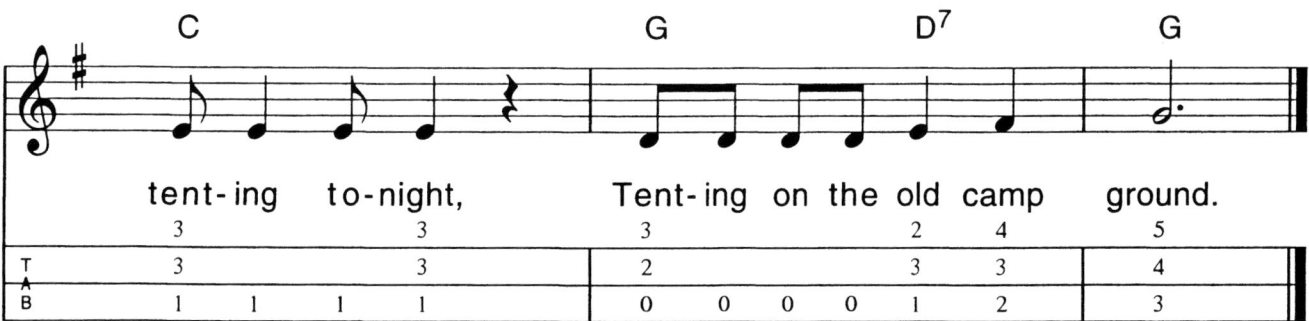

We're tenting tonight on the old camp ground,
Give us a song to cheer
Our weary hearts, a song of home
And friends we loved so dear.

CH
Many are the hearts that are weary tonight,
Wishing for the war to cease;
Many are the hearts that are looking for the right,
To see the dawn of peace.
Tenting tonight, tenting tonight,
Tenting on the old camp ground.

We've been tenting tonight on the old camp ground,
Thinking of days gone by,
Of the loved ones at home that gave us a hand,
And the tear that said, "Good-bye."

We are tired of war on the old camp ground,
Many are dead and gone
Of the brave and true who left their home,
Others been wounded long ago.

We've been fighting tonight on the old camp ground,
Many are lying near;
Some are dead, and some are dying,
Many are in tears.

As the Civil War dragged on and on, both the North and the South found they could agree on two things: singing William Kittredge's Tenting Tonight *and wishing for peace.*

America (My Country 'Tis of Thee)

S.F. Smith

My country, 'tis of thee, sweet land of liberty,
Of thee I sing;
Land where my father's died, land of the Pilgrims' pride,
From ev'ry mountain side
Let freedom ring.

My native country, thee, land of the noble free,
Thy name I love.
I love thy rocks and rills, thy woods and templed hills,
My heart with rapture thrills
Like that above.

Let music swell the breeze, and ring from all the trees
Sweet freedom's song.
Let mortal tongues awake, Let all that breathe partake,
Let rocks their silence break,
The sound prolong.

Sometime before 1831, the Reverend Samuel Frances Smith composed these words to one of America's best-loved songs. The melody had been previously been used for the British anthem God Save Great George, Our King.

It's love, oh love
Oh careless love.

Songs of the Restless Heart

Aura Lee

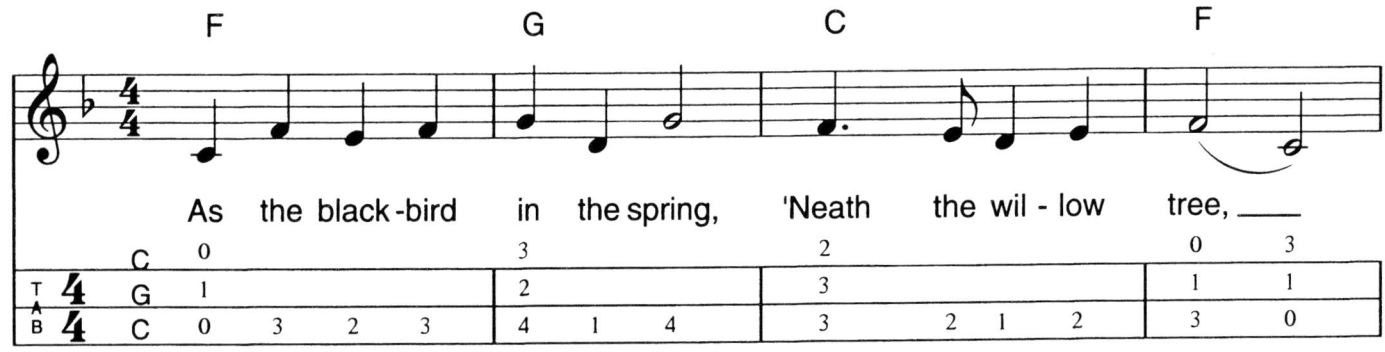

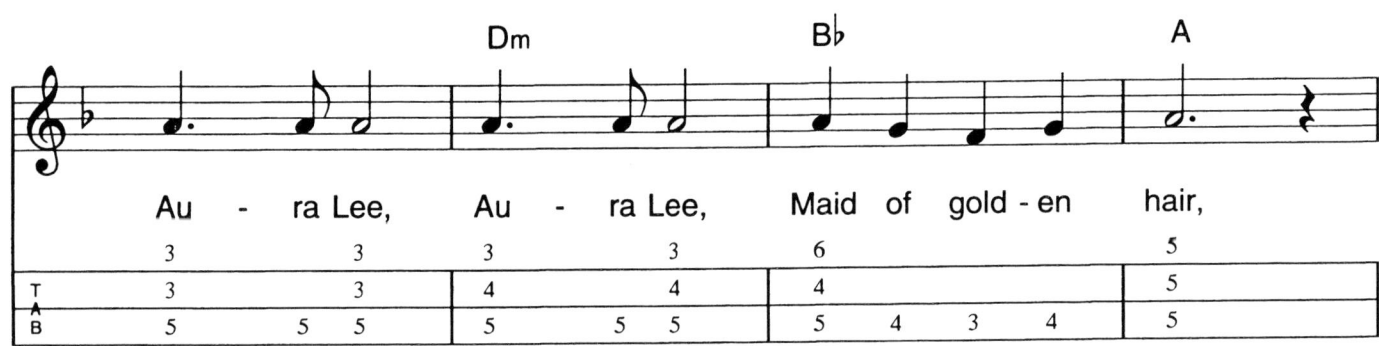
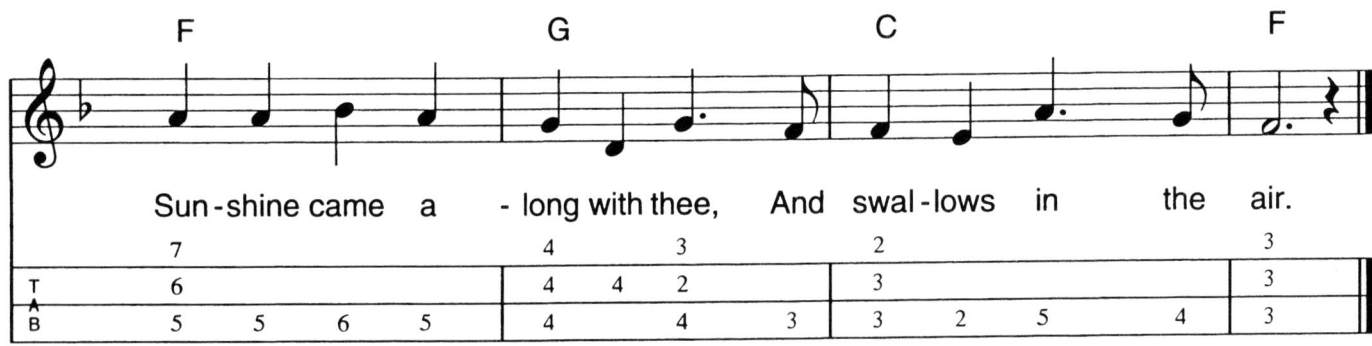

As the blackbird in the spring,
'Neath the willow tree,
Sat and piped, I heard him sing;
Singing Aura Lee.
Aura Lee, Aura Lee,
Maid of golden hair,
Sunshine came along with thee,
And swallows in the air.

In thy blush the rose was born,
Music when you spoke.
In thine eyes the glow of morn'
Into splendor broke.
Aura Lee, Aura Lee,
Birds of crimson wing.
Never songs have sung to me
As in that bright, sweet spring.

When mistletoe was green,
'Mid the winter's snows,
Sunshine in thy face was seen,
Kissing lips of rose,
Aura Lee, Aura Lee,
Take my golden ring;
Love and light return with thee,
And swallows with the spring.

*A tender old love song that has endured in both the folk and popular music worlds.
Its haunting melody deserves to be better known with these original words.*

Beware, Oh Take Care

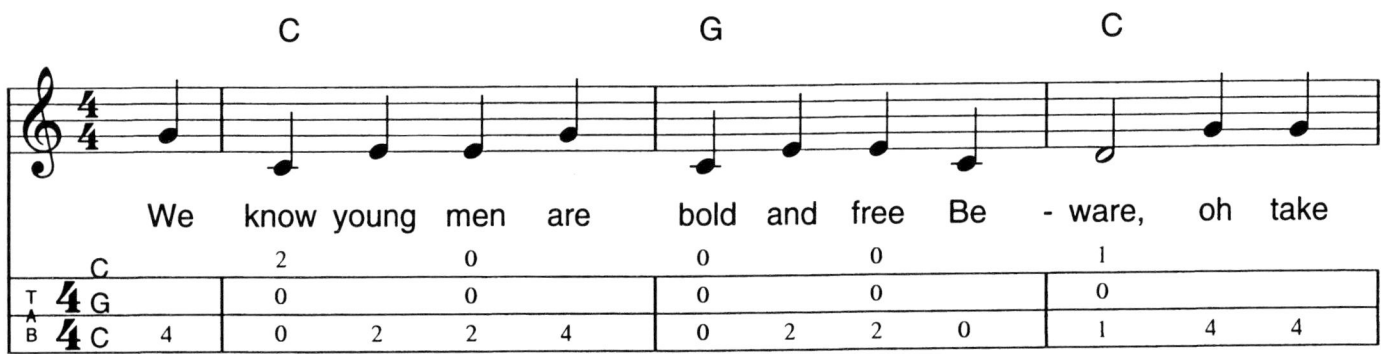

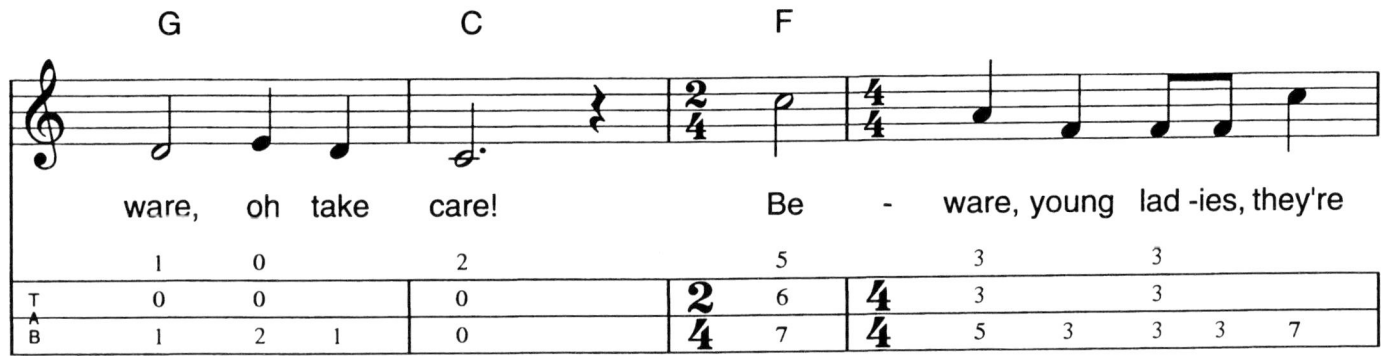

We know young men are bold and free,
Beware, oh take care,
They tell you they're angels but they're devils, you see,
Beware, oh take care.

CH
Beware young ladies, they're fooling you.
Trust them not, they're fooling you,
Beware young ladies, they're fooling you;
Beware, oh take care.

They smoke, they chew, they wear fine shoes,
Beware, oh take care,
But in their pocket is a bottle of booze,
Beware, oh take care.

Around their neck they wear a guard,
Beware, oh take care,
While in their pockets is a deck of cards,
Beware, oh take care.

They hold their hands up to their hearts,
They sigh, oh they sigh,
They say they love no one but you,
They lie, oh they lie.

A moral tale made popular by the singing of Blind Alfred Reed, though the song is considerably older. Fore warned is fore armed, they say.

Down in the Valley

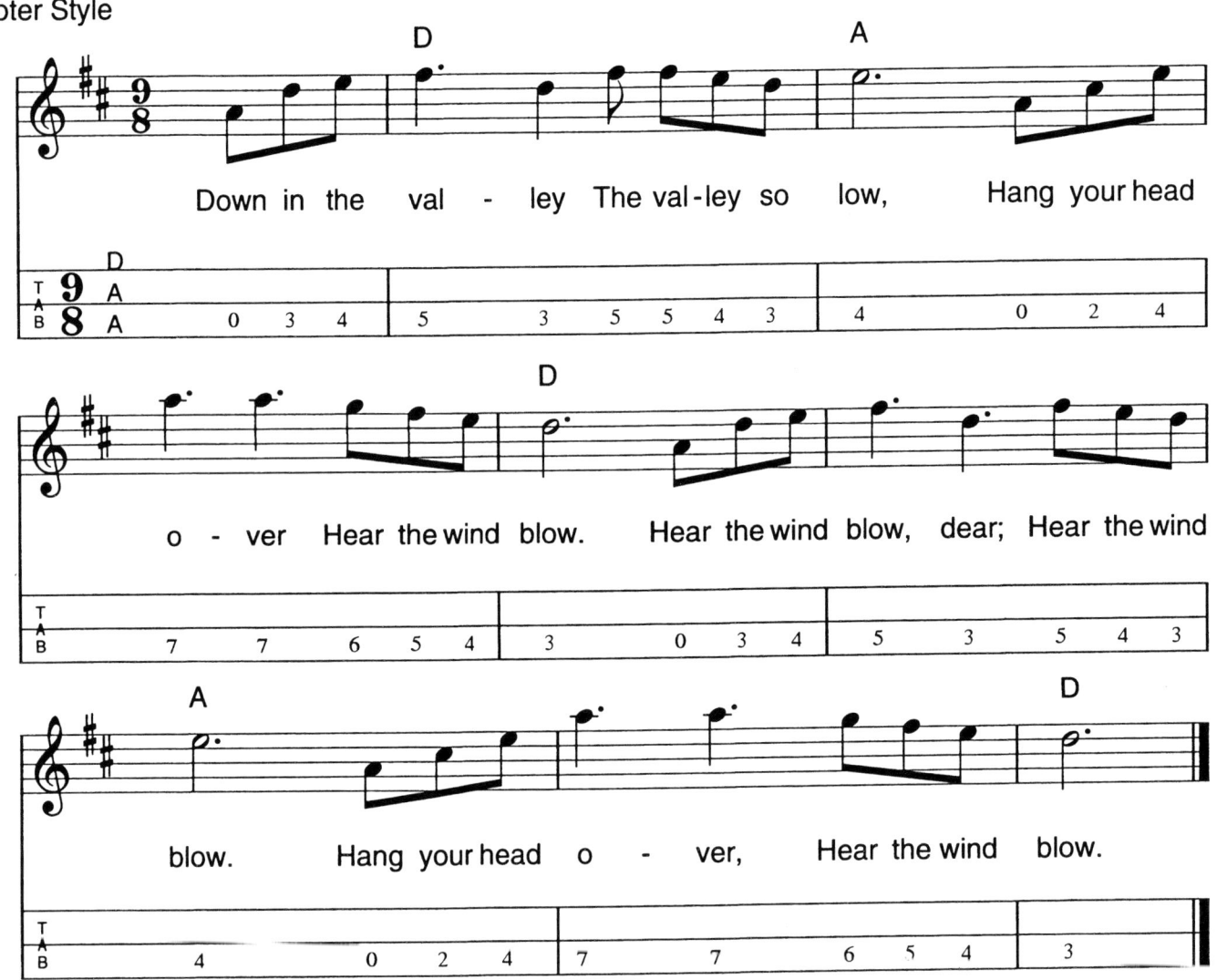

Down in the valley, the valley so low,
Hang your head over, hear the wind blow,
Hear the wind blow, dear, hear the wind blow,
Hang your head over, hear the wind blow.

Roses love sunshine, violets love dew,
Angels in heaven, know I love you.
Know I love you, dear, know I love you
Angels in heaven, know I love you.

Write me a letter, of only three lines,
Answer my question, "Will you be mine?"
Will you be mine?, dear, will you be mine?
Answer my question, "Will you be mine?"

If you don't love me, love whom you please,
But hold me close, dear, give my heart ease.
Give my heart ease, dear, give my heart ease.
While there is time, love, give my heart ease.

One of the simplest, and most lovely, of American folksongs. "Angels in heaven know I love you."

Wedding Dress

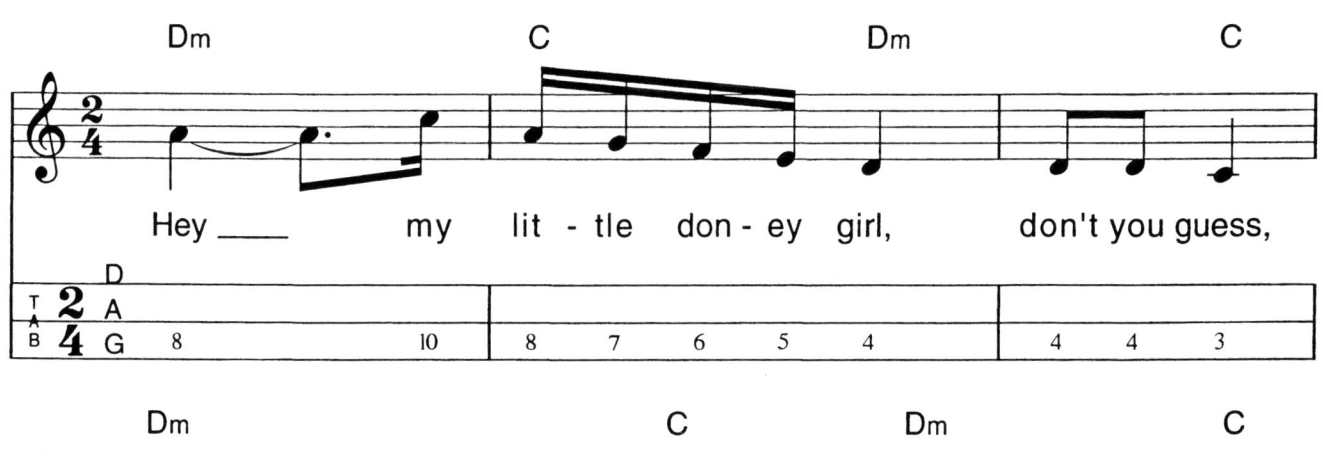
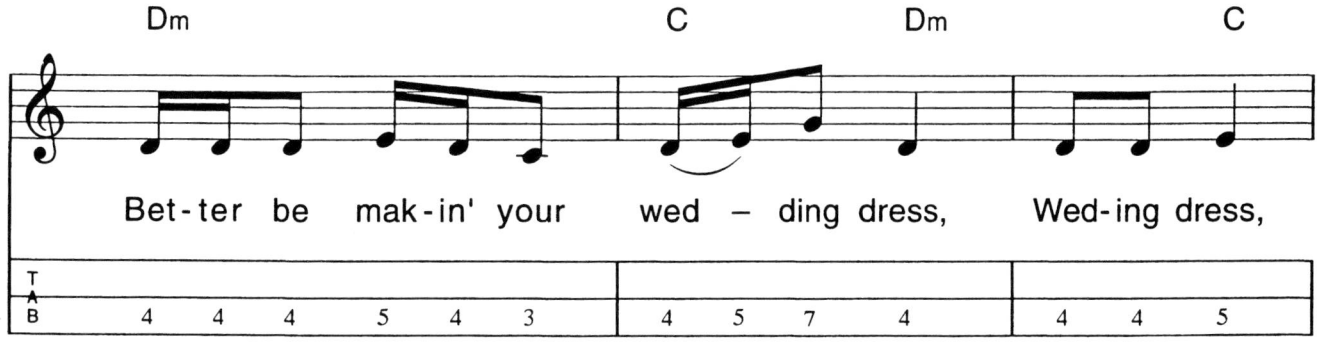

Hey my little doney gal, don't you guess.
Better be making your wedding dress,
Wedding dress, wedding dress,
Better be making your wedding dress.

Well, it's already made, trimmed in red,
Stitched all around with a golden thread,
Golden thread, golden thread,
Stitched all around with a golden thread.

Well, it's already made, trimmed in green,
Prettiest thing you ever seen.
Ever seen, ever seen,
Prettiest thing you ever seen.

Well, it's already made, trimmed in white.
Gonna be married on Saturday night.
Saturday night, Saturday night,
Gonna be married on Saturday night.

Well, she wouldn't say yes, she wouldn't say no;
All she'd do is sit and sew.
Sit and sew, sit and sew,
All she'd do is sit and sew.

I learned this American banjo song years ago from an English folk group. I've no idea what a doney (rhymes with bone-y) girl might be. The mode is Dorian, sometimes called Mountain Minor.

My Bonnie lies over the ocean,
My Bonnie lies over the sea,
My Bonnie lies over the ocean,
Oh, bring back my Bonnie to me.

   CH
   Bring back, bring back,
   Oh bring back my Bonnie to me, to me.
   Bring back, bring back,
   Oh bring back my Bonnie to me.

Oh, blow, ye winds, over the ocean,
Oh, blow, ye winds, over the sea,
Oh, blow, ye winds, over the ocean,
And bring back my Bonnie to me.

Last night as I lay on my pillow,
Last night as I lay on my bed,
Last night as I lay on my pillow,
I dreamed that my Bonnie was dead.

Another of those ubiquitous songs from my school days, where it was saddled with a different set of words altogether. It really is quite a lovely song and deserves to be sung more than it is currently.

On Top of Old Smoky

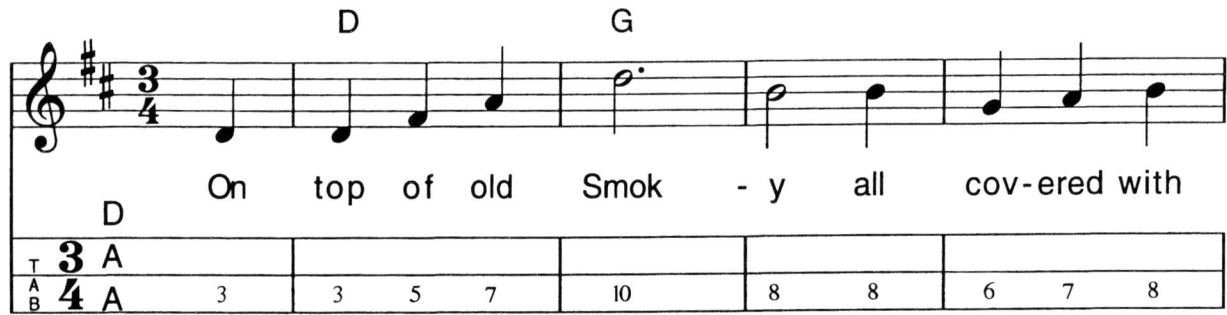

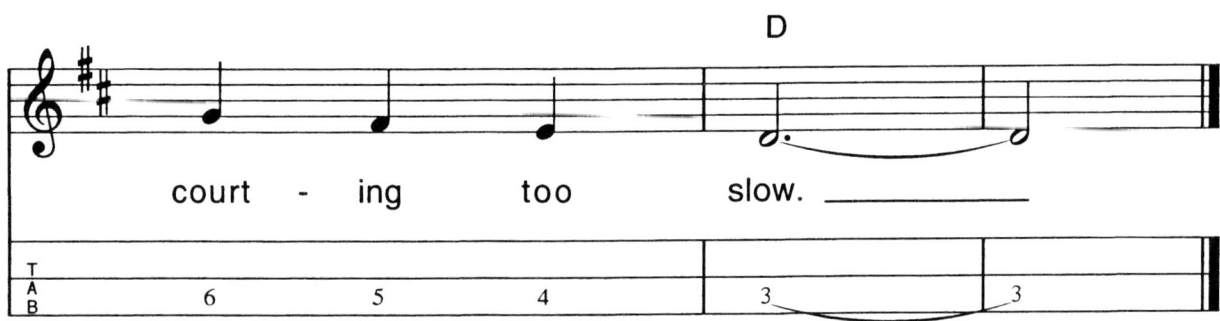

On top of old Smoky, all covered with snow,
I lost my true lover by courting too slow.

For courting's a pleasure and parting is grief,
But a false hearted lover is worse than a thief.

A thief will just rob you of all that you save,
But a false hearted lover will lead to the grave.

The grave will decay you, and turn you to dust;
But not one in a million, a poor girl can trust.

They'll kiss you and squeeze you and tell you more lies,
Than raindrops from heaven, or stars in the sky.

They'll swear that they love you, your heart they will please,
But as soon as your back's turned, they'll love who they please.

I wrote him a letter, in rosy red lines,
He sent it back to me, all twisted in twine.

"Your parents don't like me, and mine is the same,
If I'm wrote in your book, love, please blot out my name."

"I'll go on to Georgia, and write you my mind,
My mind is to marry, and leave you behind."

Your horses are hungry, come feed them on hay,
Come sit down here by me as long as you stay.

"My horses ain't hungry, they won't eat your hay,
So fare well forever, I'll feed on the way."

As sure as the dew drops fall on the green corn,
Last night I was with him, tonight he is gone.

Like many too-well-known songs, this beautiful Appalachian lament has become almost invisible today. Almost everybody can sing the first verse but how many have ever heard the whole sad story? Notice how many of the verses are shared with other songs; it's a sure sign of a song that was sung often.

There's More Pretty Girls Than One

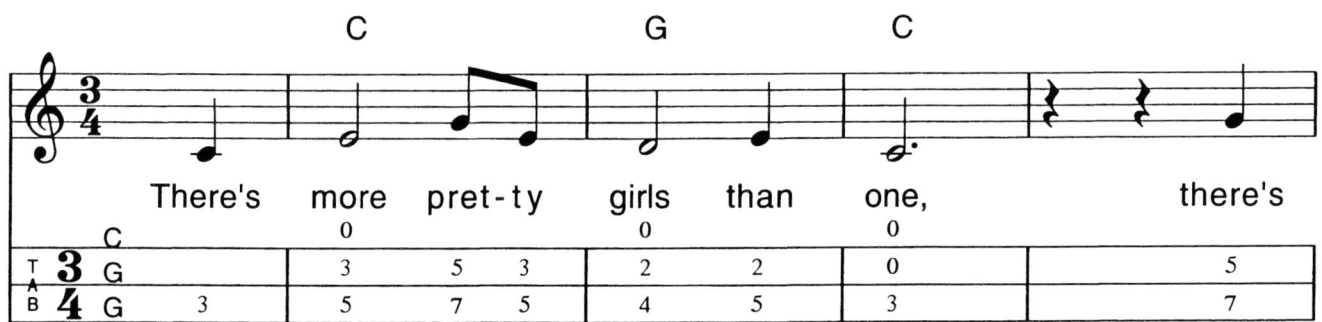
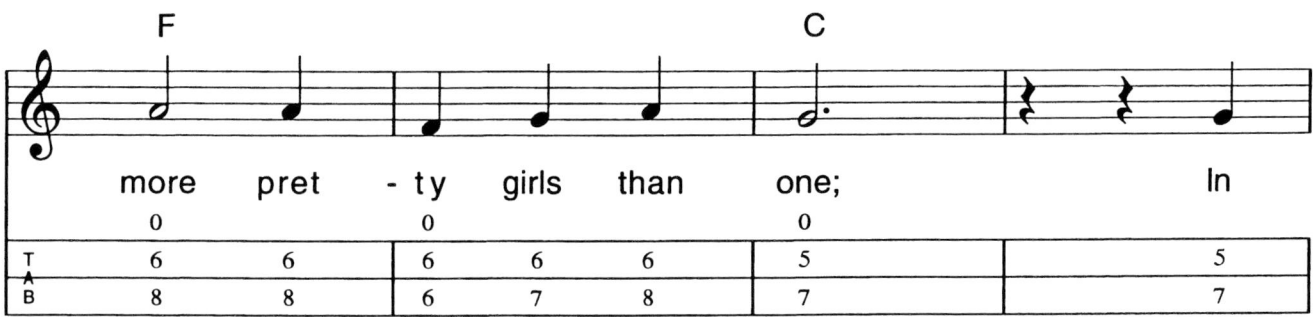
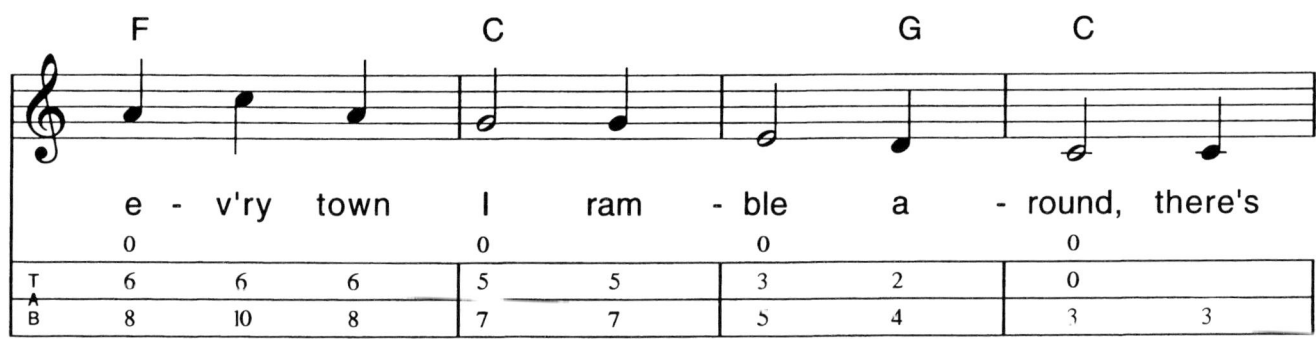

There's more pretty girls than one,
There's more pretty girls than one.
In ev'ry town I ramble around,
There's more pretty girls than one.

My mama told me one night,
She gave me good advice,
"You'd better stop your ramblin' around,
And marry you a wife."

I asked your mother for you,
She said that you were too young,
I'm sorry that ever I saw your face,
I wish you never was born.

There's more pretty girls than one,
There's more pretty girls than one,
There's more pretty girls, than one, two three,
There's more pretty girls than one.

Goin' down that lonesome road.
Hang your head and cry,
For thinkin' about those pretty li'l girls,
And wishin' that I could die.

Another brokenhearted love song. Although I've heard lots of versions from the Appalachians, it has also been collected in Utah, California and other parts of the West.

The Buggerboo

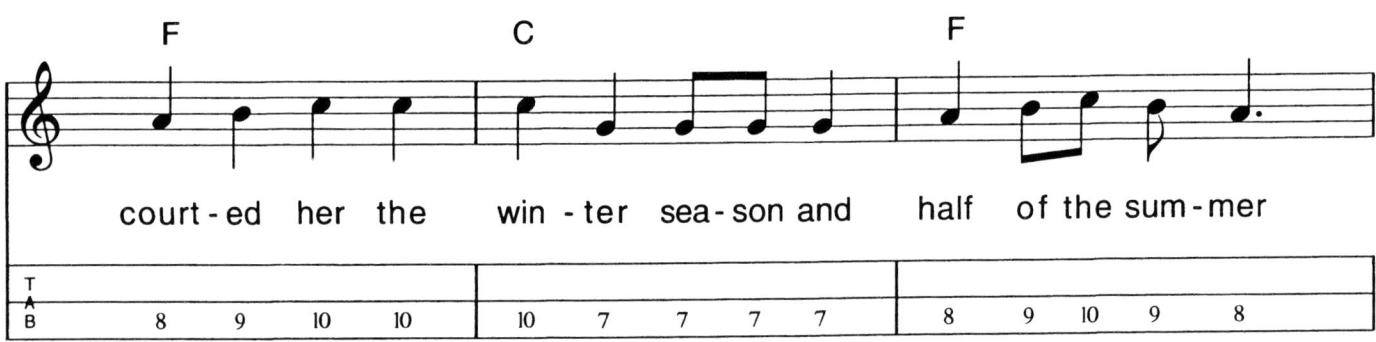
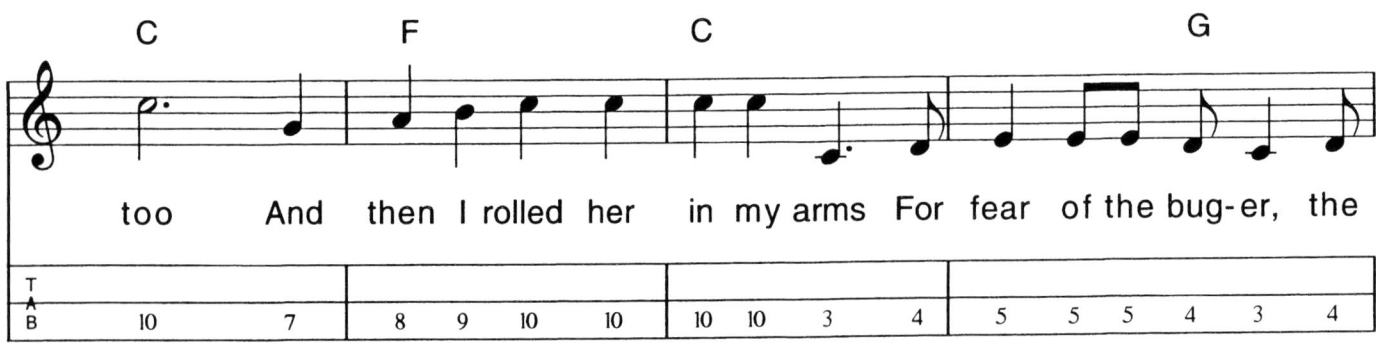

bug-ger, the bug-ger, For fear of the bug-ger - boo.

When I was young and a bachelor they called me a roving blade.
All the harm I ever did was to court a pretty fair maid.
I courted her the winter season and part of the summer, too.
And I rolled her in my arms for fear of the bugger,
the bugger, the bugger
For fear of the buggerboo.

My love came to my bedside when I lay fast asleep,
My love came to my bedside and bitterly she did weep.
She wrung her hands and tore her hair,
Sayin', "Johnny, what shall I do?"
Says I, "My love jump into bed, for fear of the bugger,
the bugger, the bugger
For fear of the buggerboo."

All the fore part of that night we spent in sport and fun,
And in the last part of the night our sorrow it begun.
I never told her of the night nor never intended to,
But every time the baby cries, I think of the bugger,
the bugger, the bugger
I think of the buggerboo.

A likely story. This implausible tale has been collected in England, the Southeast, and the Intermountain West, with only slight variations in text and tune.

Careless Love

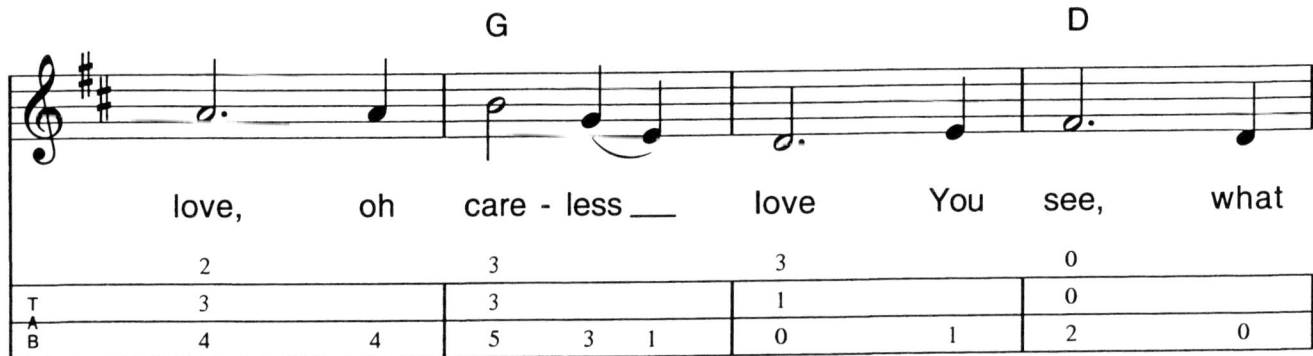
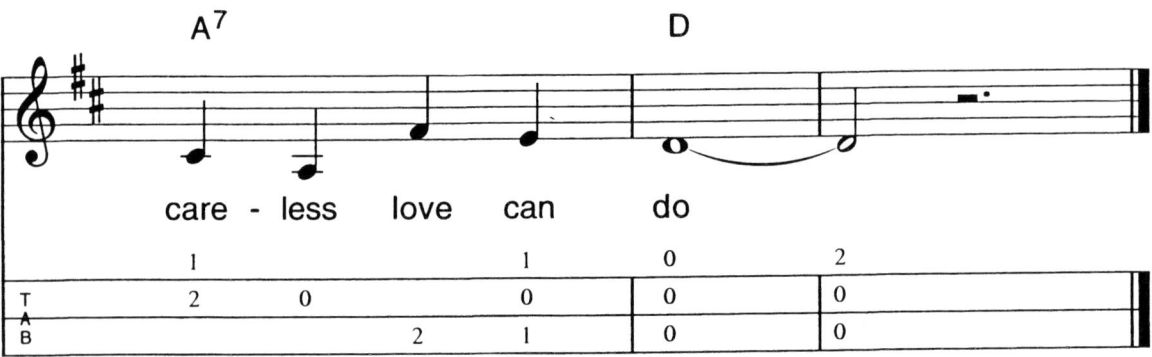

It's love, oh love, oh careless love,
Love, oh love, oh careless love,
Love, oh love, oh careless love,
You see, what careless love can do.

When I wore my apron low,
When I wore my apron low,
When I wore my apron low,
You followed me through rain and snow.

Now my apron strings won't pin,
Now my apron strings won't pin,
Now my apron strings won't pin,
You pass my door and you won't come in.

How I wish that train would come,
How I wish that train would come,
How I wish that train would come,
Take me back where I come from.

You see what careless love will do,
You see what careless love will do,
You see what careless love will do,
Make you leave your mama, leave your papa, too.

A staple of the New Orleans marching band tradition, this is one of the all-time classics.
You can sing it sweet or bluesy as the mood strikes you.

The Riddle Song

I gave my love a cherry without a stone,
I gave my love a chicken without a bone,
I gave my love a ring that has no end,
I gave my love a baby with no cryin'.

How can there be a cherry without a stone?
How can there be a chicken without a bone?
How can there be a ring that has no end?
How can there be a baby with no cryin'?

A cherry, when its bloomin', it has no stone;
A chicken ,when it's peepin', it has no bone,
A ring, when its a rollin', it has no end,
A baby, when its sleepin', has no cryin'

Among the best known and best loved of all Appalachian folksongs. Riddling songs are some of the oldest ballads in the European and Anglo-American traditions. Often the young woman or young man must outwit a would be murderer, or even the Devil himself. In another type, the lover is given a set of seemingly impossible tasks to complete in order to win a betrothed.

The Wagoner's Lad

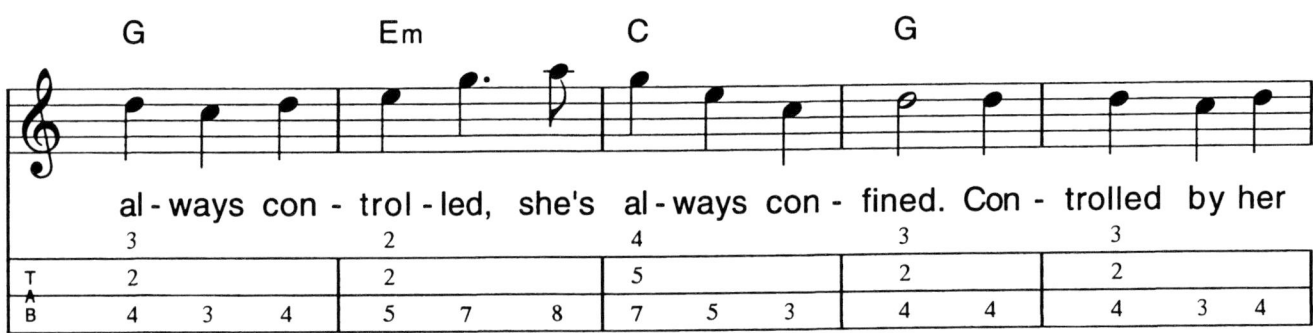

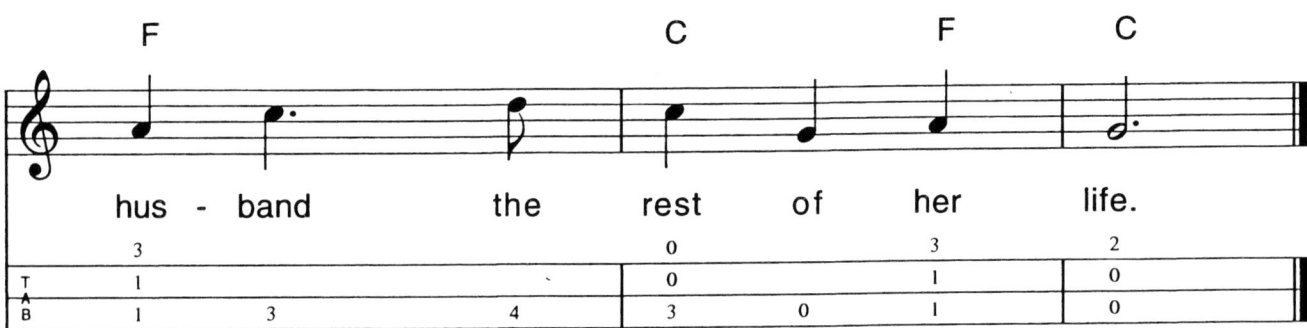

Oh, hard is the fortune of all woman kind,
She's always controlled, she's always confined.
Controlled by her parents until she's a wife,
A slave to her husband the rest of her life.

I am a poor girl, my fortune is bad,
I've always been courted by the wagoner's lad,
He courted me daily by night and by day,
And now he is loaded and going away.

"Your parents don't like me because I am poor,
They say I'm not worthy to enter their door;
I work for my living, my money's my own,
And them that don't like me can leave me alone."

Your horses are hungry, go feed them some hay.
Come sit down beside me as long as you'll stay.
"My horses ain't hungry, they won't eat your hay,
So fare you well, darling, I'll feed on my way."

Your wagon needs greasing, your whip is to mend,
Come sit down beside me as long as you can.
"My wagon is greasy, my whip's in my hand,
So fare you well, darling, no longer to stand."

Young men who traveled for a living; be they soldiers, sailors, cowboys or circuit riders; always seemed to leave a trail of broken hearts. This lovely ballad may be the source for some of the various verses common to many different American folk songs such as I'm a Rambler, I'm a Gambler *and* On Top of Old Smoky.

Oh, Can't You Hear That Turtle Dove

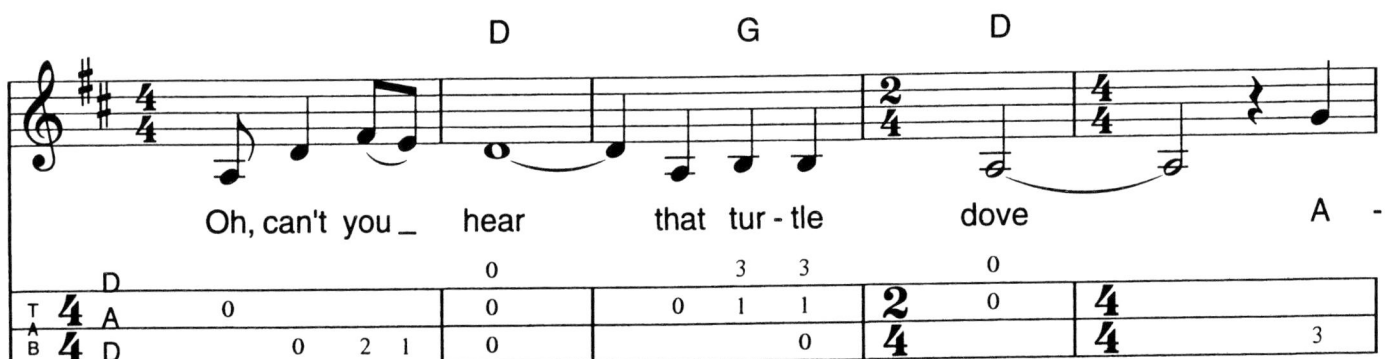
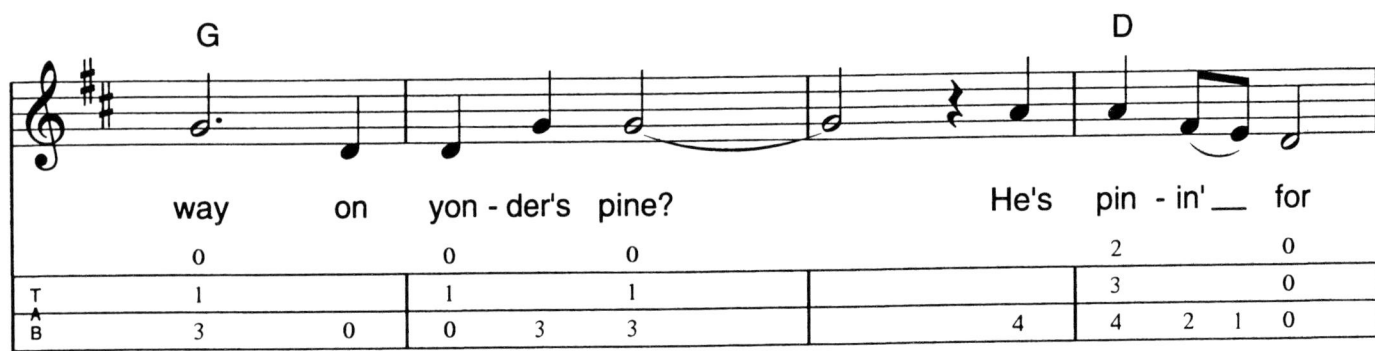
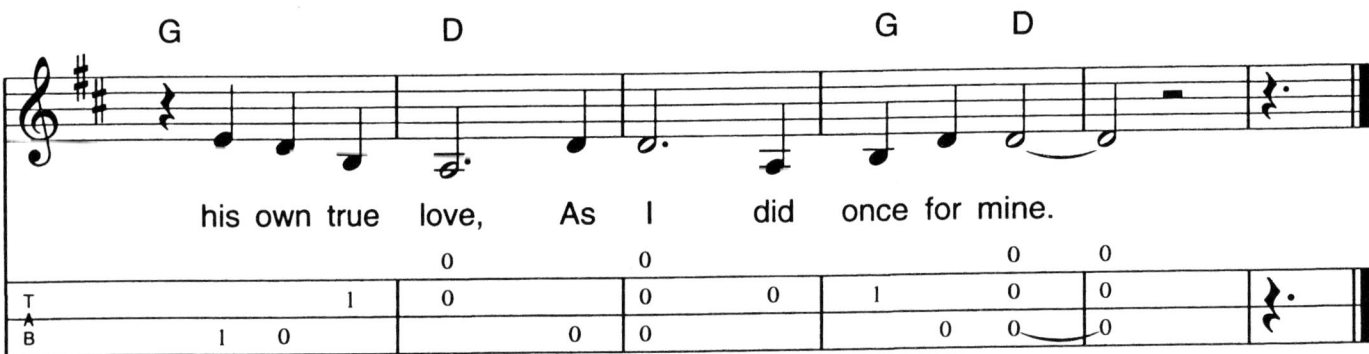

Oh, can't you hear that turtle dove,
Away on yonder's pine?
He's pinin' for his own true love,
As I did once for mine.

I'm goin' away and I ain't coming back,
And if I'm gone a hundred years;
This heart of mine will never know peace
Till I'm in your arms again.

And who will shoe your foot my love;
And who will glove your hand?
And who will kiss your red ruby lips
While I'm in a foreign land?

My mama will shoe my foot, my love.
My papa will glove my hand;
Ain't a man on earth will kiss my lips,
While you're in a foreign land.

I'll put my right foot in my stirrup
Take my bridal in my hand;
It's fare thee well, my own true love;
I'm bound for a foreign land.

Oh, can't you hear that turtle dove,
Away on yonder's pine?
He's pinin' for his own true love,
As I did once for mine.

Another variation on the "Who will shoe your pretty little foot" theme that also shows up in
Don't Let Your Deal Go Down. *I think this is one of the prettiest of all mountain love songs.*
The sparse dulcimer arrangement is meant to mimic the twists and turns of an unaccompanied singer,
hence the long pauses and slightly irregular meter.

Old Dog Tray

Stephen Foster

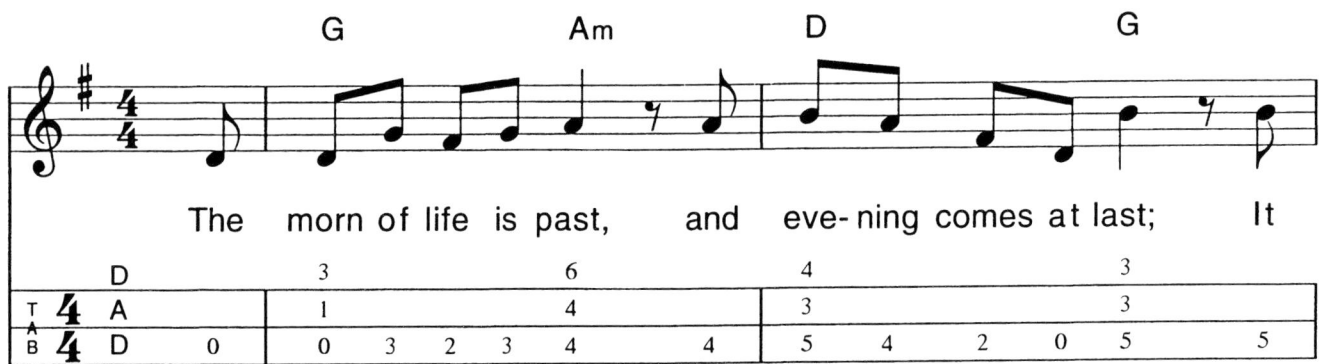

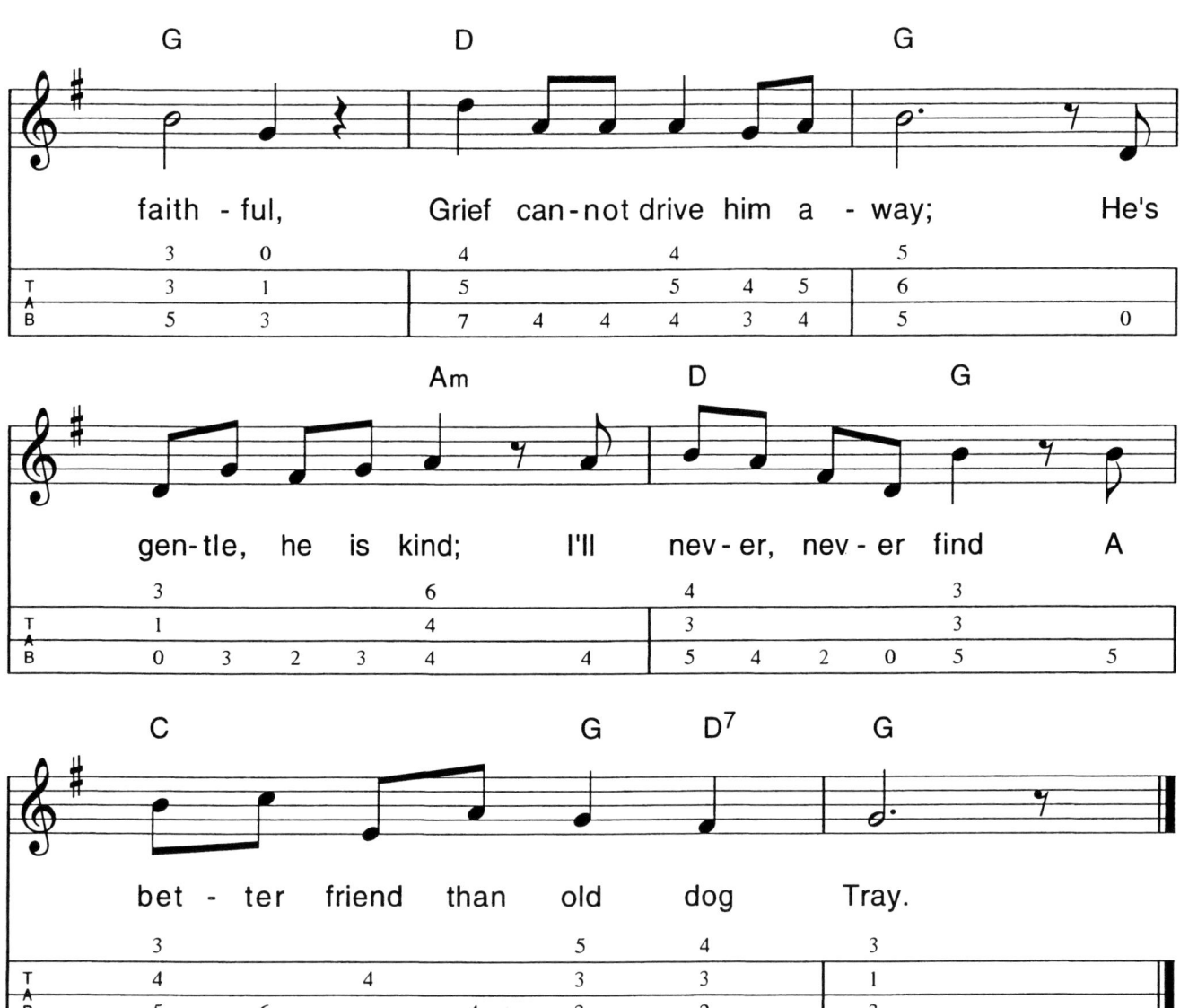

The morn' of life is past; and evening comes at last;
It brings me a dream of a once happy day,
Of merry forms I've seen upon the village green,
A-sporting with my old dog Tray.

CH
Old dog tray's ever faithful,
Grief cannot drive him away;
He is gentle, he is kind;
I'll never, never find a better friend than old dog Tray.

When thoughts recall the past, his eyes on me are cast;
I know that he feels what my breaking heart would say,
Though he cannot speak, I'll vainly, vainly seek
A better friend than old dog Tray.

*Anyone who would question the inclusion of this song has obviously never owned a dog!
Steven Foster wrote this tribute to his long-departed friend in 1853.*

Silver Threads Among The Gold

Hart P. Danks and Eben Rexford.

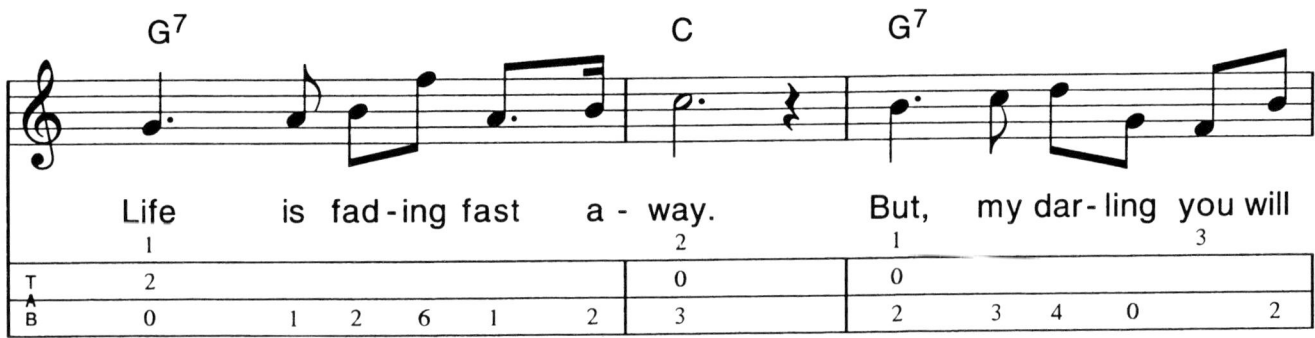

Silver Threads Among The Gold

Darling, I am growing old,
Silver threads among the gold,
Shine upon my brow today,
Life is fading fast away;
But my darling you will be, will be,
Always young and fair to me,
Yes, my darling you will be,
Always young and fair to me.

   CH
   Darling I am growing old,
   Silver threads among the gold.

When your hair is silver white,
And your cheeks no longer bright
With the roses of the May,
I will kiss your lips and say:
Oh, my darling, mine alone, alone,
You have never elder grown.
Yes, my darling, mine alone,
You have never elder grown.

Love can never more grow old.
Locks may lose their brown and gold,
Cheeks may fade and hollow grow,
But hearts that love will know
Never, never, winter's frost and chill,
Summer's warmth is in them still;
Never winter's frost and chill,
Summer's warmth is in them still.

Love is always young and fair.
What to us is silver hair,
Faded cheeks or steps grown slow,
To the heart that beats below?
Since I kissed you, mine alone, alone,
You have never older grown;
Since I kissed you mine alone,
You have never elder grown.

Quite possibly the greatest among the many sentimental heart songs penned at the end of the 19th Century, Silver Threads Among the Gold *was set to music around 1870 by Hart P. Danks from a poem written by Eben Rexford.*

Behind the barn, down on my knees,
Singin' Polly Wolly Doodle all the day
I thought I heard a chicken sneeze
Singin' Polly Wolly Doodle all the day

Just for Fun

Polly Wolly Doodle

Well I went downtown for to see my Sal
Singin' Polly Wolly Doodle all the day
My Sal she is a spunky gal
Singin' Polly Wolly Doodle all the day

CH
Fare thee well, fare thee well
Fare the well my fairy fay,
For I'm going to Louisiana for to see my Susiana
Singin' Polly Wolly Doodle all the day

There's a grasshopper sittin' on a railroad track
Singin' Polly Wolly Doodle all the day
A-pickin' his teeth with a carpet tack
Singin' Polly Wolly Doodle all the day

Behind the barn, down on my knees,
Singin' Polly Wolly Doodle all the day
I thought I heard a chicken sneeze
Singin' Polly Wolly Doodle all the day

He sneezed so hard with the whoopin' cough
Singin' Polly Wolly Doodle all the day
That he sneezed his head and tail clean off!
Singin' Polly Wolly Doodle all the day

Ever hear a chicken sneeze?

The Crawdad Song

You get a line and I'll get a pole, honey;
You get a line and I'll get a pole, babe;
You get a line and I'll get a pole
And we'll go down to the crawdad hole,
Honey, baby mine.

Yonder comes a man with a sack on his back, honey;
Yonder comes a man with a sack on his back, babe.
Yonder comes a man with a sack on his back,
He's got more fish than he can pack,
Honey, baby mine.

Whatcha gonna do when the lake runs dry, honey?
Whatcha gonna do when the lake runs dry, babe?
Whatcha gonna do when the lake runs dry,
Sit on the bank and watch the crawdads die.
Honey, baby mine.

What the duck say to the drake, honey? (Quack quack!)
What the duck say to the drake, babe? (Quack quack!)
What the duck say to the drake,
There ain't no crawdads in this lake.
Honey, baby mine.

It doesn't matter whether you call 'em crawdads, crayfish, mudbugs or crawfish – they sure taste good.

Quit Kickin' My Dog Around

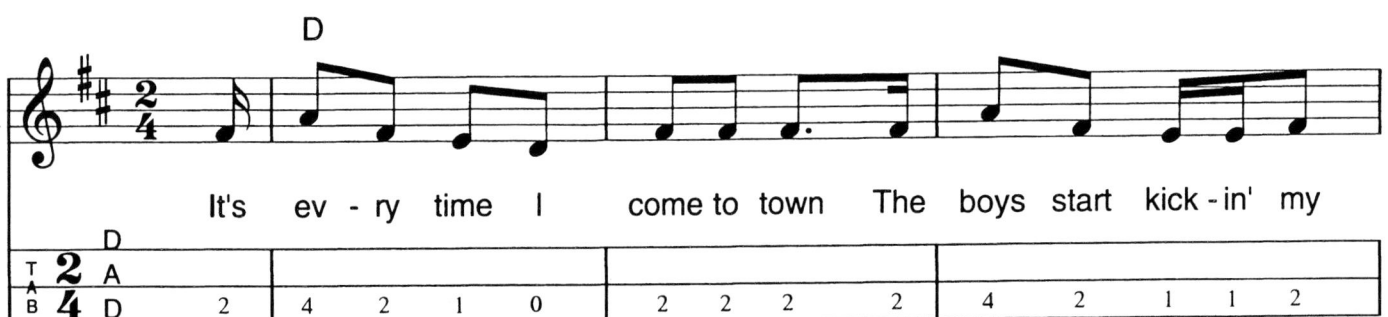
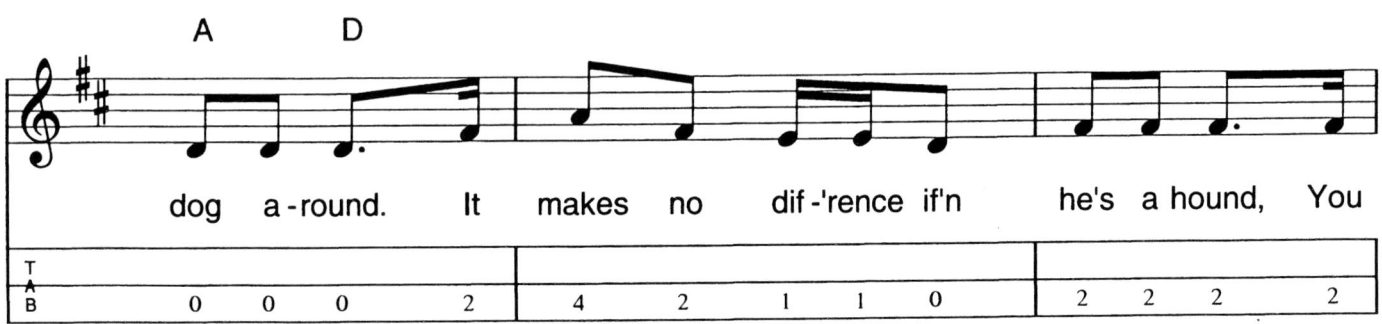

It's every time I come to town
The boys start kickin' my dog around.
It makes no difference if'n he's a hound,
You gotta quite kickin' my dog around.

Me and Lem Brigs and old Bill Brown
Took a load of corn to town,
My old Jim dog, onery ol' cuss,
He just naturally followed us.

As we drove past old Johnson's store,
A passel of yaps come out the door.
Jim, he scooted behind a box
With all them fellers thowin' rocks.

They tied a can 'round old Jim's tail
And chased him past the county jail.
That just naturally made us sore;
Lem, he cursed and Bill, he swore.

Me and Lem Briggs and old Bill Brown
Lost no time in gettin' down.
We wiped them fellers on the ground.
For kickin' my old dog, Jim, around.

Jim saw his duty there and then;
He lit into them gentlemen;
He sure mussed up the courthouse square
With rags and meat and hide and hair!

So every time I come to town
The boys start kickin' my dog around.
Makes no difference if'n he's a hound,
You gotta quite kickin' my dog around.

Rough and tumble rural poetry at it's best.

Rueban and Rachel

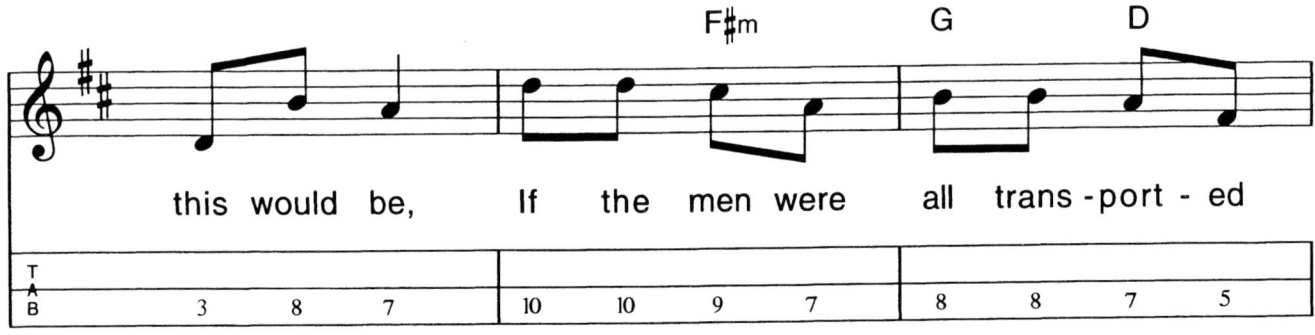
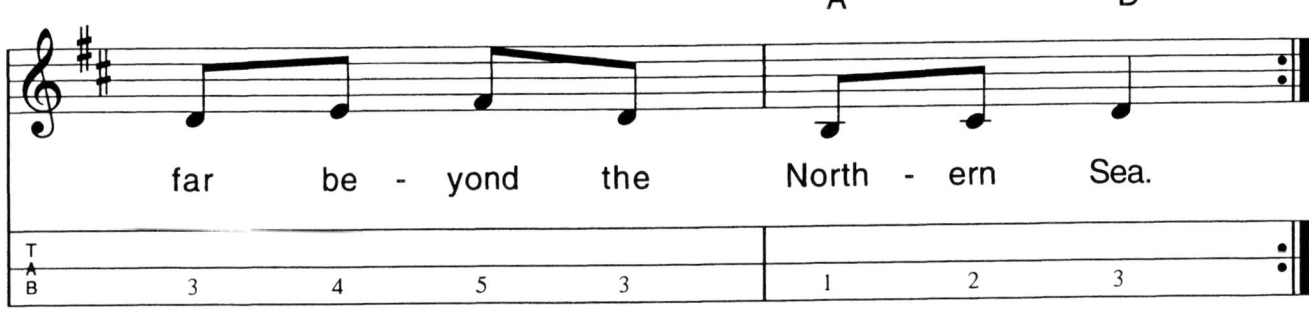

Rueban, Rueban, I've been thinking,
What a grand world this would be,
If the men were all transported
Far beyond the Northern Sea.

Rachel, Rachel, I've been thinking
Men would have a merry time,
If at once they were transported
Far beyond the salty brine.

Rueban, Rueban, I've been thinking,
Life would be so easy then,
What a lovely world this would be
If there were no tiresome men.

Rachel, Rachel, I've been thinking
If we went beyond the seas,
All the girls would follow after
Like a swarm of bumble bees.

Rueban, Rueban, I've been thinking
What a fine life girls would lead
If they had no boys around them,
None to tease them, none to heed.

Oh my goodness gracious, Rachel,
What a strange world this would be,
If the men were all transported
Far beyond the Northern Sea.

This teasing song has been a favorite for generations of school children.
Quite a few parodies have made it into the folk tradition, only a few of which are fit to print.

Froggie Went a-Courtin'

Froggie went a-courtin' and he did ride, *Uh huh!*
Froggie went a-courtin' and he did ride
A sword and pistol by his side, *Uh huh!*

He rode till he came to Miss Mousie's den,
And said, Miss Mousie, are you within?

He said, "Miss Mousie, will you marry me?
And, oh so happy we will be."

"Without my Uncle Rat's consent,
I would not marry the President."

Uncle Rat laughed till he shook his sides
To think Miss Mousie would be a bride.

Where will the wedding be?
'Way down yonder in a hollow tree.

What will the wedding supper be?
Two green beans and a black-eyed pea!

Believe it or not, this song is ancient.
Some versions go into great detail about the wedding held "way down yonder in a hollow tree."

Fod

214

I went down to the turnip patch,
Too ri too ri fol da dinky di do
I went down to the turnip patch,
(Spoken) *Fod!*
I went down to the turnip patch
To see if my old hen had hatched,
Too ri la day

When I got there I told my dream
Too ri too ri fol da dinky di do
When I got there I told my dream
Fod!
When I got there I told my dream
All the eggs had hatched and the chickens weaned.
Too ri la day

I went down to the meetin' house,
To see that preacher jump and shout.

The woodchuck strummed a banjo song,
Up jumped the skunk with his britches on!

The woodchuck and skunk got into a fight,
It stunk so bad it put out the light!

I saw a flea throw a tree,
In the middle of the sea.

Some years back I performed at an international gathering of folk singers and traditional musicians held in a little town in Ireland. Singers from all over Europe and the British Isles agreed that Fod was the stupidest song they'd ever heard. Score one for our side.

Turkey in the Straw

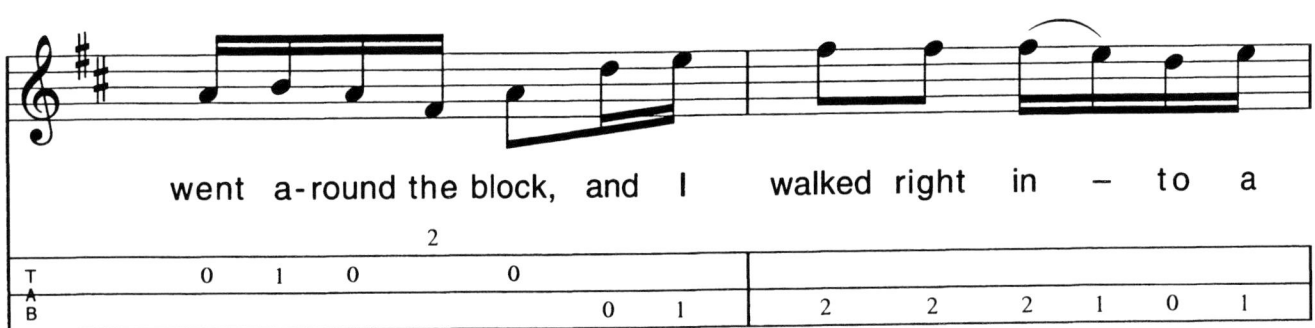

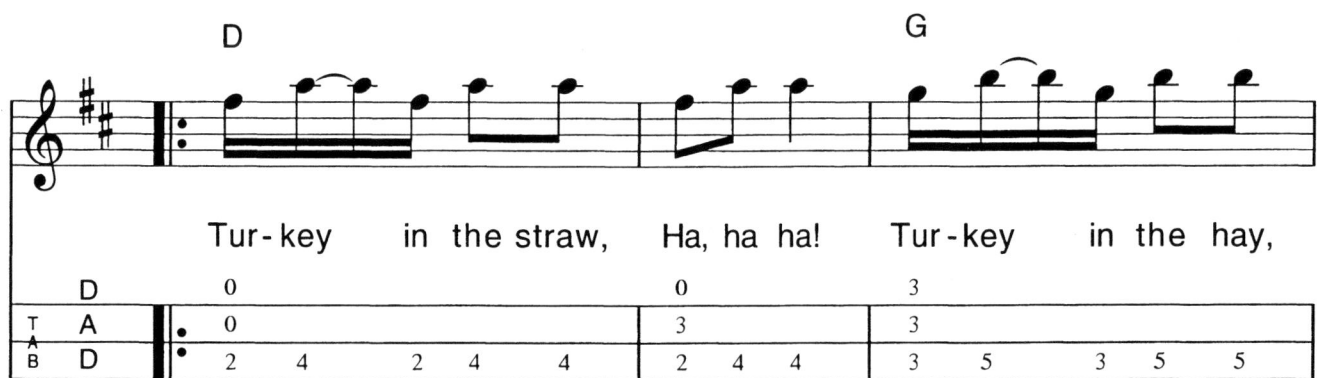

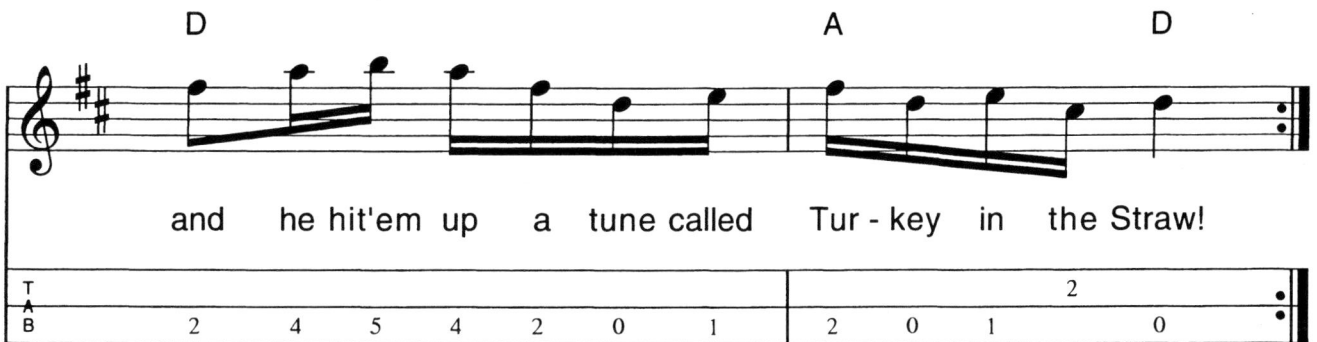

Well, I went around the corner and I went around the block
And I walked right into a doughnut shop;
I fetched me a doughnut right out of the grease
And I handed the lady a five-cent piece.

She looked at the nickel and she looked at me;
She said, "This nickel's no good to me.
There's a hole in the middle that goes all the way through!"
I said, "There's a hole in your doughnuts, too."

    CH
Turkey in the straw, ha, ha, ha!
Turkey in the hay, hey, hey, hey!
The bullfrog danced with his brother-in-law
And he hit 'em up a tuned called Turkey in the Straw!

If frogs had wings and snakes had hair and automobiles went running through the air;
If watermelons grew on a huckleberry vine, we'd all have winter in the summertime.

Clementine

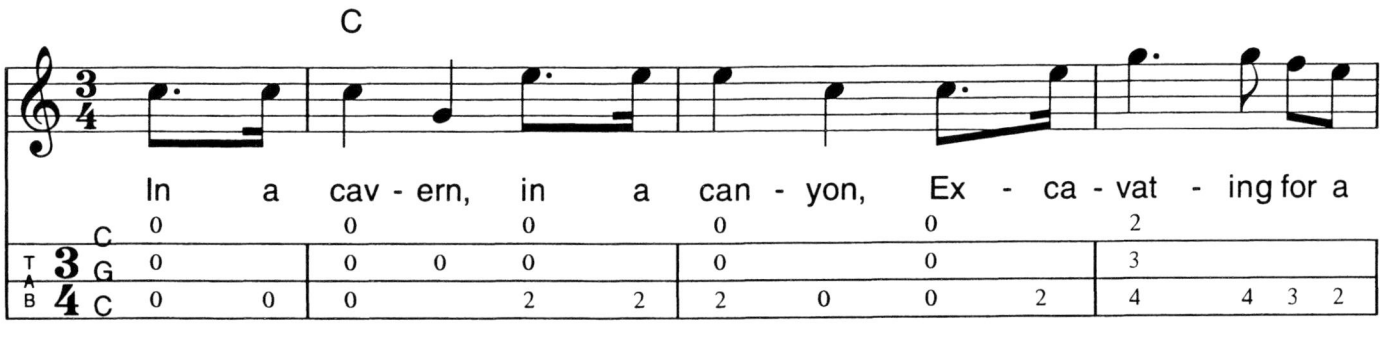
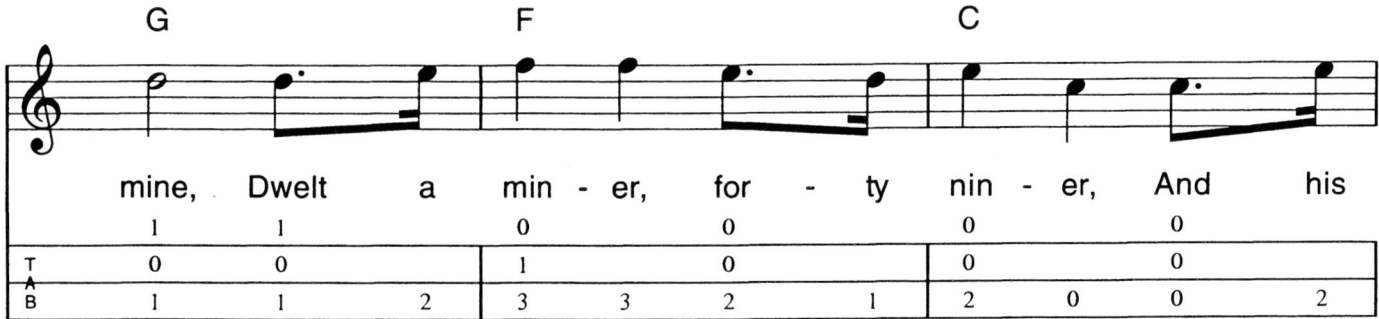
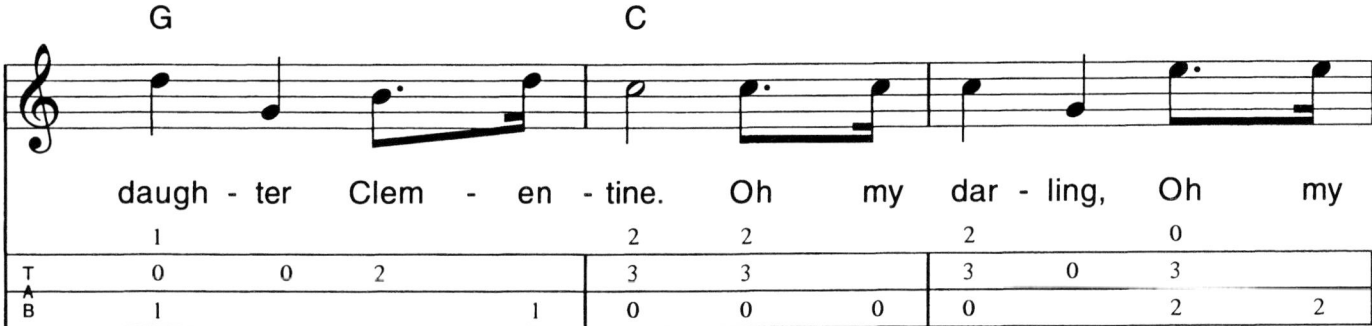

In a cavern in a canyon
Excavating for a mine;
Dwelt a miner, forty-niner
And his daughter, Clementine.

> CH
> Oh my darling, Oh my darling,
> Oh my darling, Clementine,
> You are lost and gone forever,
> Dreadful sorry, Clementine

Light she was, just like a fairy,
And her shoes were number nine,
Herring boxes, without topses,
Sandals were for Clementine

Drove she ducklings to the water
Every morning just at nine,
Struck her foot upon a splinter
Fell into the foaming brine.

Ruby lips above the water,
Blowing bubbles soft and fine.
Alas for me, I was no swimmer,
So I lost my Clementine.

How I missed her, how I missed her,
How I missed my Clementine,
Till her kissed her little sister
And forgot my Clementine.

Some songs take on a life of their own.
Try to imagine an old western movie without some grizzled geezer working a pickax to this simple melody.

I Wish I Was a Mole in the Ground

I wish I was a mole in the ground;
I wish I was a mole in the ground.
Was a mole in the ground, I'd root this mountain down,
I wish I was a mole in the ground.

I wish I was a lizard in the spring;
Wish I was a lizard in the spring.
I was a lizard in the spring I could hear my darlin' sing;
I wish I was a lizard in the spring.

Annie wants a nine-dollar shawl;
Annie wants a nine dollar shawl.
When I come 'round the hill with a twenty-dollar bill,
It's Annie wants a nine dollar shawl.

Daddy, where you been so long?
Daddy, where you been so long?
When I come 'round the hill with a twenty-dollar bill,
It's "Daddy, where you been so long?"

This haunting old-time mountain song has deep roots.
Simple on the surface, it expresses a profound sense of longing and restlessness.

Old Dan Tucker

Noter Style
Daniel Emmett

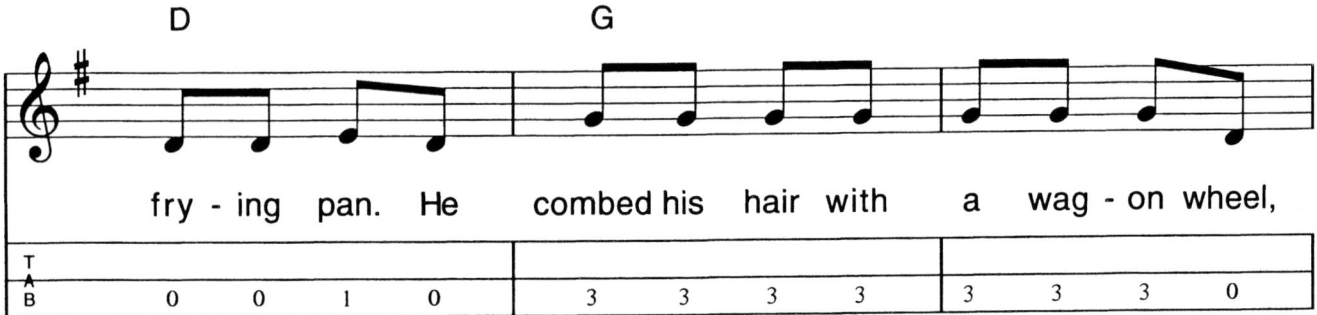
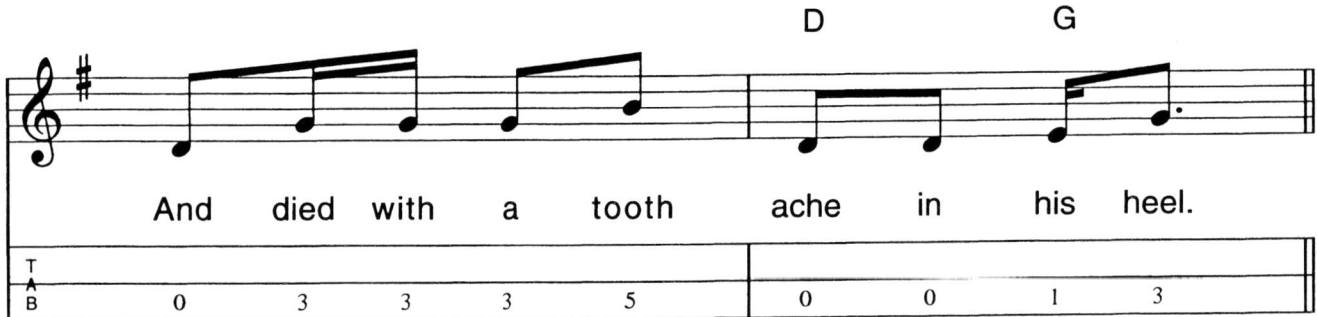

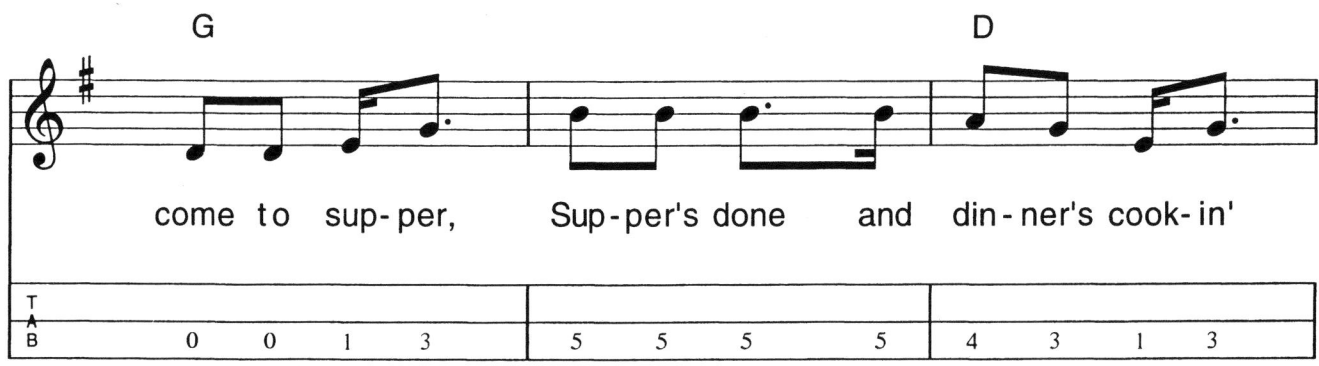

Old Dan Tucker was a fine old man,
He washed his face in the frying pan,
Combed his hair with a wagon wheel
And died with a toothache in his heel.

   CH
Get out the way, Old Dan Tucker;
You're too late to come to supper,
Supper's done and dinner's cookin',
Old Dan Tucker just stand there lookin'.

Old Dan Tucker and I fell out;
What do you think it was all about?
He borrowed my old sittin' hen
And never brought her back again.

When Old Dan Tucker comes to town
He swings those ladies all around,
Swings them right, he swings them left,
He swings the one he likes the best.

Old Dan Tucker he got drunk,
He fell in the fire and he kicked up a chunk;
Red hot coals fell in his shoe,
And good-gawd-a-mighty how the ashes flew!

Another masterpiece by minstrel songwriter Dan Emmett, the composer of Dixie.
How can you get a toothache in your heel, anyway?

Little Liza Jane

I've got a house in Baltimore,
Little Liza Jane.
Streetcars run up to my door,
Little Liza Jane.

> CH
> Hey, Little Liza,
> Little Liza Jane.
> Hey, Eliza,
> Little Liza Jane

Boston carpets on the floor,
Little Liza Jane;
Silver knocker on the door,
Little Liza Jane.

You got a nickel I got a dime,
Little Liza Jane;
We can be happy all of the time,
Little Liza Jane.

Yonder comes Sally with her new shoes on,
Little Liza Jane;
Skippin' and dancin' and singin' this song,
Little Liza Jane.

Grab your partner by the hand,
Little Liza Jane;
And take her to the Promised Land,
Little Liza Jane.

Kids have sung this as a jump rope and play-party song for years and years.

Go Tell Aunt Rhody

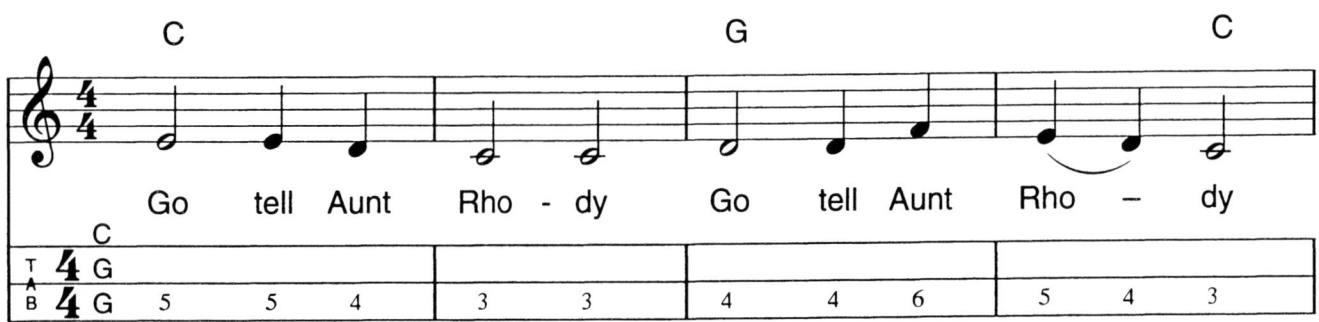

Go tell Aunt Rhody,
Go tell Aunt Rhody,
Go tell Aunt Rhody,
The old grey goose is dead.

The one she was saving,
The one she was saving,
The one she was saving,
To make a feather bed.

It died in the millpond,
It died in the millpond,
It died in the millpond,
Standing on it's head.

The gander is crying,
Because the goose is dead.

The goslings are crying,
Because the goose is dead.

Many old children's songs seem sad to us now. We tend to forget rural families depend on their animals for food, clothing and muscle power. Although the goslings are crying, Aunt Rhody will have a new feather bed.

Shoo Fly, Don't Bother Me

Frank Campbell and Wm. Reeves

This delightful children's song was a favorite of both Confederate and Union Soldiers during the Civil War.

About the Author

Like many of us, Mark Nelson was exposed to American folk music as a young child through school, summer camp and the playground songs of his classmates: "My Bonnie has tuberculosis..." And, again like many of us, he didn't know it *was* folk music until a bunch of college-educated singers with guitars and earnest expressions started singing about lonesome graves and long black veils in the early 1960's.

Fortunately he wasn't permanently damaged by the folk scare of the Sixties. Mark nonetheless took up the Appalachian dulcimer and began exploring traditional music from many cultures. He took first place at the National Dulcimer Championships in Winfield, Kansas in 1979 and began a recording career that has included albums, books and instructional videos. His wide-ranging interest in and knowledge about a number of different musical idioms has made him an in-demand recording artist, teacher and concert performer throughout the United States, Canada and Europe.

Mark lives in southern Oregon's Applegate Valley. These days he divides his time between recording, writing and performing on the one hand and keeping the cat happy on the other. Sometimes the cat requires both hands.

Author's Bibliography and Discography

Books and CD Sets from Mel Bay Publications

    The Complete Collection of Celtic Music for the Appalachian Dulcimer
    Scottish Airs and Ballads for Appalachian Dulcimer
    Learn to Play Hawaiian Slack Key Guitar (with Keola Beamer)

Videos (Lark in the Morning, available from Mel Bay Publications)
    Beginning Appalachian Dulcimer

Recordings
    Fiddle Tunes for Dulcimer – The Rights of Man (Kicking Mule Records)
    After The Morning (Kicking Mule Records)
    Southern Light (Flying Fish Records)
    The Faery Hills (Wizmak Productions)
    Autumn (Wizmak Productions)
    Masters of the Mountain Dulcimer (Sue Trump Productions)
    Slack Key Solos and Duets (Acme Arts)
    The Water is Wide (Acme Arts)

You may contact Mark @ Acme Arts/P.O. Box 967/Jacksonville OR 97530
www.Mark-o.com

Alphabetical Song Index

A
Acres of Clams 72
All Are Talking of Utah 162
All Night, All Day 148
Amazing Grace 134
Alsea Girls 69
America (My County 'Tis of Thee) 176
Aura Lee 178

B
Banks of the Ohio 22
Barb'ry Allen 18
The Battle Hymn of the Republic 68
Beulah Land 76
Beware, Oh Take Care 180
Blood Red Roses 106
Boatman Dance 90
Bonnie Black Bess 116
The Buggerboo 190
Bury Me Not on the Lone Prairie 75

C
Camptown Races 118
Careless Love 192
Chickens Are a-Crowin' 58
Cindy 50
Clementine 218
Cold Rain and Snow 48
The Crawdad Song 208
Cripple Creek 52
The Cuckoo 42

D
Dakota Land 77
Darlin' Cory 113
The Devil's Questions 34
Dixie 170
Don't Let Your Deal go Down 128
Down in the Valley 182
The Drunken Sailor 102

E
Eating Goober Peas 158
Erie Canal 98
The E-Ri-E 104

F
The Farmer's Curst Wife 24
Fennario 26
Fod 214
Follow the Drinking Gourd 172
Frankie and Johnnie 114
Froggie Went a-Courtin' 213

G
The Girl I Left Behind Me 154
The Glendy Burke 92
Go Tell Aunt Rhody 226
The Greenland Whale Fishery 110
Groundhog 44

H
Hallelujah, I'm a Bum 126
Handsome Molly 121
Haul Away, Joe 86
He's Got the Whole World in His Hands 133
Hold On 137
Home on the Range 70

I
I'm a Rambler I'm a Gambler 120
I'm on My Way 146
I Wish I Was a Mole in the Ground 220
In the Good Old Colony Days 62

J
Jack o' Diamonds 122
Jenny Fair Gentle Rosemarie 16
Jimmy Crack Corn 124
John Henry 84

K
Kansas Boys 68
The King's Daughter Fair 20

L
The Lady of York 19
Lady Mary 32
Let My People Go 36
The Little Brown Bulls 88
Little David, Play on Your Harp 132
Little Liza Jane 224
Little Mattie Groves 36
Little Old Sod Shanty 80

M
My Bonnie Lies Over the Ocean 184
My Country, Tis of Thee 176

N
Nearer, My God, to Thee 150
Nobody Knows the Trouble I've Seen 144

O
Oh Can't you Hear that Turtle Dove 198
Oh, Death 54
Old Dan Tucker 222
Old Dog Tray 200
Old Joe Clark 56
Omie, Let Your Bangs Hang Down 47
On Top of Old Smoky 186
One Morning in May 30

P
Pie in the Sky 108
Polly Wolly Doodle 206
Poor Wayfaring Stranger 138

Q
Quit Kickin' My Dog Around 210

R
Red River Valley 61
The Riddle Song 194
Rueben and Rachel 212

S
Same Old Man 46
Shady Grove 39
The Shantyman's Life 96
Shenandoah 94
Shoo, Fly, Don't Bother Me 227
Silver Threads Among the Gold 202
Simple Gifts 140
Sourwood Mountain 40
The Sow Took the Measles 66
Steal Away 142
Sweet Betsy From Pike 78

T
Tenting Tonight 174
The Texas Rangers 166
There's a Little Wheel a-Turnin' 152
There's More Pretty Girls Than One 188
Tom Dooley 43
Turkey in the Straw 216
The Two Sisters 28

U
The Unquiet Grave 23

W
The Wagoner's Lad 196
Wedding Dress 183
When First Unto This Country 60
When Johnny Comes Marching Home 156
Whoopee Ti Yi Yo 100
Wondrous Love 130

Y
Yankee Doodle 160
The Yellow Rose of Texas 164
The Young Man Who Wouldn't Hoe Corn 64